I0795704

The Campus History Series

Framingham
State College

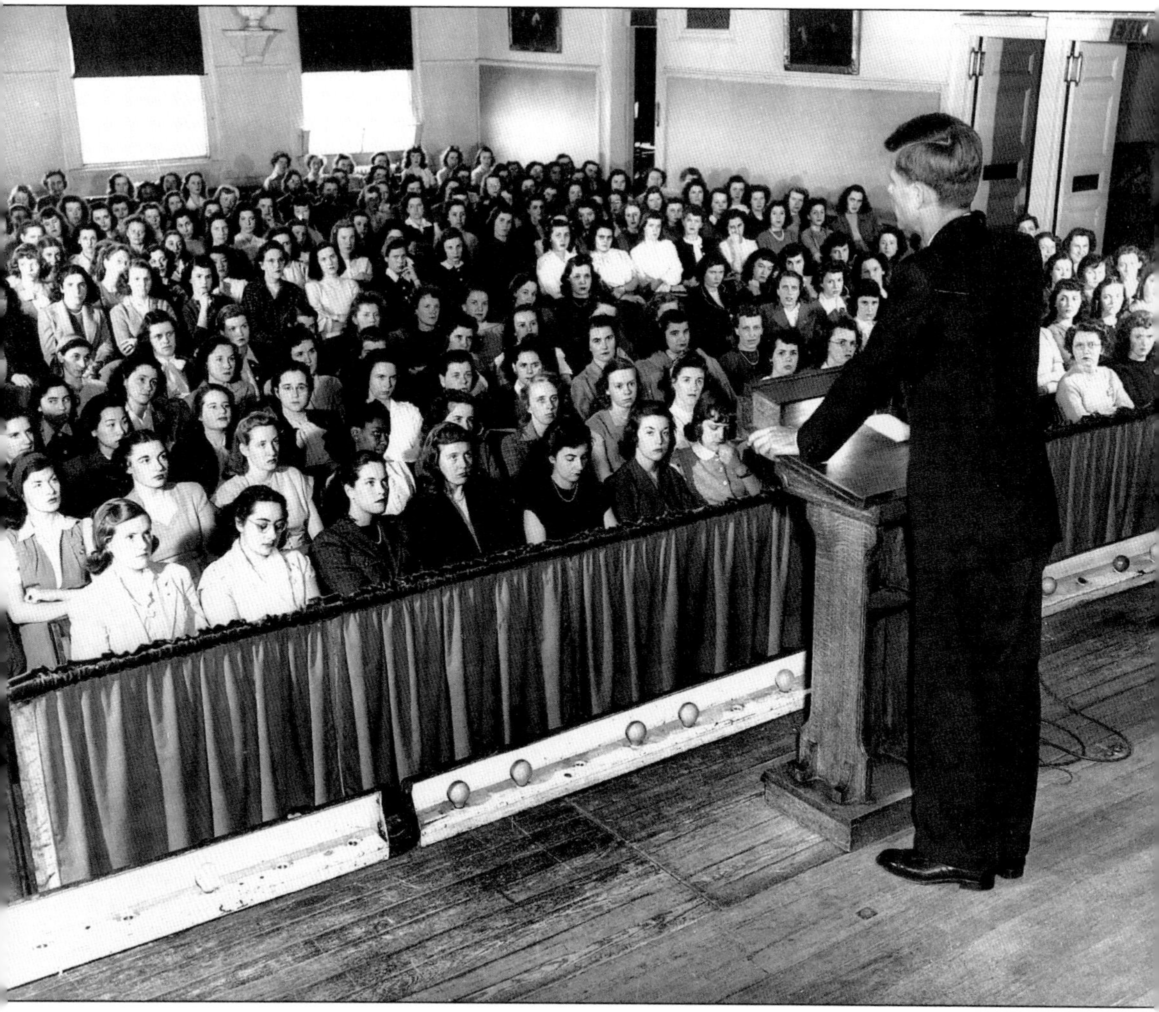

JFK Addresses the Student Body, 1946. John F. Kennedy, newly returned from World War II, was just starting his political career when he spoke to the women of Framingham State. His career would carry him to the House of Representatives, the Senate, and the presidency. (*Look Magazine* Collection, JFK Library, Boston.)

The Campus History Series

FRAMINGHAM STATE COLLEGE

R. MARC KANTROWITZ AND MARIANNE LARSON

ARCADIA PUBLISHING

Copyright © 2003 by R. Marc Kantrowitz and Marianne Larson.
ISBN 978-0-7385-1242-6

Published by Arcadia Publishing
Charleston, South Carolina

Printed in the United States of America

Library of Congress Catalog Card Number: 2003105618

For all general information, contact Arcadia Publishing:
Telephone 843-853-2070
Fax 843-853-0044
E-mail sales@arcadiapublishing.com
For customer service and orders:
Toll-free 1-888-313-2665

Visit us on the Internet at www.arcadiapublishing.com.

This book is dedicated to the men and women of Framingham State College, past and present, who made the school what it is today. As we rush into the future, we should not forget the hard work and dedication of those who walked on these same grounds over a century earlier. On a more personal level, to Rosie, Diane, Cindy, Chrissy, and Stella, who made it all that much better.

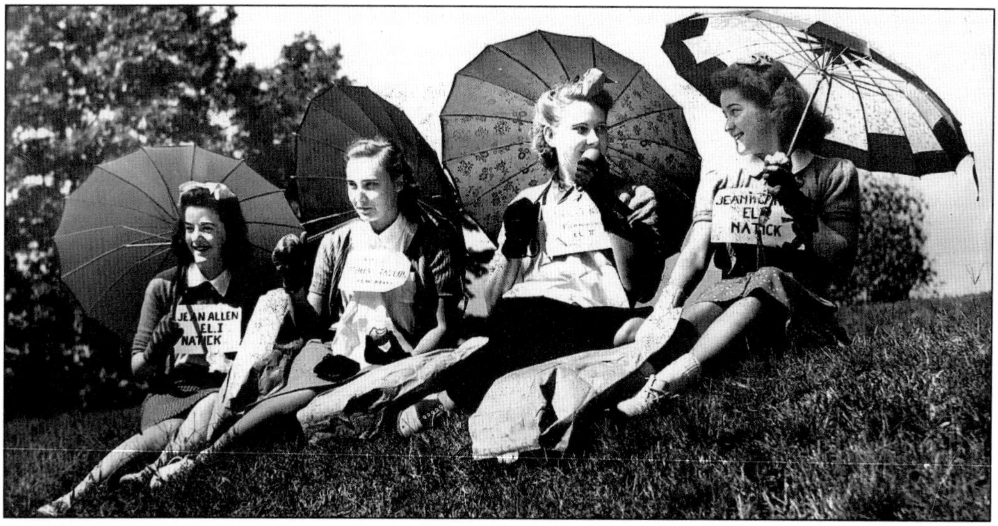

Freshmen Orientation, September 28, 1940. The school was entering its second century. Its graduating class routinely exceeded 100 students. Incoming freshmen were subject to good-natured and innocent ribbing, as demonstrated here.

Contents

ACKNOWLEDGMENTS

If it were not for the full cooperation of the administration, faculty, and staff of Framingham State College, this book would never have been written. We wish to thank the following people: President Helen L. Heineman; Martha Flinter, Director of the International/Study Abroad programs, who served as our liaison with the school; Tom Kelley, Athletic Director; Teresa Pagliuca, Multimedia Coordinator; Philip Dooher, Vice President of Enrollment Management and Dean of Admissions; Bonnie Mitchell, Director of Library Services; Margaret Storch, Director of College Publications; Rachel Lucking, Director of Student Involvement; Bob Richards, President of the Alumni Association; and Peter Desmarais, Sports Information Director. A very special thank-you must go to Chris Carden, Special Collections Librarian-Archivist, whom we bothered and peppered with questions and demands—all of which he responded to in a friendly, timely, and knowledgeable manner. Outside of the college, we wish to thank Amanda Slater, Kelly Trainor, Gina Demetrio, Monique Duarte; and our editors at Arcadia Publishing—Jill Anderson, Jessica Engstrom, Amy Sutton, Brendan Cornwell, Will Willoughby, and Pam O'Neil.

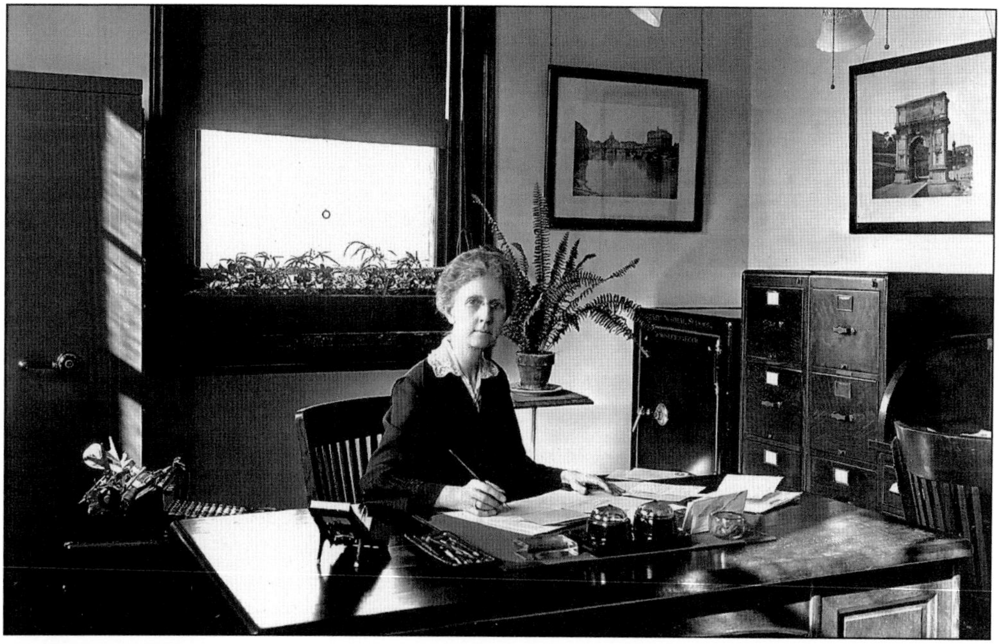

EVA HEMENWAY. Eva Hemenway was the secretary-treasurer of the school from 1918 to 1931. She was the mother of Vera Hemenway, a member of the faculty. This photograph was taken in her office on the second floor of May Hall, facing Crocker and Horace Mann Halls.

INTRODUCTION

The school now known as Framingham State College was established in 1839 as the Normal School, from the French école normale (model school). The school was the first public institution for the education of teachers in the United States. Initially located in Lexington, it relocated to West Newton in 1844, and, finally, to Framingham in 1853.

When members of the Massachusetts legislature were originally asked to appropriate funds for the creation of the Normal School, they balked. Edmund Dwight, a wealthy textile businessman and member of the Massachusetts Board of Education, stepped in and pledged $10,000 on the condition that his gift be matched. It was. An educational uprising was on the horizon.

According to P. Bradley Nutting, Framingham State College history professor, "The school was considered the beginning of a 'second' American Revolution which would train new teachers in how to instruct in basic subjects and likewise inculcate proper moral behavior, including temperance, industry, and civic responsibility."

On July 3, 1839, a day that was marked by a heavy rainstorm, the Normal School opened its doors in the historic town of Lexington and three students showed up: Sarah Hawkins, Maria Smith, and Hannah Damon. Fortunately, the number of students quickly grew, and the Class of 1840 found 25 students enrolled.

Initially, the school was reserved solely for women, in marked contrast to the European models that housed men. There were many reasons for the difference, most notably the feeling that a school should be nurturing, much like the home, in which women created the acceptable environment. There was also the economic reality that women were paid less than men.

The school's student body grew to 31 and then to 60. With money always a serious concern, and the need to find new quarters to address its growing numbers, the school was forced to relocate. West Newton provided an acceptable facility at a discounted price, reportedly $1,500, and in the mid-1840s, Lexington bade its school a sad farewell. Not surprisingly, the same considerations led to the school again moving, this time to its final location.

Beginning a long history of cooperation, the town of Framingham donated a six-acre piece of land on Bare Hill in Framingham Centre and pledged $2,500. The Boston and Albany Railroad pledged an additional $2,000, and the state legislature appropriated another $6,000, giving the Massachusetts Board of Education a total of $10,500 to construct a new school building. On December 15, 1853, the Normal School Building was dedicated and officially opened its doors.

Over the years, the school has grown, in all imaginable ways. Throughout its history, its focus has been on providing a high-quality education to its students, always responding to the changing needs of society. Many buildings have been constructed and upgraded since the school's founding.

In the fall of 2002, there were 5,950 students enrolled, with the residence halls providing a home for 1,500 of them. Continuing its history of innovation, Framingham State College became the first public college in New England to implement a wireless laptop capability for entering freshmen. Despite its growth and expansion, the college retains the appearance of a traditional

New England campus, with a beautiful pedestrian-only zone providing a peaceful quad in the heart of the campus.

Under the leadership of the college's 14th president, Dr. Helen Heineman, the mission statement of the college continues to prioritize teacher education and preparation, although it has expanded to include nutrition, dietetics, and food technology; advanced technology; and business and its applications across the disciplines—all supported by a strong liberal arts foundation.

In the pages that follow, live the lives of the students and teachers—from 1839 to the present—who are Framingham State College.

Bibliography and Resource Information

The following served as resources: *Pioneers in Education*, published by the Historical Publication Subcommittee of Framingham State College in 1989; *Historical Resume of the Alumnae Association, 1839–1964*; the school newspaper, the *Gatepost*; the school yearbook, the *Dial*; literature from the school; and the memories of those who were kind enough to speak with us. With this in mind, we recognize that memories fail and that earlier written articles might contain errors. If any errors have found their way into this printed book, we apologize and ask that you contact and correct us via e-mail (Lawman926@aol.com).

One

The Early Years

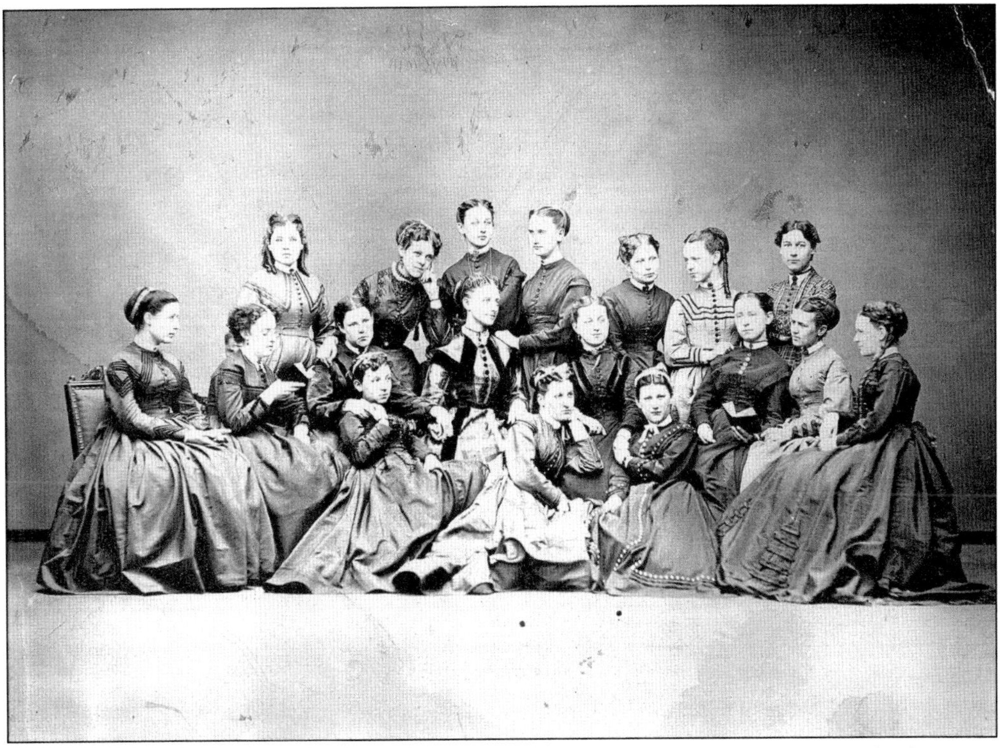

The Class of 1868. The Class of 1868 included Maria Adams, Abbie Albee, Abbie Aldrich, Emma Aldrich, Ellen Boynton, Florence Brett, Emily Damon, Marian Dewing, Helen Dunn, Ella Gibbs, Emma Goldthwaite, Eliza May, Lucy Merriam, Harriet Northrop, Mary Richardson, Abbie Turner, Martha Whitney, and Anna Wood.

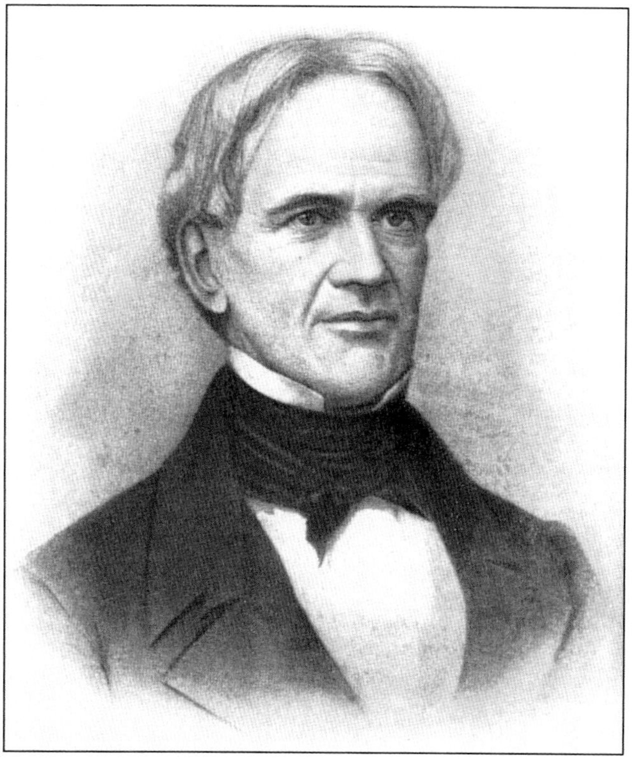

Horace Mann (1796–1859). So concerned was he about the cause of higher education that he left his powerful position as Massachusetts Senate president to become the Commonwealth's first secretary of the Massachusetts Board of Education. He, along with Edmund Dwight and Cyrus Peirce, is most responsible for the creation of the first normal school, which eventually became Framingham State College.

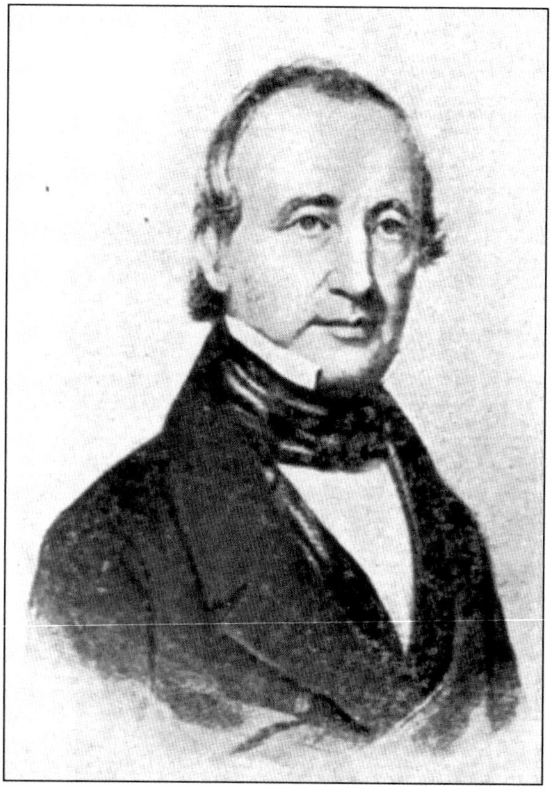

Edmund Dwight. It took all of the persuasive powers of Horace Mann to convince businessman and philanthropist Edmund Dwight that he should contribute to the creation of the normal school concept. So moved was Dwight that he challenged the legislature to match his gift of $10,000, which it did. Dwight Hall, the main administration building, is named after him (see pages 30–31).

Cyrus Peirce. Fr. Cyrus Peirce (pronounced purse) was the first principal of the Normal School. At age 49, he left his job as headmaster of a school in Nantucket to assume the challenging duties of creating the Normal School. Had he failed, the cause of public higher education would have suffered a serious setback.

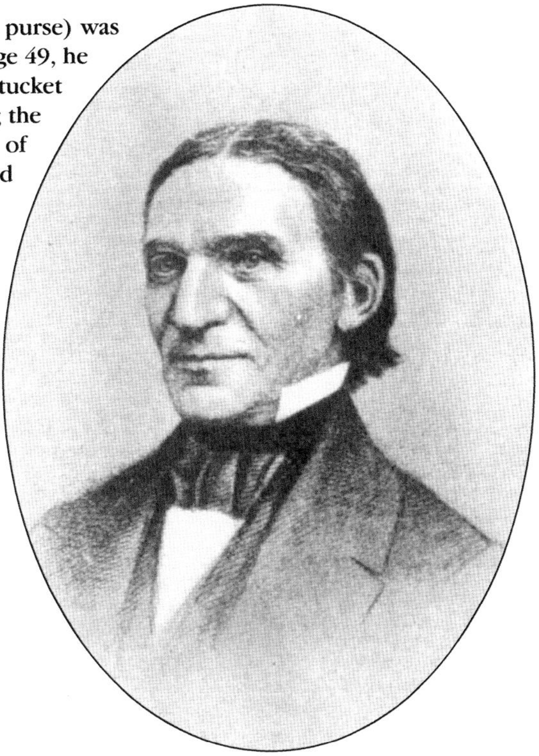

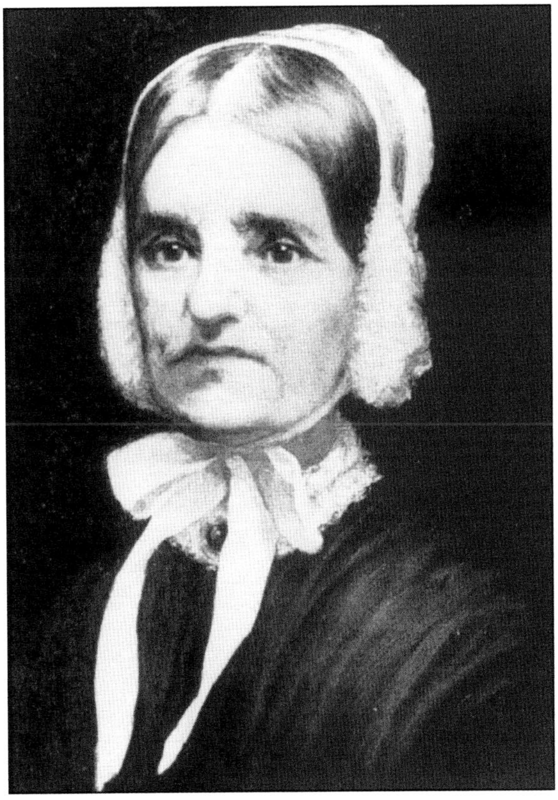

Harriet Coffin Peirce. Part of a large Quaker family, the wife of Cyrus Peirce was a descendent of the earliest settlers on Nantucket. She was related to feminists and suffragettes Lucretia Coffin Mott and Martha Coffin Wright. She was a student of Peirce when he taught on Nantucket. They married in 1816, and with him, she administered a school on the island from 1831 to 1837 and, later, the Normal School.

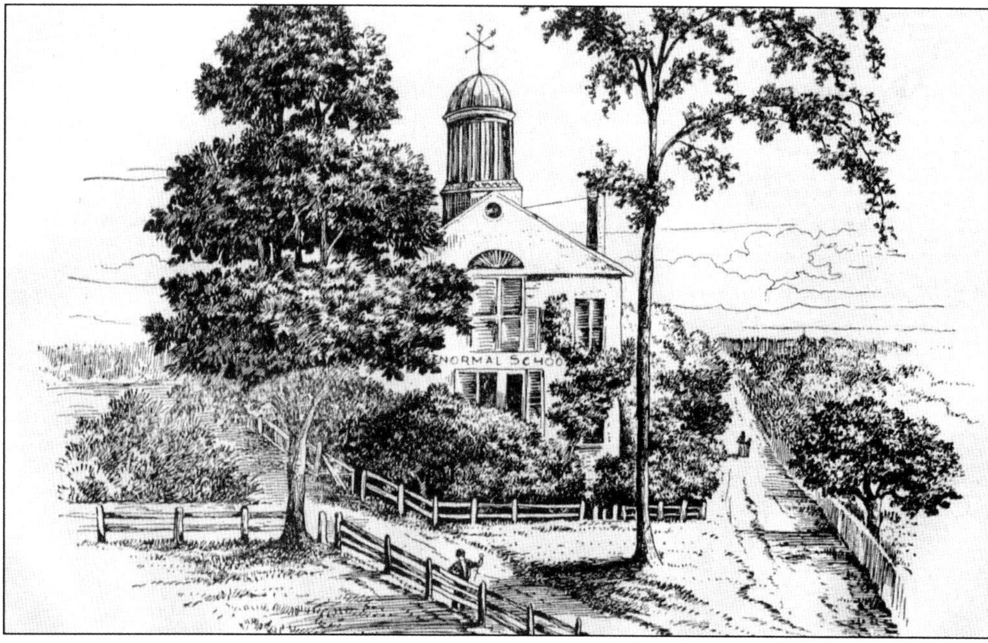

The Lexington Site, 1839. The Normal School opened on July 3, 1839. Only three young women, Sarah Hawkins, Maria L. Smith, and Hannah Damon, registered that first day. Fortunately, others came forward, and the Class of 1840 found itself filled with 25 female students. In 1844, due to space limitations, the school relocated to West Newton.

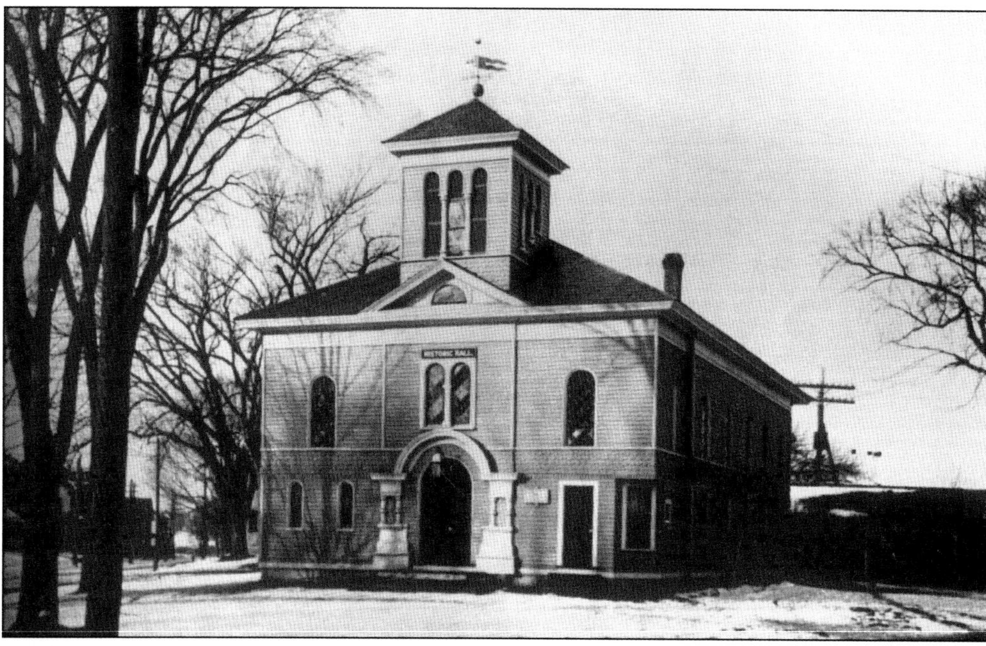

The Site, c. the Early 1900s. The building, which opened in 1823, originally housed the Lexington Academy. Various entities used the location following the Normal School's move to West Newton. The building has undergone changes over the years, as indicated in this photograph. Today, it is a Masonic hall, still standing in Lexington Center near the common. It is listed on the National Register of Historic Places.

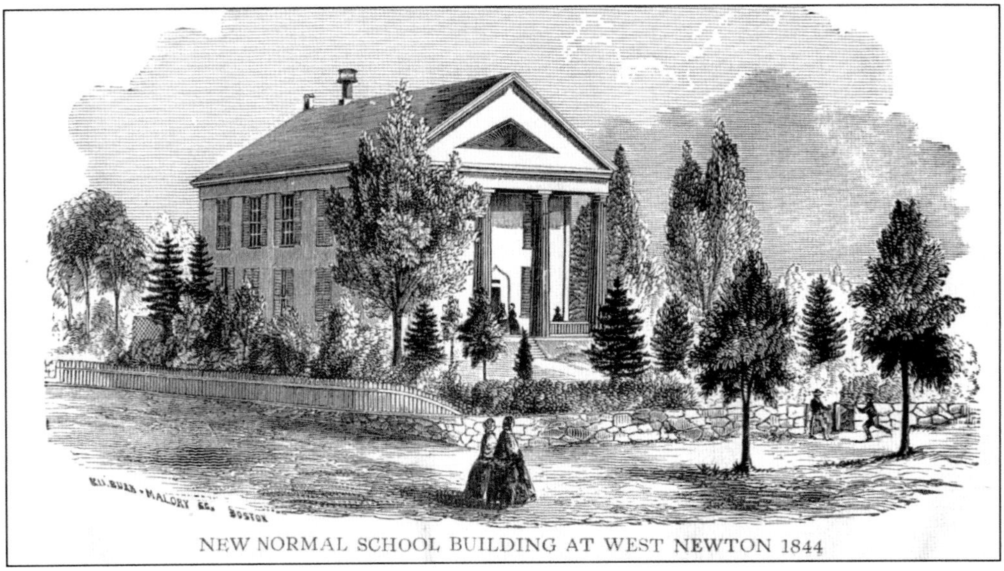

The West Newton Schoolhouse, 1844. Fr. Cyrus Peirce, who had grown ill, was replaced in Lexington by Samuel J. May. When Peirce recovered, May stepped down and Peirce returned to a new school location with an increased enrollment. Peirce resigned a second and final time in 1849.

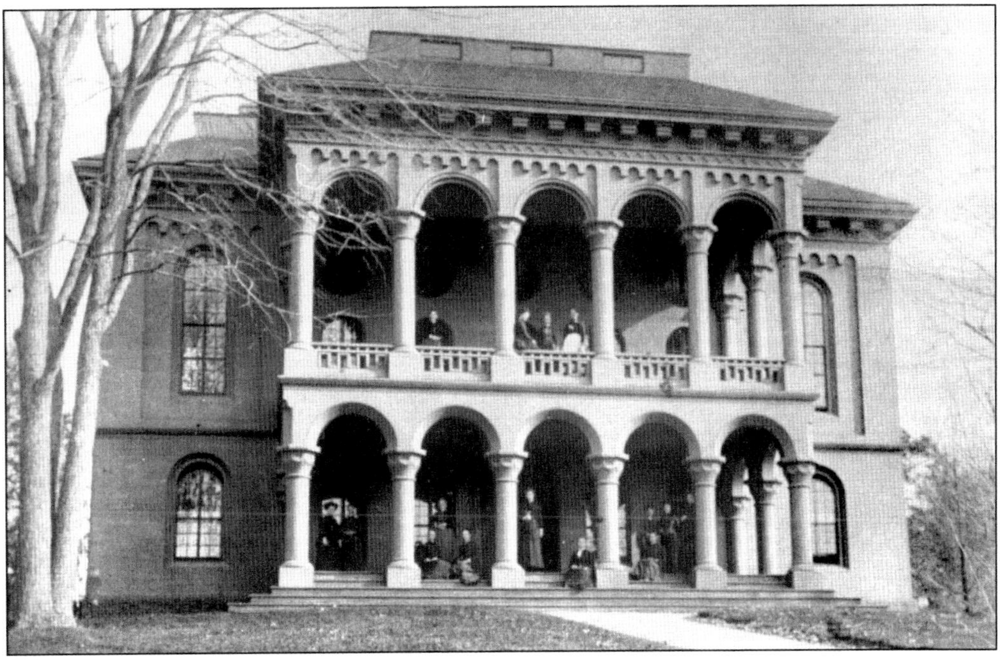

The Normal School Building, 1853–1889. The first building constructed on the Framingham campus has been referred to as the Normal School, the Normal School Building, and Normal Hall. The structure housed classrooms and the administration, and was located on the present site of May Hall. Eventually, a dormitory was built in 1869, which was also called Normal Hall. Shortly after the dormitory was built, so were May and Crocker Halls. When construction started on May Hall in 1888, the Normal School Building was moved north of its original site and set up on timbers as a temporary facility that was described as "uncomfortable beyond expression." After May Hall opened in 1889, the Normal School Building was demolished.

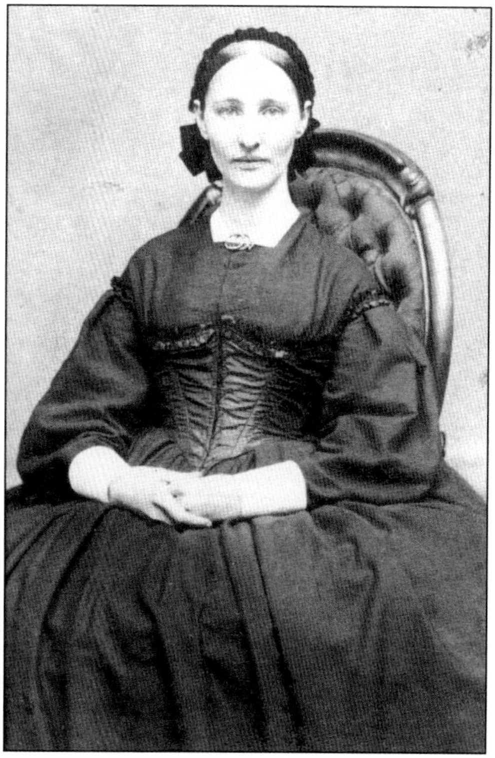

Lavinia Brown, Class of 1864. This was a typical graduation portrait for those successfully completing the course of study. In 1864, the school celebrated its 25th anniversary. While it should have been a happy time, it was not—the horror of the Civil War saw to that.

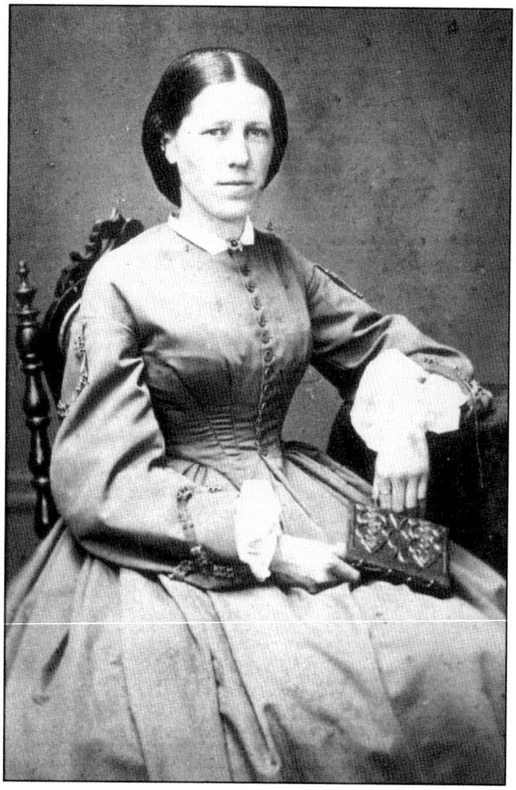

Ellen Brown, Class of 1864. A classmate of Lavinia Brown, Ellen Brown joined the ranks of the relatively few women in the nation who graduated from college during this time period. Still rarer were female professors. The Normal School produced three notable college teachers during this time period, including Maria Eaton (Class of 1867), who became a professor of chemistry at Wellesley College in 1877.

Two

THE BUILDINGS AND THE PEOPLE BEHIND THEM

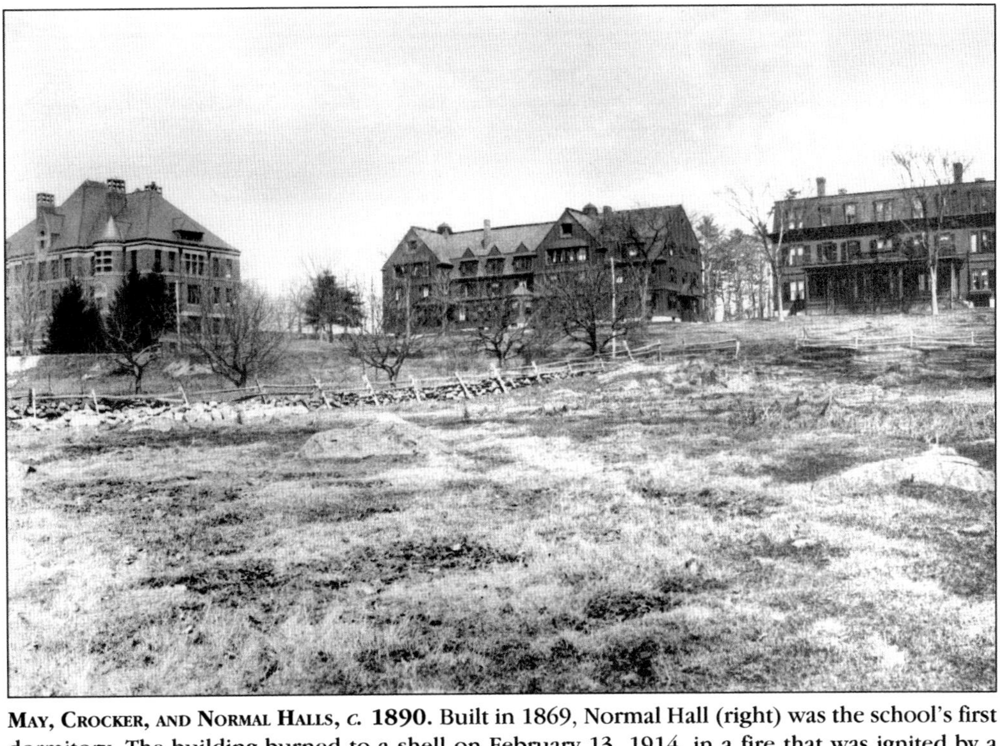

MAY, CROCKER, AND NORMAL HALLS, *C.* 1890. Built in 1869, Normal Hall (right) was the school's first dormitory. The building burned to a shell on February 13, 1914, in a fire that was ignited by a defective fireplace chimney in the principal's quarters. Normal Hall was demolished in 1919 and replaced by a new dormitory, Horace Mann Hall, in 1920. The other two halls—Crocker (center), built in 1886, and May, built in 1889—remain today.

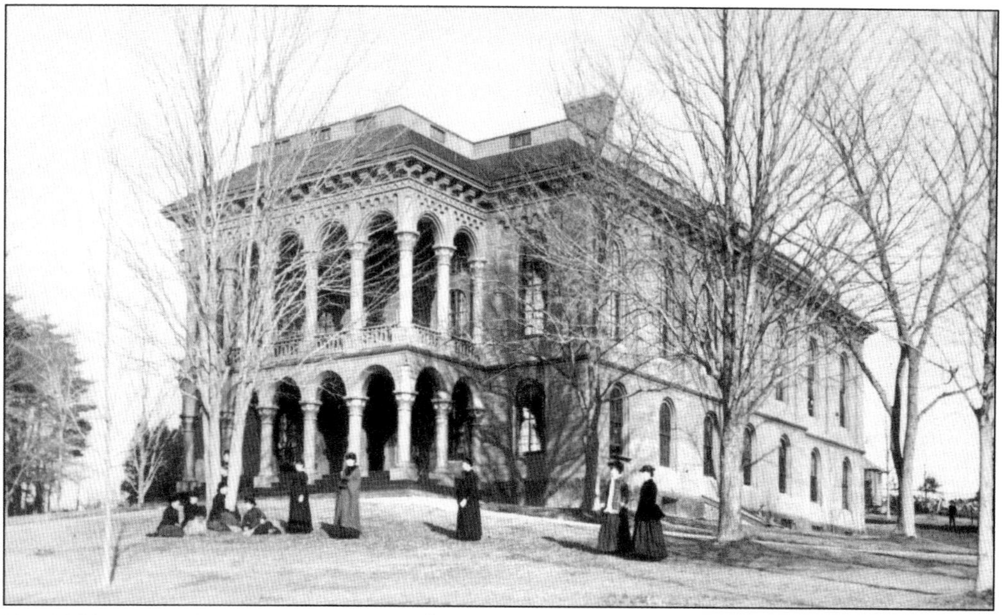

The 1853 Normal School Building, c. 1860. Designed by Alexander Rice Esty, a prominent local architect, the building opened on December 15, 1853. At the time, there were no dormitories, so students had to take up residence in nearby private homes or commute to school, many of them by train. The shortage of student housing was remedied when the first dormitory was opened in 1869.

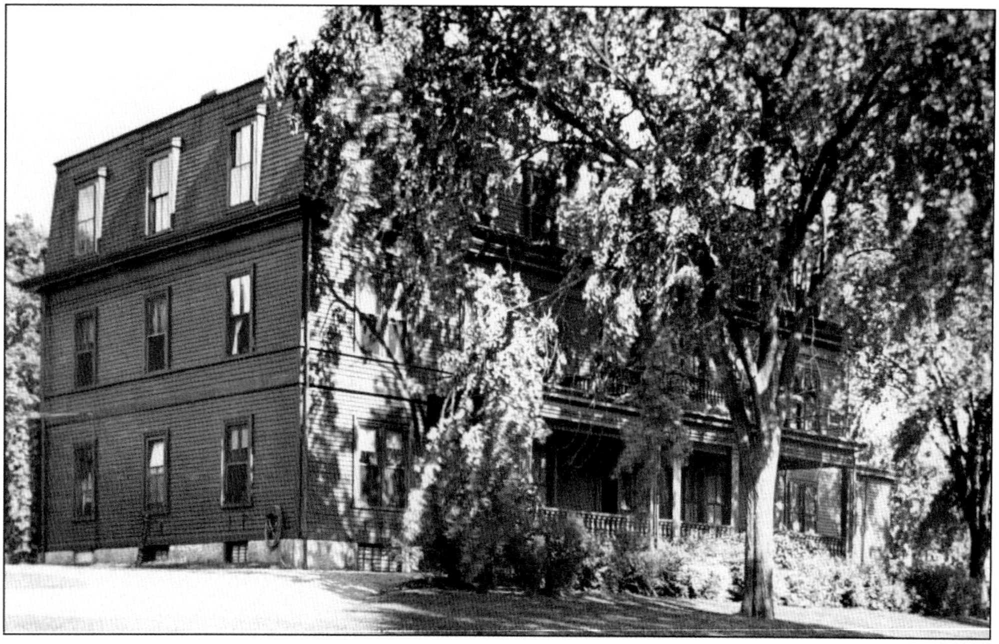

The 1869 Normal Hall (Dormitory). To avoid confusion between two buildings which, at various times, have been called Normal Hall, the 1853 building should be referred to as the Normal School Building, while the 1869 dormitory, pictured above, should be called Normal Hall. The school's first on-campus housing for students, Normal Hall burned down in 1914. Horace Mann Hall stands on this site today.

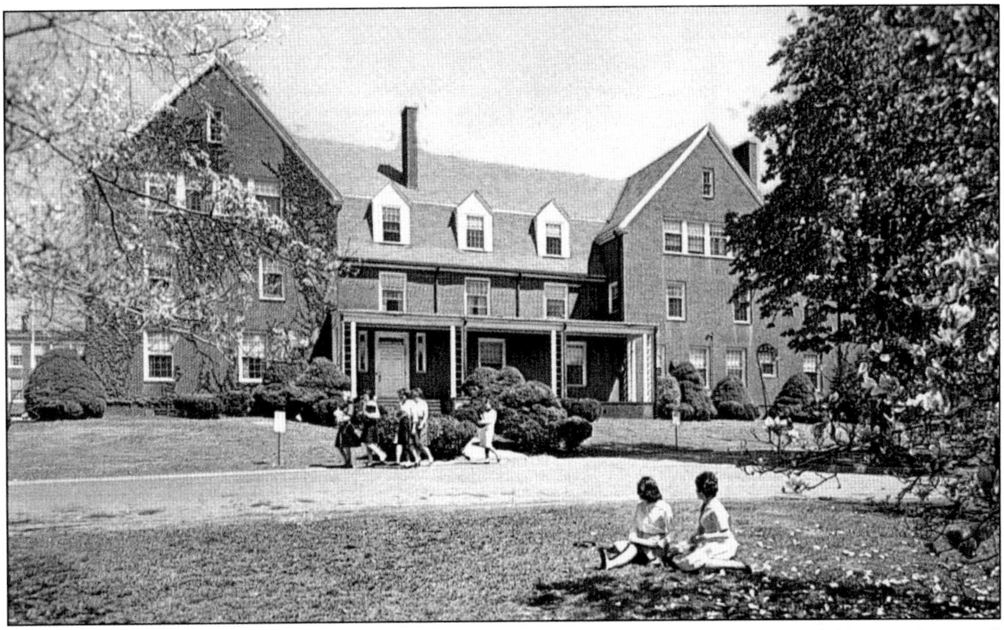

Crocker Hall, 1963. Built in 1886 as an additional dormitory to Normal Hall, Crocker Hall included space for faculty residences. Originally a timber structure, it was severely damaged by a fire on Christmas Eve 1887. It was rebuilt and reopened in February 1889. It was again heavily damaged during the Hurricane of 1938. No longer a dormitory, Crocker Hall today houses faculty offices, including the Departments of Economics and Business Administration, Sociology and Psychology, and Philosophy.

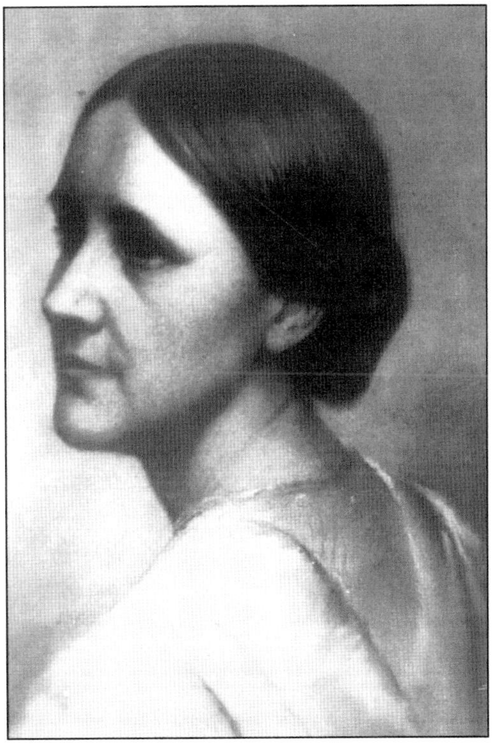

Lucretia Crocker. Crocker Hall bears the name of this Class of 1850 graduate. Lucretia Crocker was a member of the faculty for several years thereafter and, subsequently, taught mathematics and astronomy at Antioch College in Ohio, as well as in Boston. In 1873, she was elected to the Boston School Board, and eventually, she became the first woman to be the supervisor of Boston Public Schools. She also served as a member of the Board of Supervisors of the Horace Mann School for the Deaf.

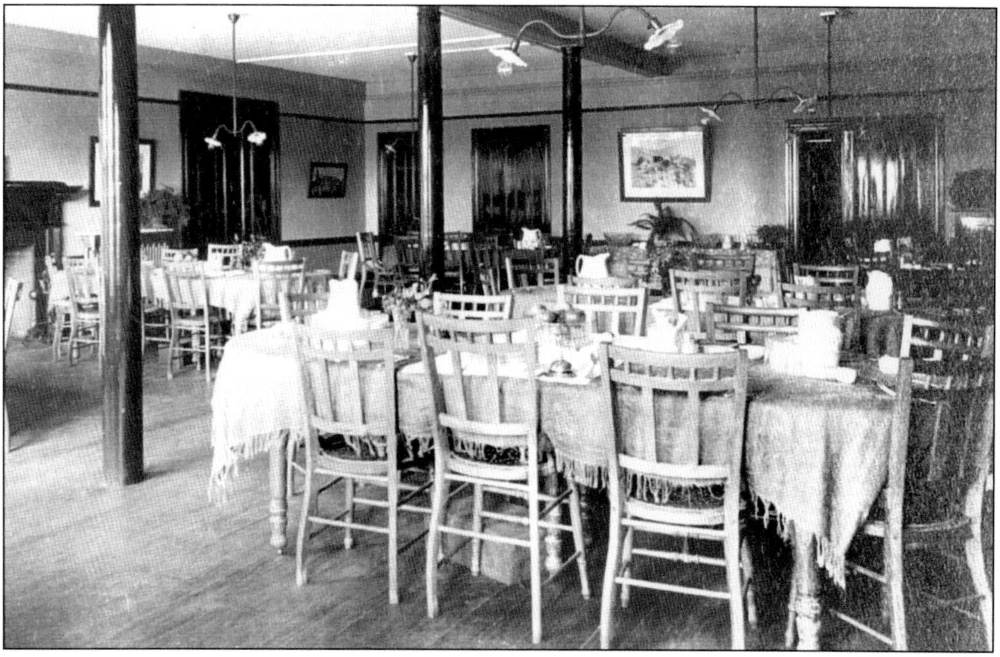

THE DINING ROOM, C. THE 1890s. Crocker Hall provided sleeping and eating accommodations for its students. In 1898, the Household Arts Department was established in May Hall.

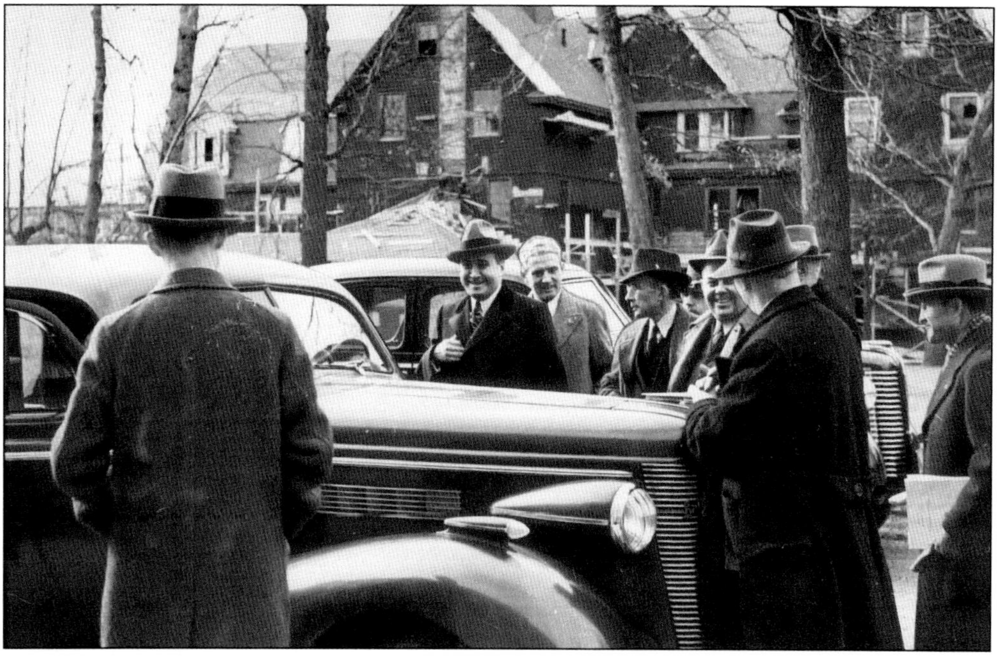

THE HURRICANE OF 1938. In September 1938, the New England region was struck by a ferocious storm that caused great destruction. Numerous campus buildings were damaged, including Crocker Hall. Paul Dever (center, smiling with hat), state attorney general, surveys the damage with college president Martin F. O'Connor (behind Dever). Dever was investigating companies accused of overcharging for storm-damage repairs. He went on to become the governor of Massachusetts from 1949 to 1953 and made an unsuccessful bid for the presidency in 1952.

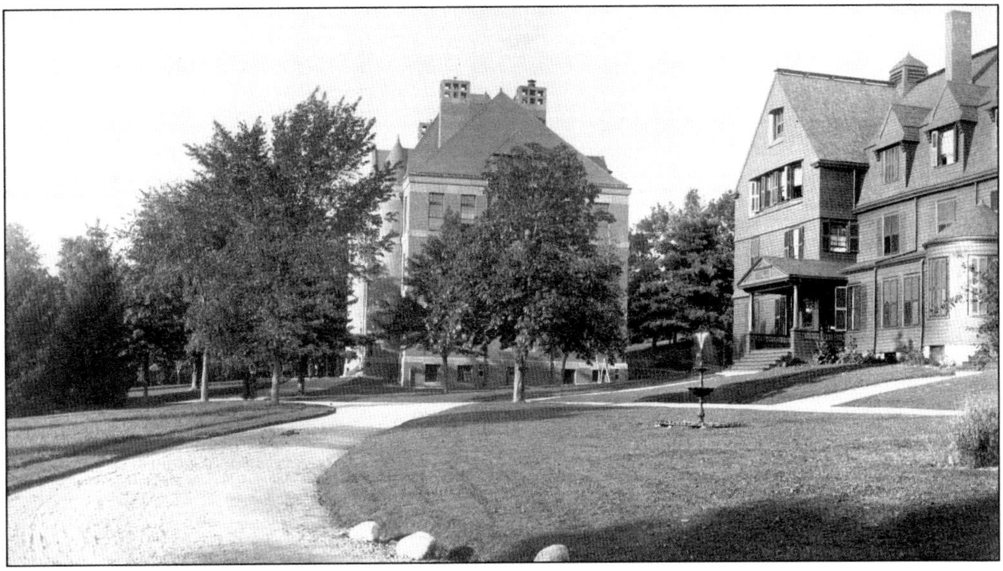

A View of May and Crocker Halls, c. 1910. This is a view from the south, where today Horace Mann Hall is located. Horace Mann replaced the Normal Hall dormitory, which burned in 1914. In 1910, the campus had a student population of 269.

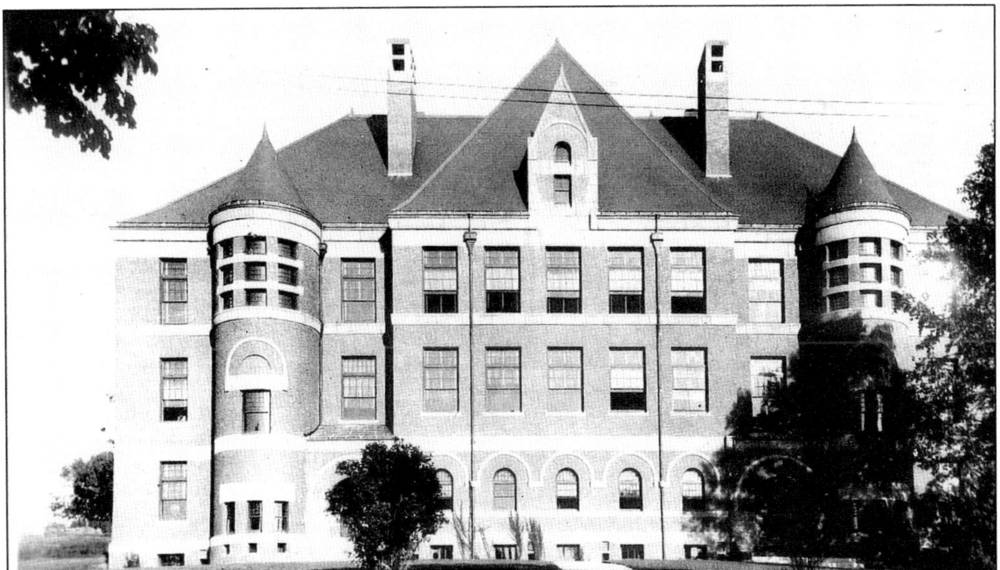

May Hall, c. 1900. As demonstrated by the number of buildings comprising the institution, the Normal School was growing. Crocker Hall, named for Lucretia Crocker, opened in 1886 and May Hall opened in 1889, and housed classrooms. In 1898, May Hall began housing the Household Arts Department, formerly the relocated Boston Normal School of Cookery.

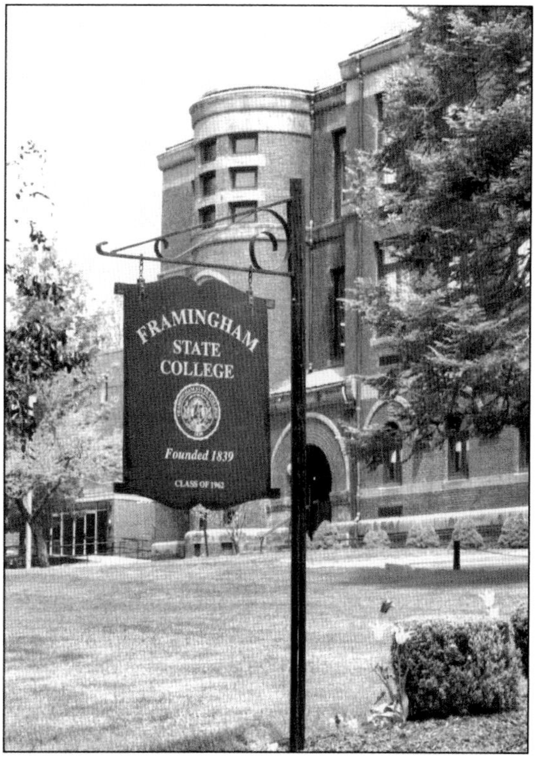

The Signpost in Front of May Hall. Abby May, the official visitor to the Normal School appointed by the Massachusetts Board of Education, was a strong advocate on behalf of the school. May Hall was named in her honor. She promoted women's rights, and with Lucretia Crocker (Class of 1850), helped advance the role of women in education. Her cousin Samuel May was the second principal of the school.

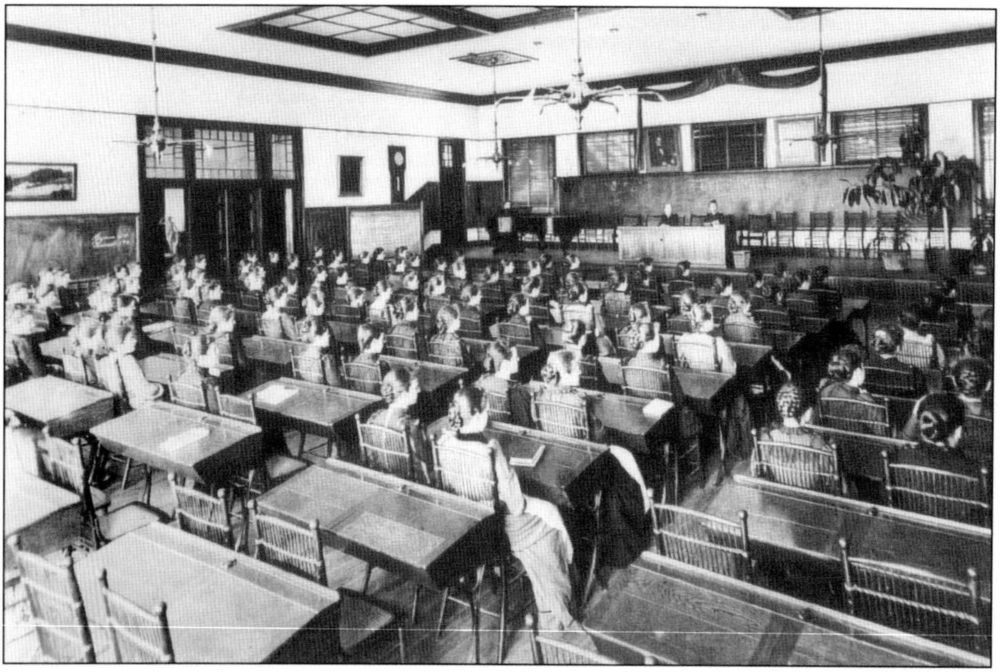

The Assembly Room, May Hall, *c.* 1890. When the school first opened in 1839, some subject areas were approached gingerly. As one administrator opined, "Some of the most vital and important details of science cannot even be alluded to before a class of ladies; [such subjects] . . . can only be taught by the lecturer in a medical school."

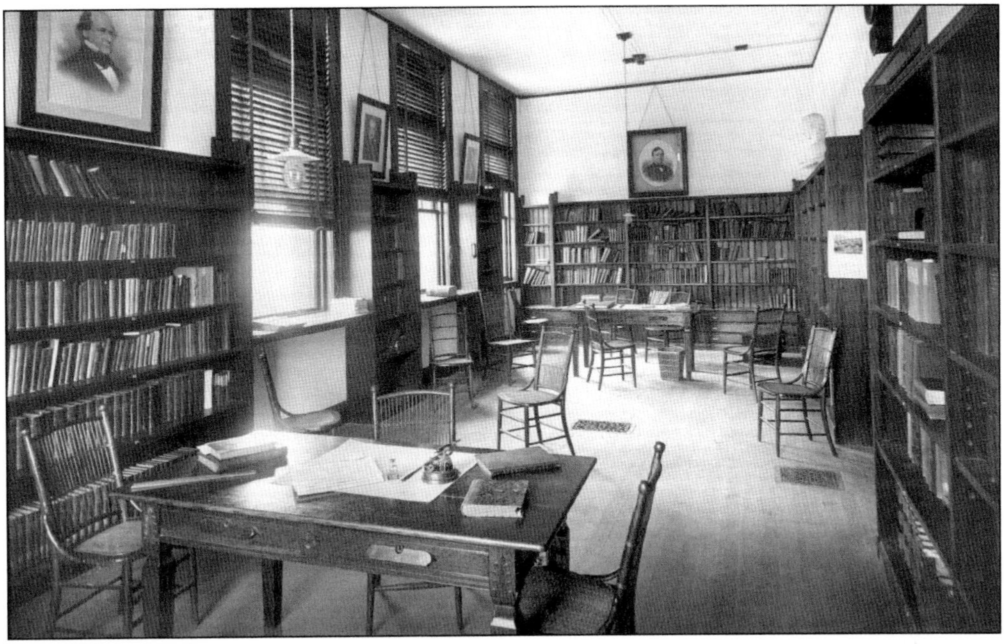

The Library, May Hall, 1892. This single room served as the college's library from 1889 to 1937, after which it was moved to Dwight Hall. Today, the Whittemore Library is housed in its own building with not only thousands of books but also technology that enables communication throughout the world.

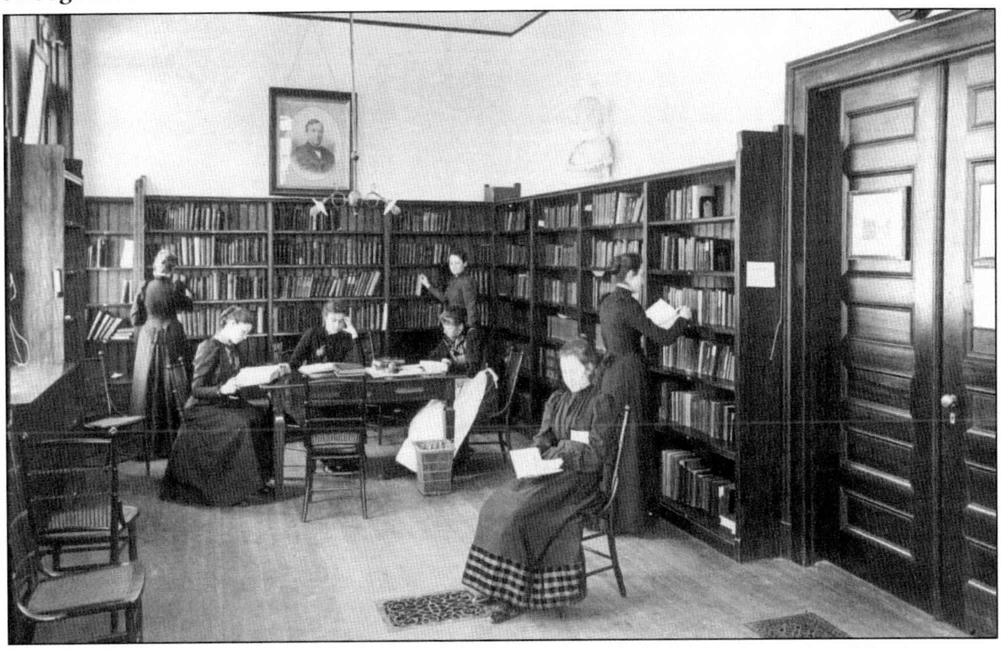

Students Using the Library, *c.* 1890. By the start of the college's 51st year, the rigors of higher education had intensified. Gone were the one-year courses, which were replaced with two-year and advanced four-year programs. The four-year program included courses in advanced algebra, geometry, trigonometry, surveying, chemistry, physics, and botany. Languages included Latin, French, German, and Greek.

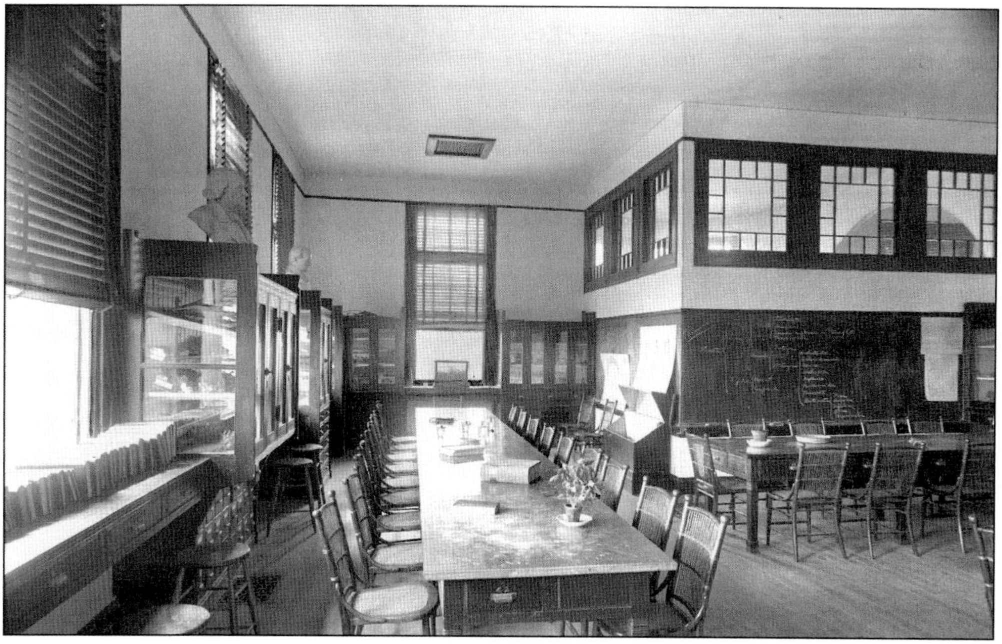

The Biology Room, May Hall, 1892. At the very start of the school, its first principal, Cyrus Peirce, was not only an administrator but a teacher as well. He eschewed the stick, believing it counterproductive in disciplinary matters. A teacher's goal was to instill in students the excitement of knowledge as a reward in and of itself.

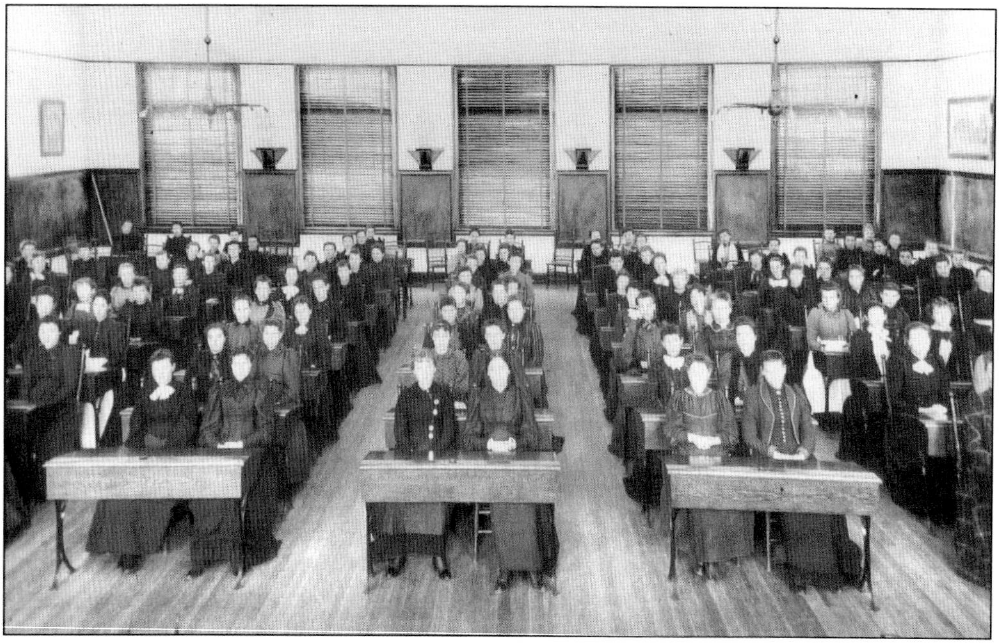

A Lecture Room in May Hall. The school day often started at 8:45 a.m. and ended at 1:45 p.m. from Tuesday through Saturday. At the outset, prayer and Scriptures were taught and sung. Each class period was approximately 55 minutes long, and after classes, the students were expected to engage in physical exercise for at least one hour. Dinner was at 5:30 p.m., followed by a two-hour study period, from 7:00 p.m. to 9:00 p.m. The school day ended at 10:00 p.m.

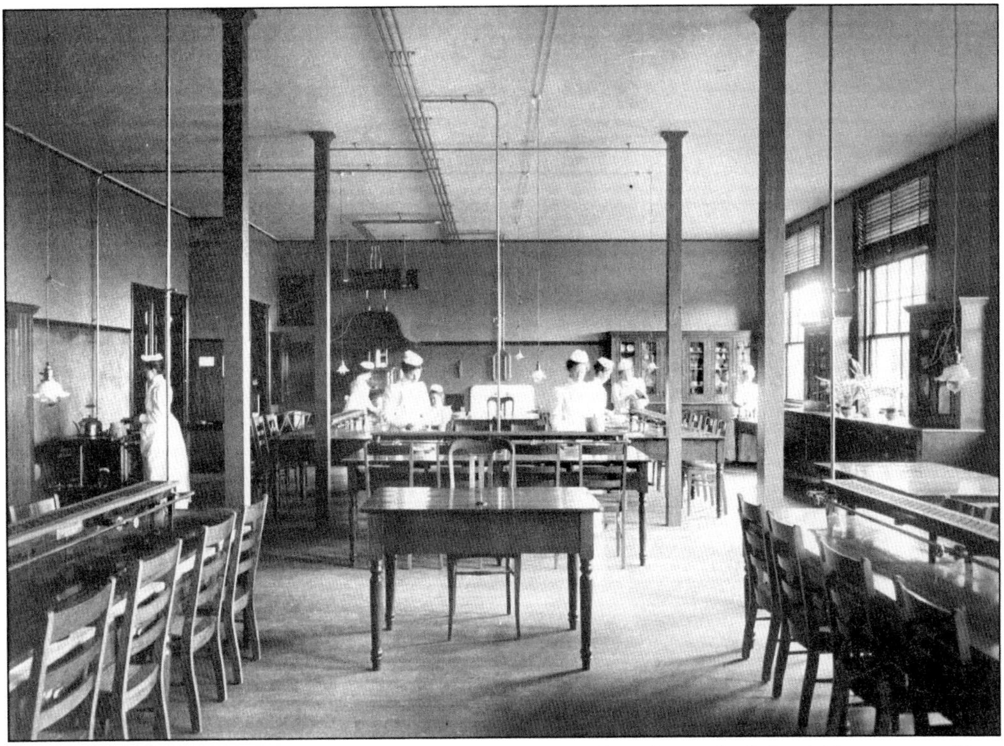

Cooking Class. The Household Arts program was started at the end of the 19th century. Mary Hemenway was a philanthropist who founded the Boston Normal School of Cookery in 1887. In 1898, the program moved to the Framingham campus and became the Mary Hemenway Department of Household Arts. That was the official name until 1915, when the Cooking was one part of the curriculum.

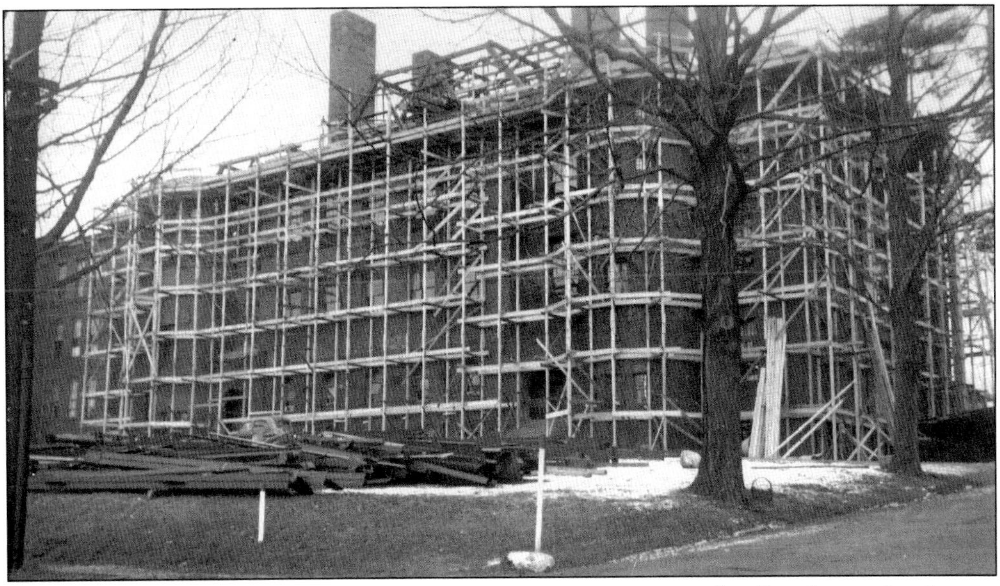

May Hall under Repair, 1939. Like other buildings on campus, May Hall suffered extensive damage caused by the Hurricane of 1938. This picture shows the extent of the repairs to the hall.

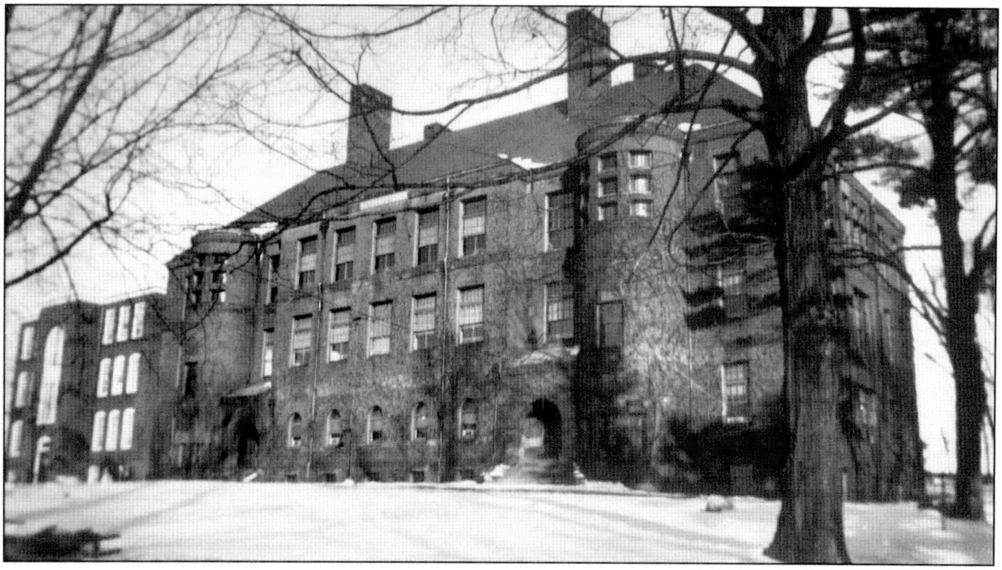

May Hall Repaired, 1940. The upper portion of the building had been severely damaged in the Hurricane of 1938. Among the repairs were new windows and a roof. The turrets, which had been a distinctive feature of the original building, were demolished.

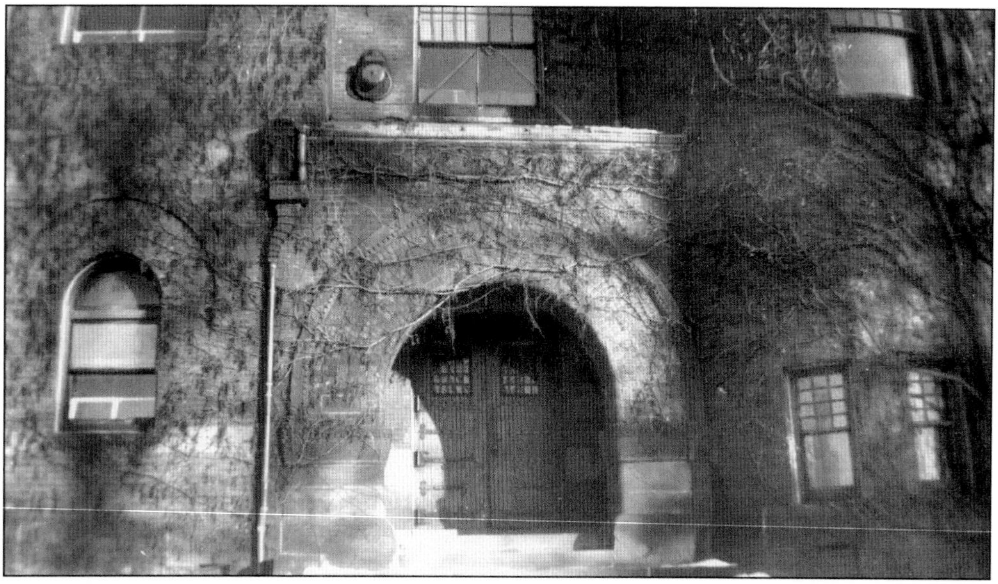

The Doorway to May Hall, 1940. May Hall had two small lunchrooms, primarily for commuters, before Peirce Hall was built in 1914. Before there was a dining area in Peirce, students who lived on campus took their meals in Crocker and Normal Halls.

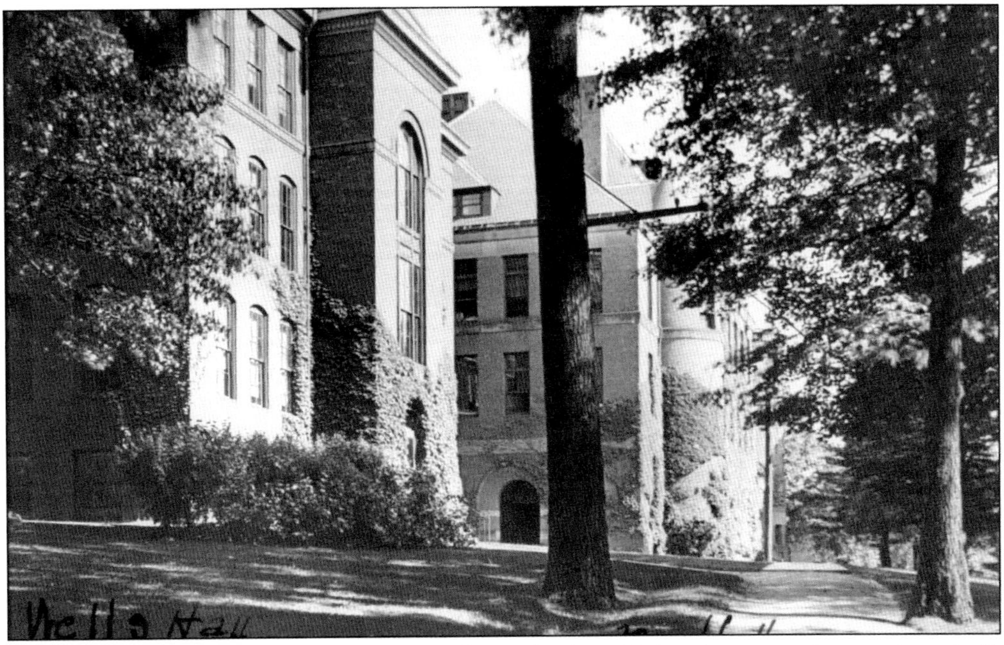

Wells and May Halls, c. 1915. Wells Hall (left) was built in 1902 and was razed approximately 60 years later. It was named for Kate Gannett Wells, who succeeded Abby May as official visitor to the Normal School.

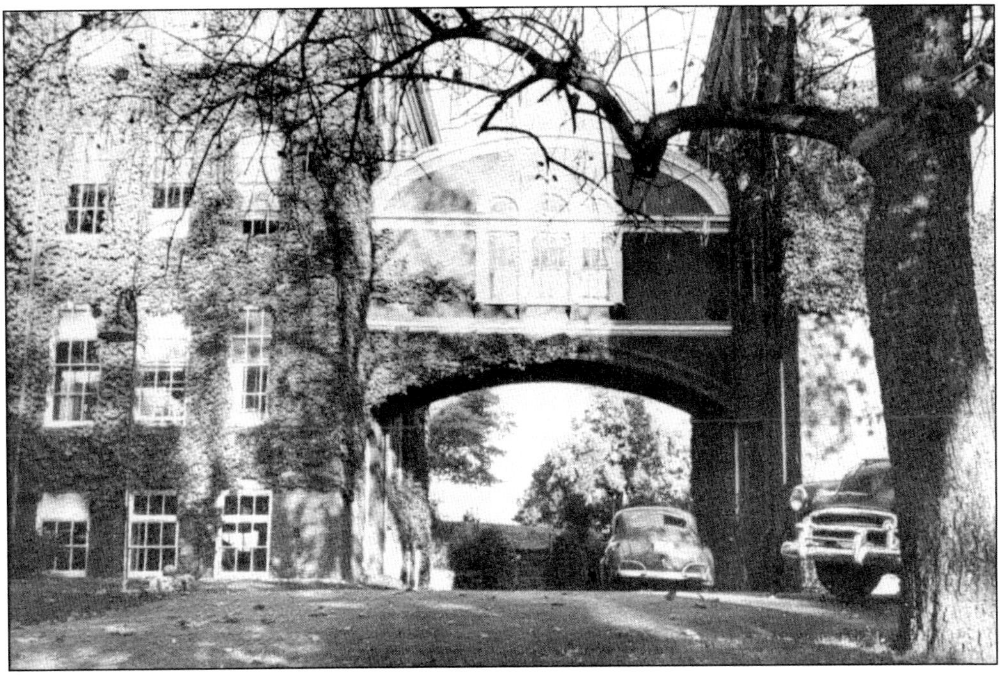

The Bridge of Sighs, c. the 1950s. This arched pedestrian bridge was frequently referred to as "the Bridge of Sighs," after the original one in Venice, Italy. This aboveground structure connected Wells Hall to the north side of May Hall; an underground tunnel also ran between the two buildings.

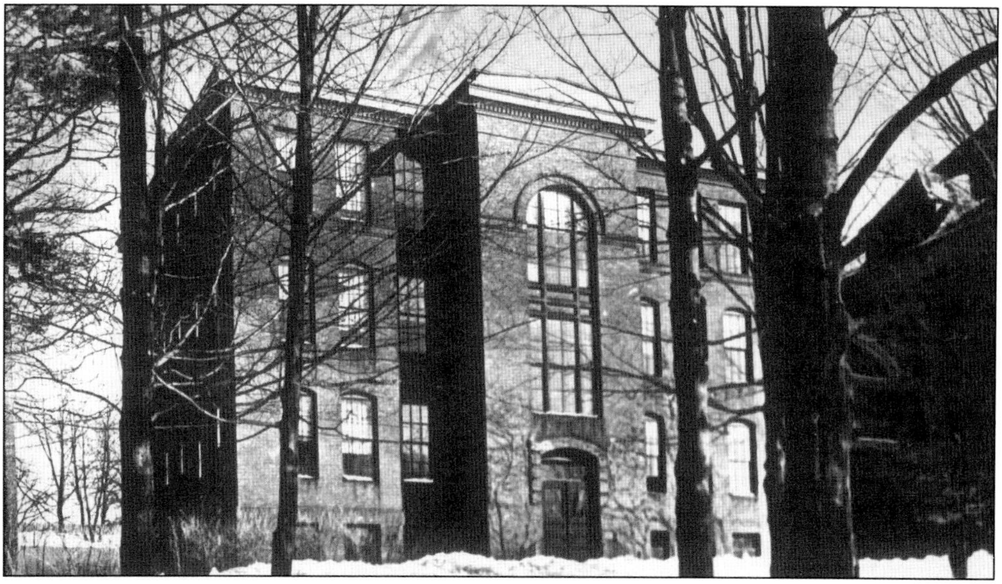

Wells Hall, the Late 1930s. Wells Hall was sparsely constructed, apparently reflecting Kate Gannett Wells's philosophy, which encouraged thriftiness. The Massachusetts Board of Education said "no simpler or more convenient building than this one has even been erected for so small a sum of money." Wells Hall added classrooms, laboratories, a gymnasium (with showers), a carpentry practice area, a large art room, and a room for a kindergarten. In 1962, it was replaced by Hemenway Hall.

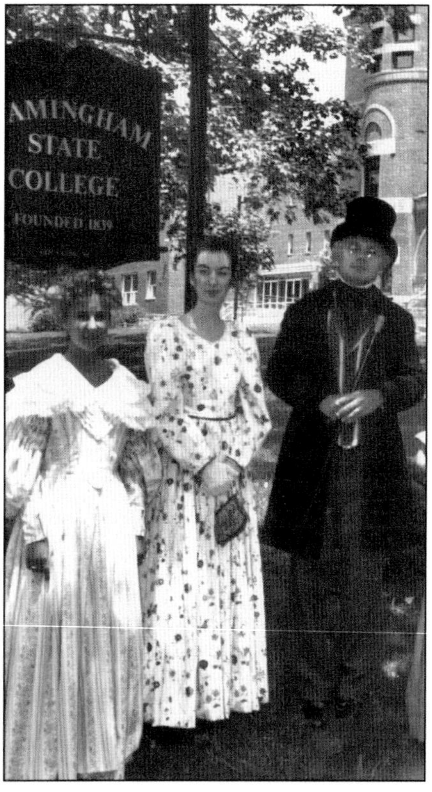

"Horace Mann." Dr. P. Bradley Nutting, a history professor at Framingham State, portrays Horace Mann at a ceremony celebrating the college's 150th anniversary in 1989. Clothing and Textile students Nancy Elizabeth Oste (left) and Brenda Lynn, both Class of 1989, join him. The attire of all three is representative of the styles at the time of the school's founding.

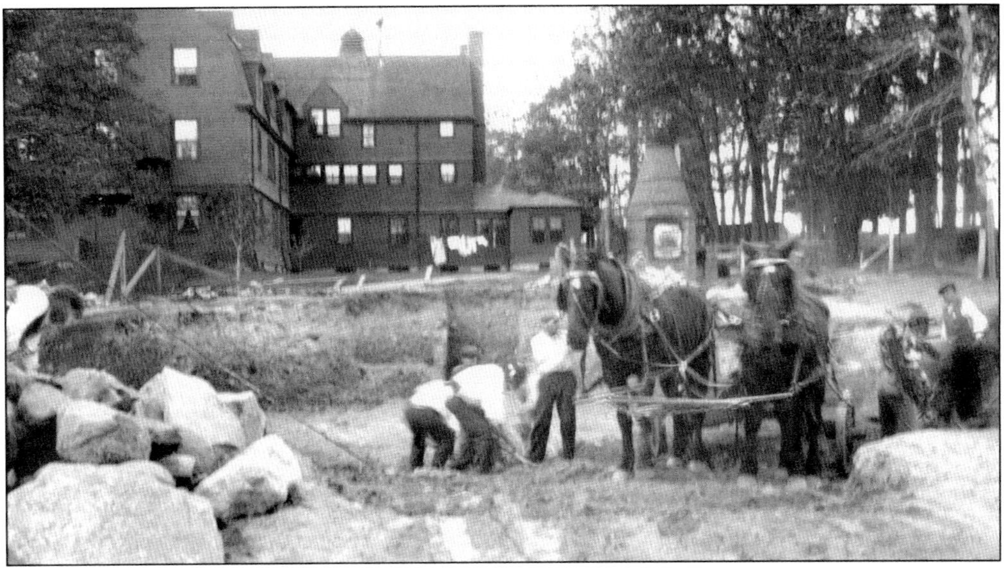

Peirce Hall, October 1914. In addition to providing housing, the building also replaced Crocker Hall as the dining facility. The dining hall moved to the D. Justin McCarthy College Center in 1976. The former dining hall space is now the home of the Center for Academic Support and Advising (CASA).

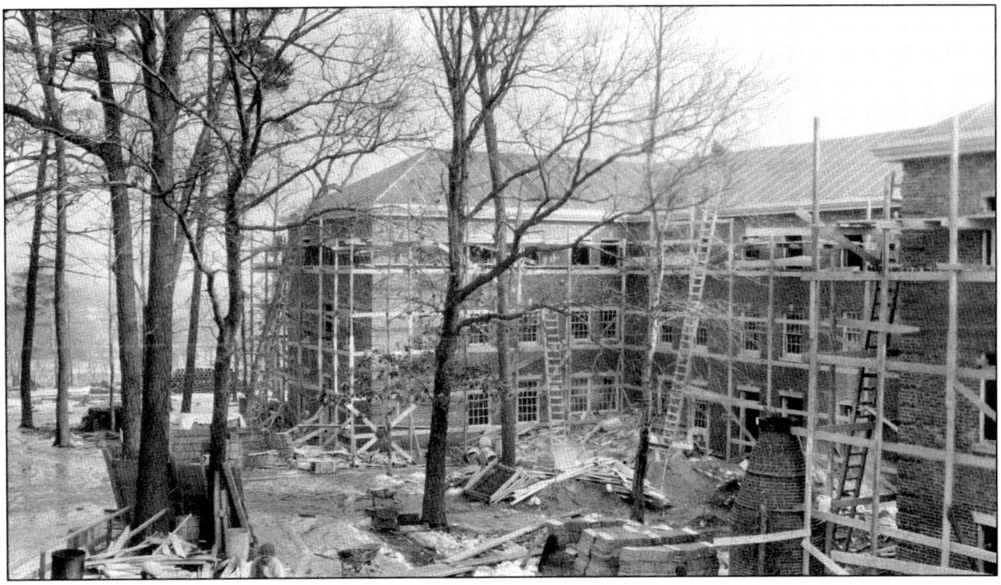

Peirce Hall under Construction, February 1915. Named for Rev. Cyrus J. Peirce (see pages 11 and 48), the first principal of the Normal School in Lexington from 1839 to 1842 and in West Newton from 1844 to 1849. Peirce Hall, built just east of the burned-out Normal Hall dormitory, replaced the latter as a residence.

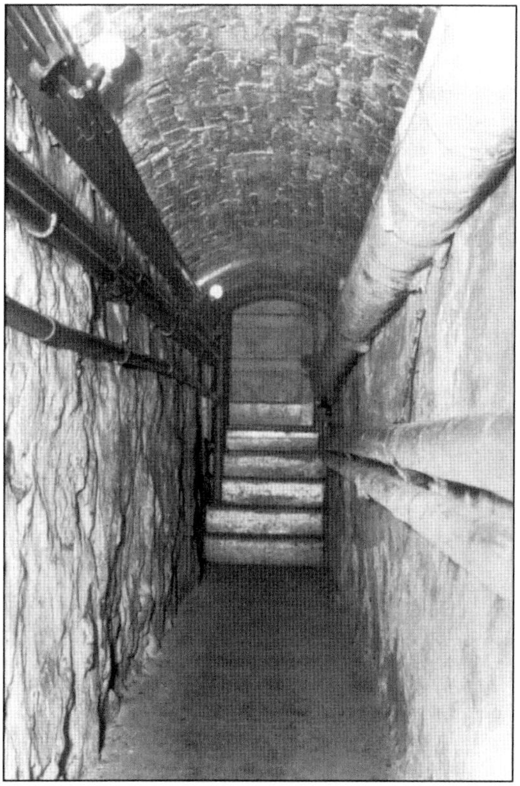

A Tunnel between the Halls. By 1920, a series of tunnels connected Wells, May, Crocker, Horace Mann, and Peirce Halls. The tunnels were three feet wide and six feet high, and were built to carry electrical and drainage pipes. Students also used them until the tunnels were eventually closed for safety reasons.

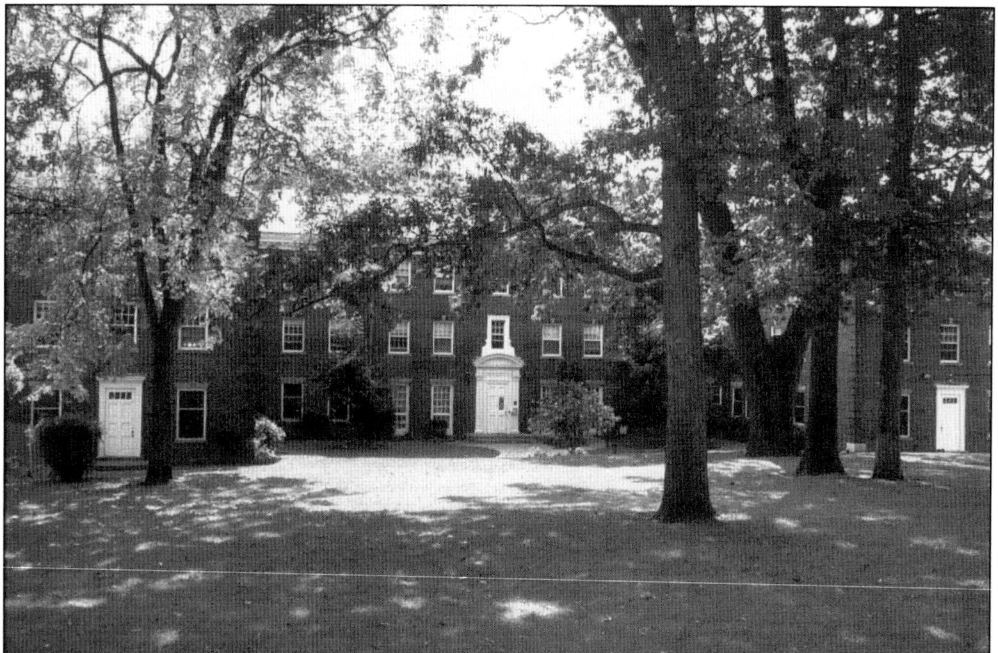

Peirce Today. Peirce is a residence hall for female students and houses the Center for Academic Support and Advising (CASA). Peirce Hall also serves as the campus mailroom and storage area.

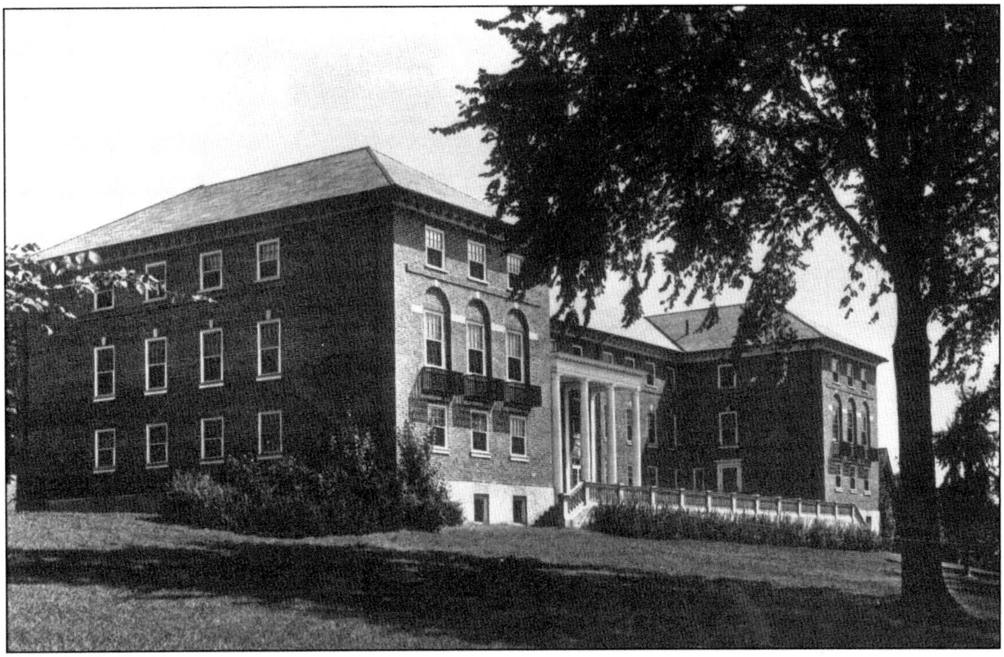

Horace Mann Hall. Opened in 1920 and still in use today, Horace Mann Hall was built on the site of the Normal School dormitory that fell victim to fire in 1914. Money was appropriated in 1917 for construction of the new hall, but due to World War I, ground was not broken until 1920. Architecturally, Horace Mann Hall is considered a sister residence to Peirce Hall, and houses primarily juniors and seniors. A portion of the building also served as the president's residence from 1920 to 1962.

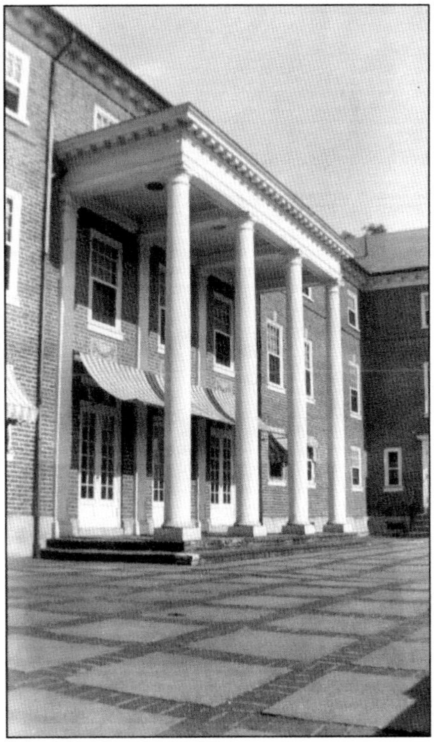

The Entrance to Horace Mann, 1939. The hall was named for Horace Mann (see page 10). Mann, (1796–1859) was an inspired Massachusetts educator, who carried the early and difficult years of the Normal School through to success. Without his leadership, schools in Massachusetts would not have opened until years later.

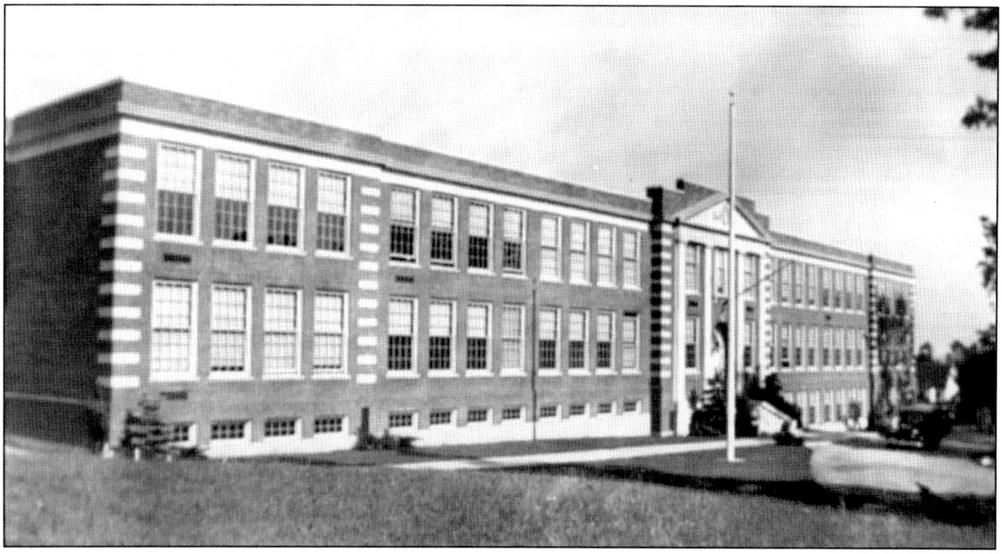

Dwight Hall, 1939. Named for Edmund Dwight (see page 10), a 19th-century philanthropist and member of the first Massachusetts Board of Education, Dwight Hall was under construction from 1935 to 1937. Dwight's contribution of $10,000 helped establish the school, and the building bearing his name houses classrooms and administrative offices. In 1955, an auditorium and gymnasium were built as a separate wing on the back of Dwight Hall. From 1937 to 1969, Dwight Hall housed the library on the second floor.

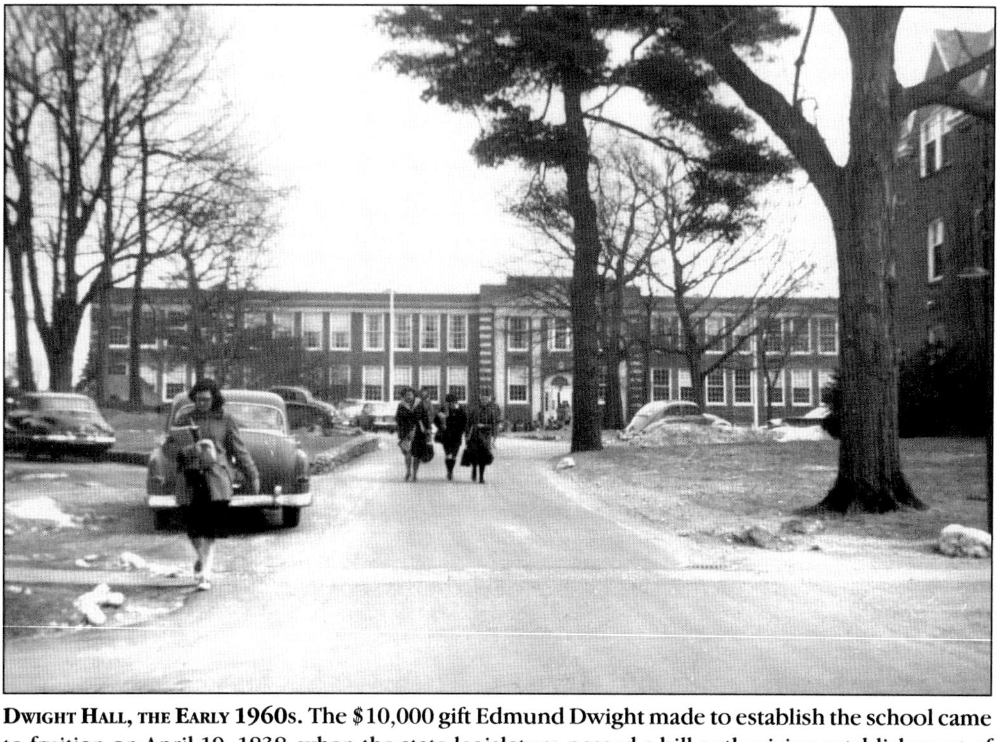

Dwight Hall, the Early 1960s. The $10,000 gift Edmund Dwight made to establish the school came to fruition on April 19, 1838, when the state legislature passed a bill authorizing establishment of the normal schools. Crocker Hall appears at the right in this photograph.

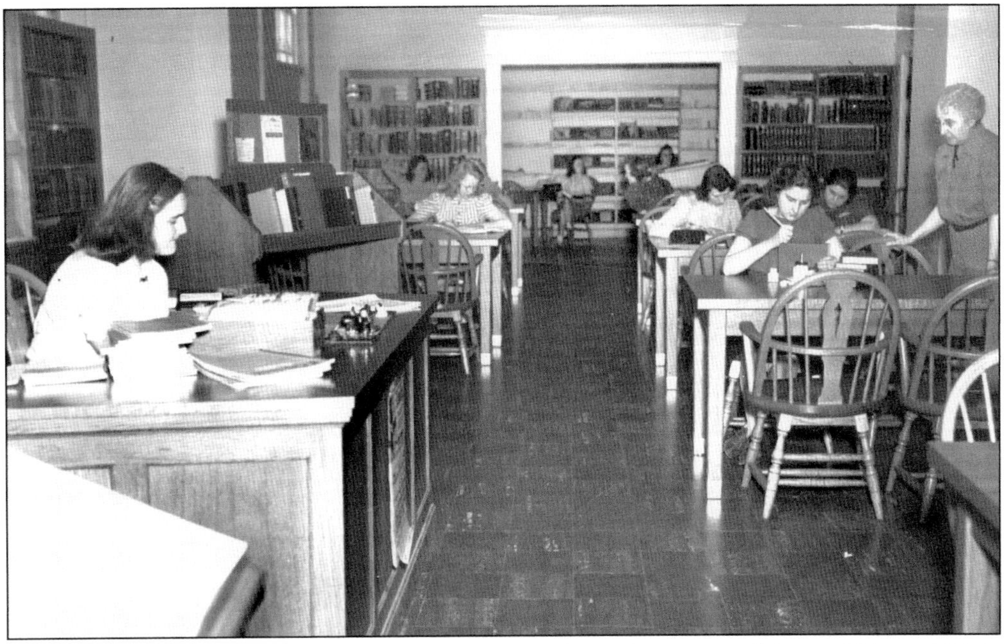

Dwight Hall Library, May 15, 1940. The library was located in May Hall from 1889 to 1937. In 1937, it moved to Dwight Hall, where it remained until 1969, when it again was moved, this time to its own building, the Whittemore Library. In this photograph, a student covers the front desk, while another binds and letters books under the watchful eye of the librarian.

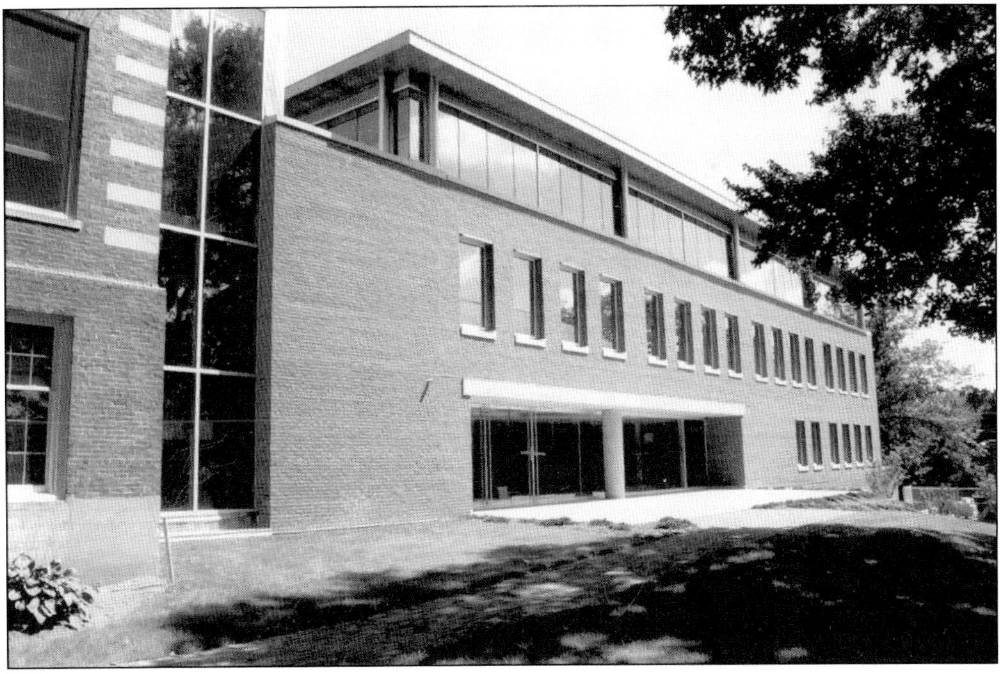

The Athletic and Recreation Center, 2003. Connected to the south side of Dwight Hall, the Athletic and Recreation Center opened in the fall of 2001. It houses a gymnasium, locker rooms, athletic training rooms and offices, as well as the college bookstore. Also featured is a fitness center, providing aerobics, conditioning, yoga, spinning, nutrition, and personal training programs.

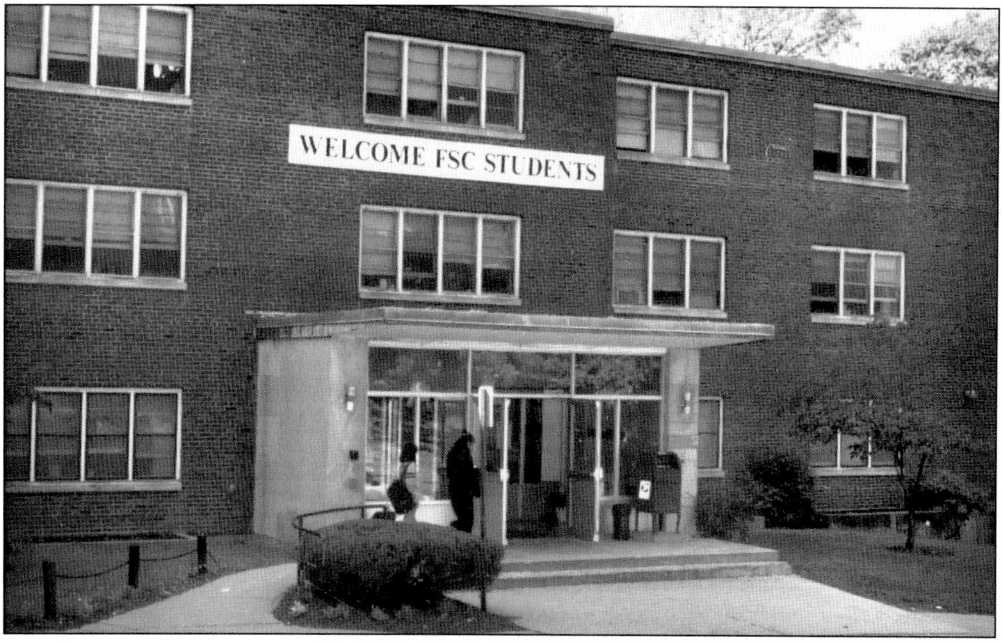

O'CONNOR HALL. Named for Martin F. O'Connor (see page 54), the president of the college from 1936 to 1961, O'Connor Hall was opened in 1961. The building currently serves as a residence hall for women and houses both the College Health Services Center and the McAuliffe Challenger Center.

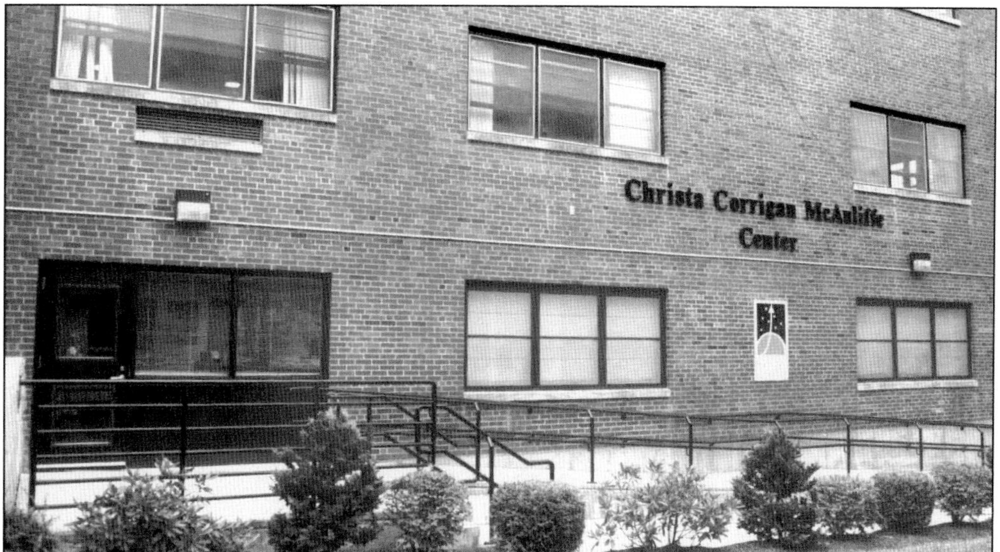

THE CHRISTA CORRIGAN MCAULIFFE CENTER FOR EDUCATION AND TEACHING EXCELLENCE. Located in the rear of O'Connor Hall, the center is affiliated with the Challenger Center for Space Science Education, a nonprofit corporation based in Alexandria, Virginia. It is a resource facility for teachers and students, kindergarten through 12th grade. It includes a simulated space station, curricula resources, and mission simulations exploring the Moon and Mars and the comets, and math, science, and technology workshops. More than 12,000 middle school students visit the center each year.

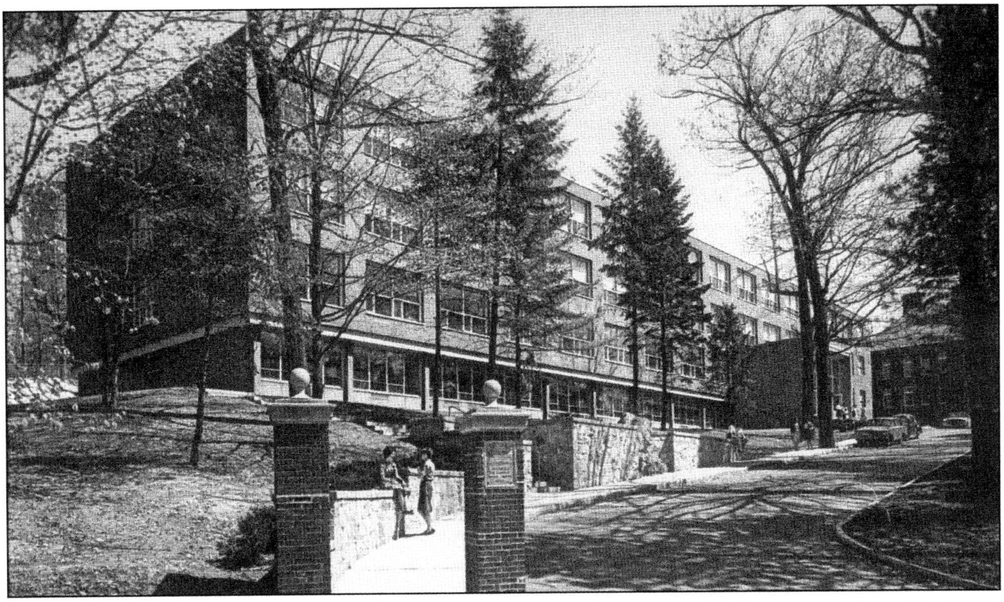

Hemenway Hall, 1964. Begun in 1960, construction on Hemenway Hall was completed in 1962. Named for Mary Hemenway, the building replaced Wells Hall and greatly expanded classroom space. It contains classrooms and laboratories for courses in biology, chemistry, clothing and textiles, consumer and family studies, earth science, food and nutrition, food science, geography, geology, mathematics, nursing, physics, and psychology. It is also the location of the Food Pilot Plant Laboratory and the Marion Scherner Leonhard Multimedia Technology Laboratory.

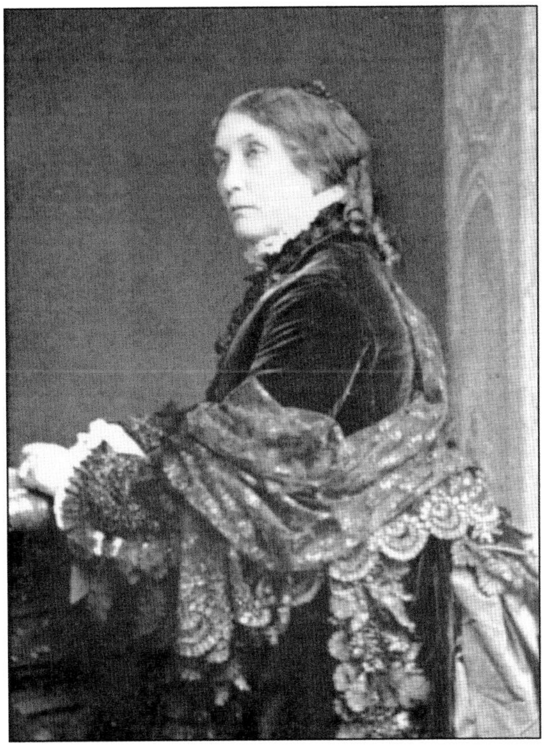

Mary Porter Tileston Hemenway. Mary Hemenway (1820–1894) was a Boston philanthropist. In 1883, she started a vocational school, and two years later, in 1885, opened the nation's first educational kitchen in a Boston public school. In 1887, she established the Boston Normal School of Cookery, which in 1898 was moved to the Normal School at Framingham and became the Mary Hemenway Department of Household Arts.

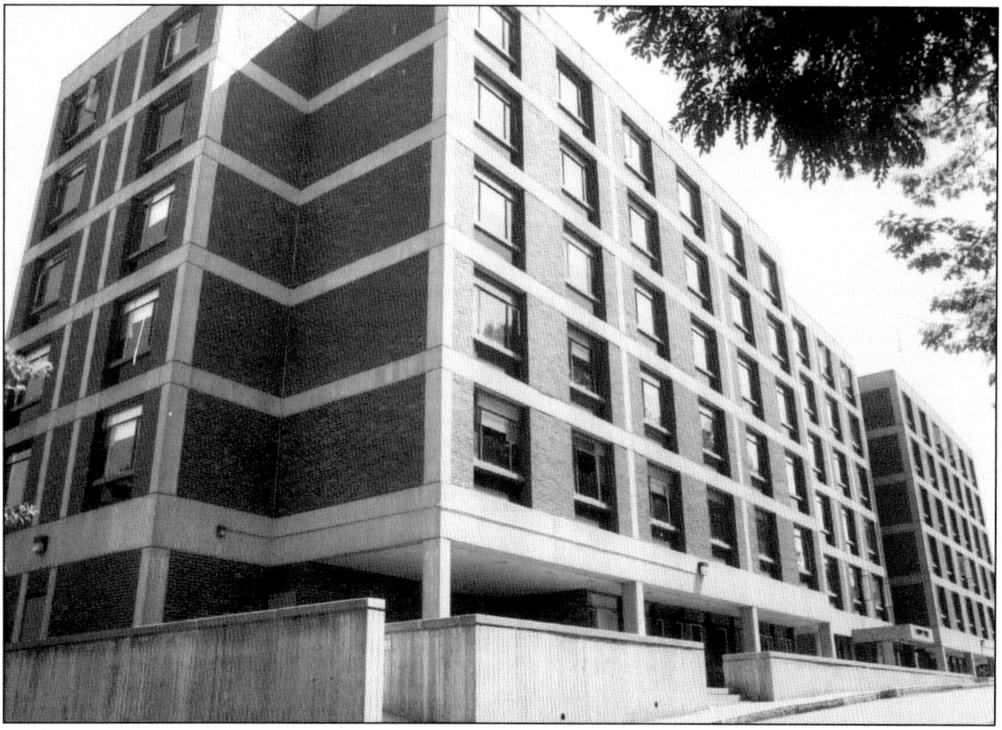

Larned Hall. Named for the former dean of women, Dorothy Larned, the facility opened in 1968. Originally a residence for women, the six-story building has housed male and female students since September 1973.

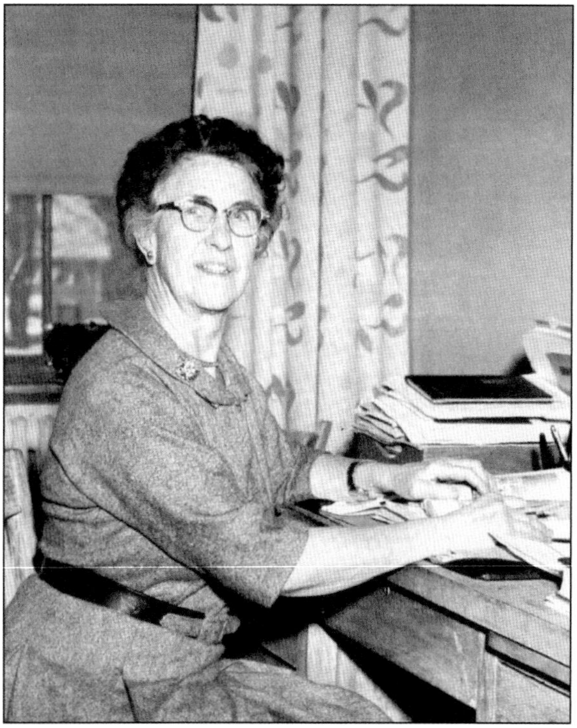

Dorothy Larned. Starting in 1929, Dorothy Larned taught French and English at the school. She served as the dean of women from 1943 to 1961, when she retired. In 1969, she spoke at the dedication of the building named for her and, in 1988, she received an honorary degree from the college.

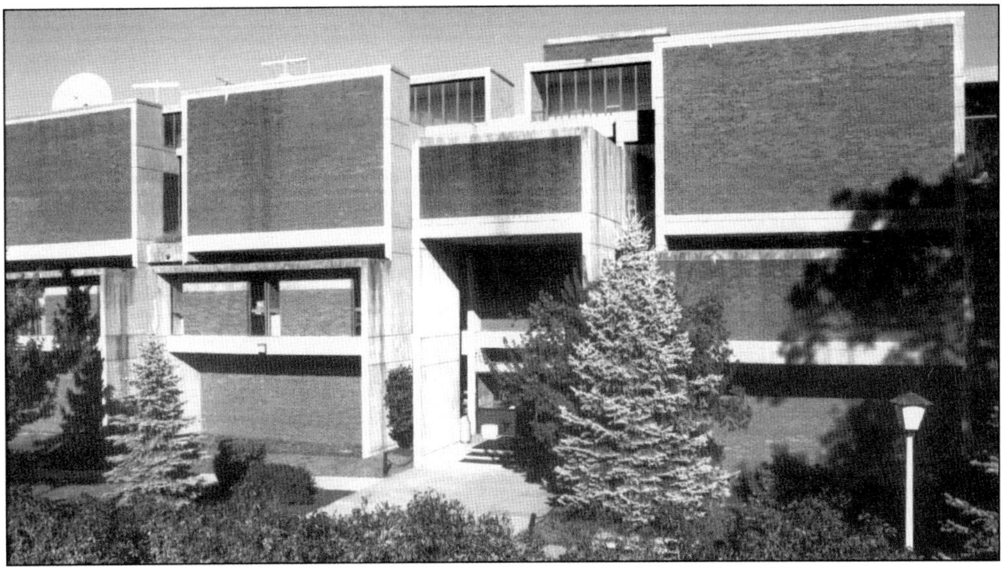

The Whittemore Library. The fourth location—following the Normal School Building, May Hall, and Dwight Hall—for the library since the school's founding, the Whittemore Library opened in 1969. Named for Henry Whittemore, the seventh principal, the seven-level structure also houses the Ellen C. Ritchie Curriculum Library, as well as the special collections and archives.

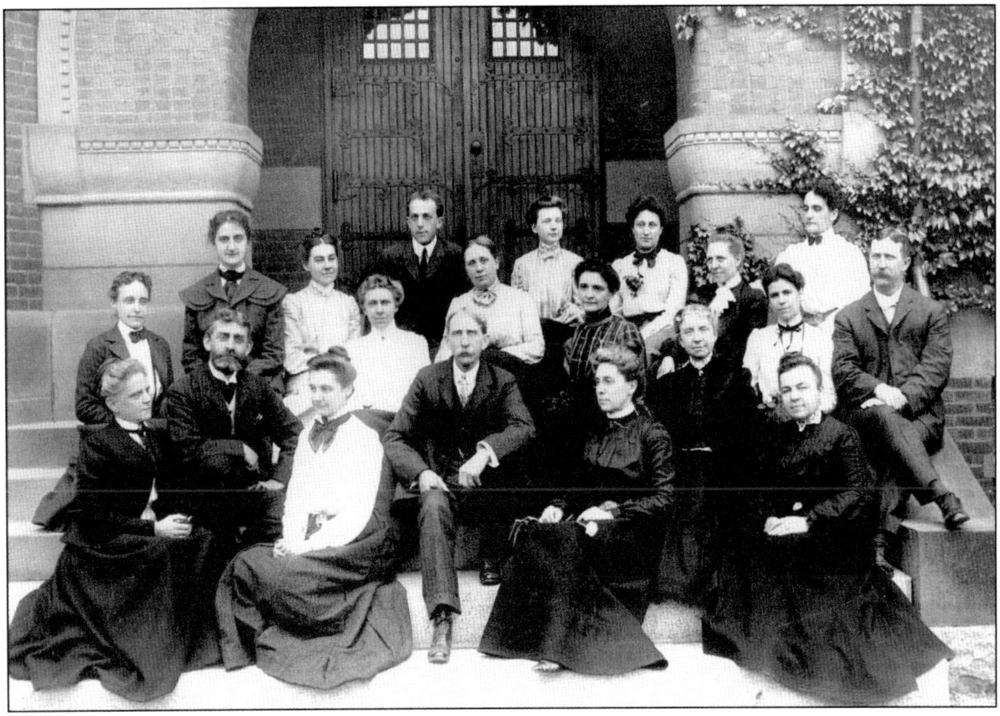

Henry Whittemore and the Faculty, in Front of May Hall, *c.* 1900. Henry Whittemore (center foreground) served as principal from 1898 to 1917, and during his tenure, the popularity and expansion of the Household Arts program grew so great that the education program was threatened with termination by the Massachusetts Board of Education. A concerted effort by the alumnae preserved the education program, which continues to this day.

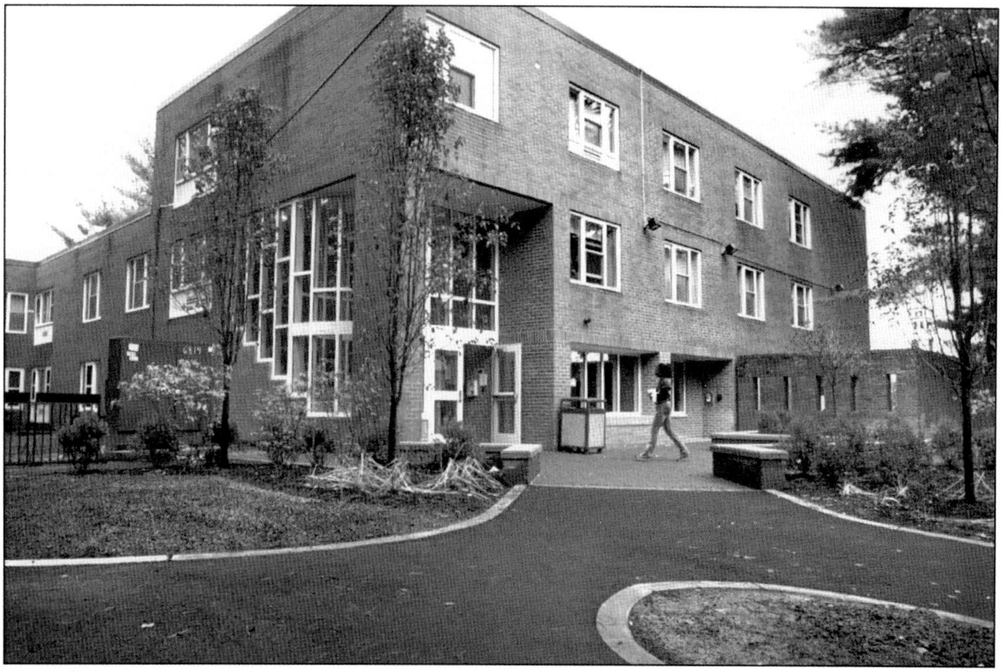

Linsley Hall. Opened in 1971, this building is named for history professor James Linsley and is located at the north end of Adams Road. Formerly an all-male residence, it is a three-story, three-winged co-ed student residence hall that was renovated in 2002.

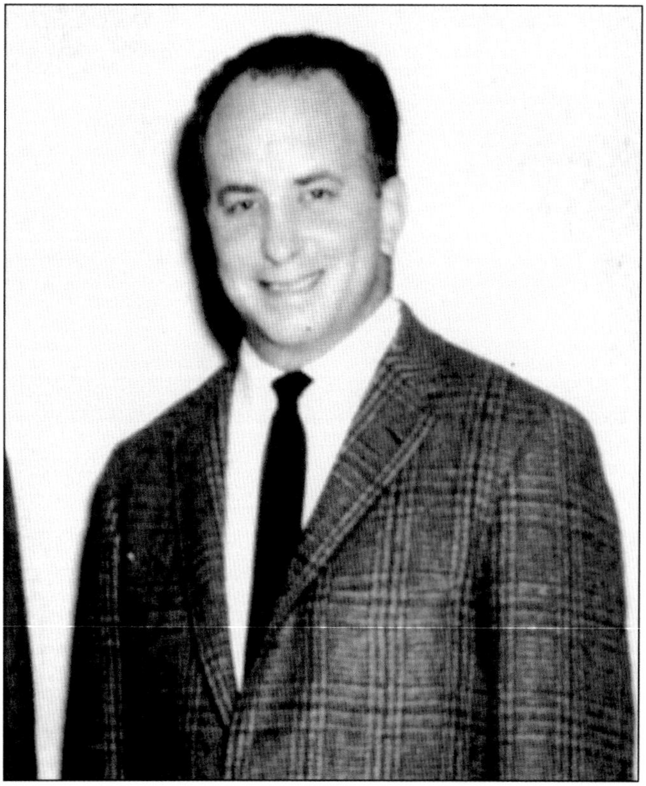

James D. Linsley. James Linsley (1936–1970) was a popular professor who taught pre–Civil War U.S. history and the history of minorities in America. Above his desk was this quote: "Generous encouragement is the necessary mental nourishment of youth, and those who withhold it from them are not only foolish but cruel. They are keeping food from the hungry." He collapsed and died while teaching a class on December 21, 1970.

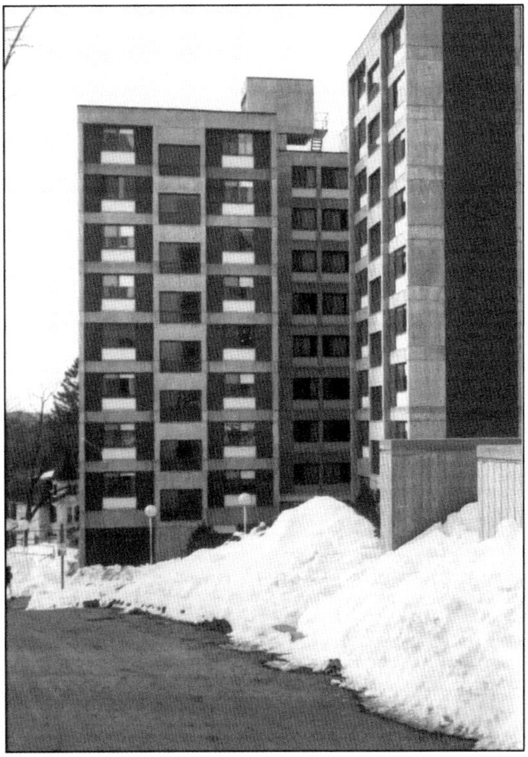

CORRINE HALL TOWERS, 1978. Opened in 1973, the 10-story Corrine Hall Towers is the largest of the school's residence halls. It also houses the Metrowest Economic Research Center, the John Stalker Institute for Food and Nutrition, and the Teachers in American Schools Overseas Program (TASO).

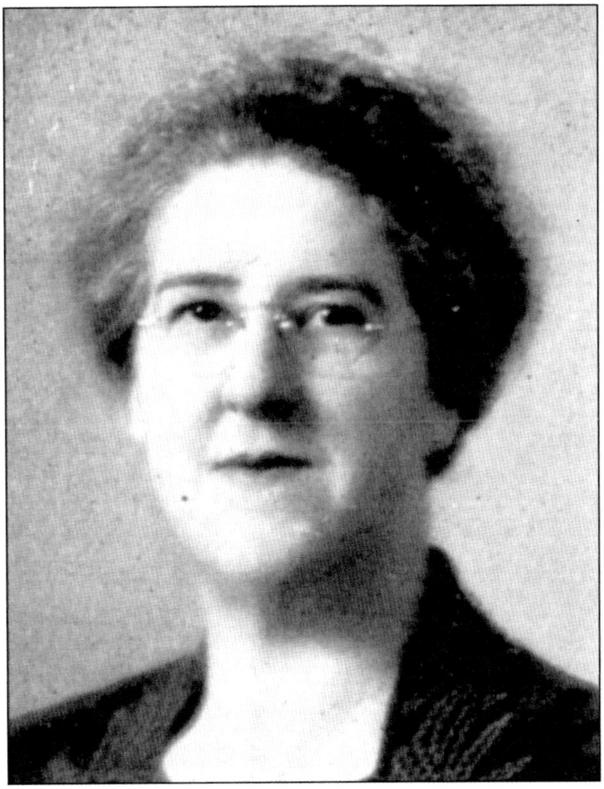

CORRINE E. HALL. Corrine Hall, Class of 1910, taught household administration and practice at the school for 33 years, from 1920 to 1953. Between 1910 and 1920, she received a bachelor's degree from Denver University and a master's degree from Columbia University. Many business and social functions were held in rooms managed and decorated by Professor Hall, whose exquisite taste and grace were evident.

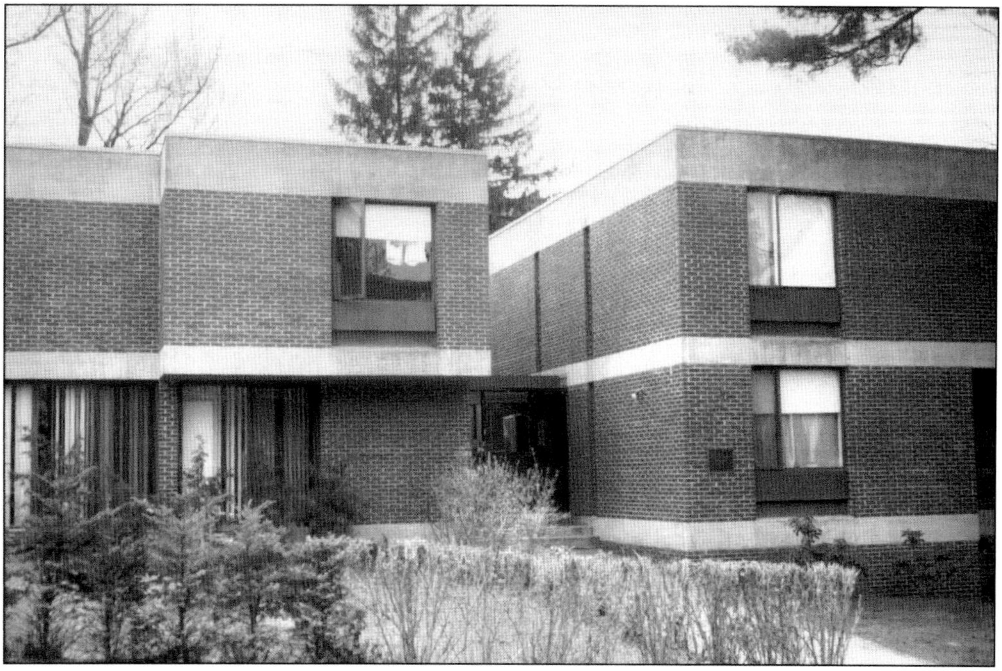

Foster Hall. Named for chemistry professor Stuart Foster, Foster Hall opened in 1973 and originally housed female students from what was the Home Economics Department. Today, it is a mixed-use building, located between O'Connor Hall and the College Center.

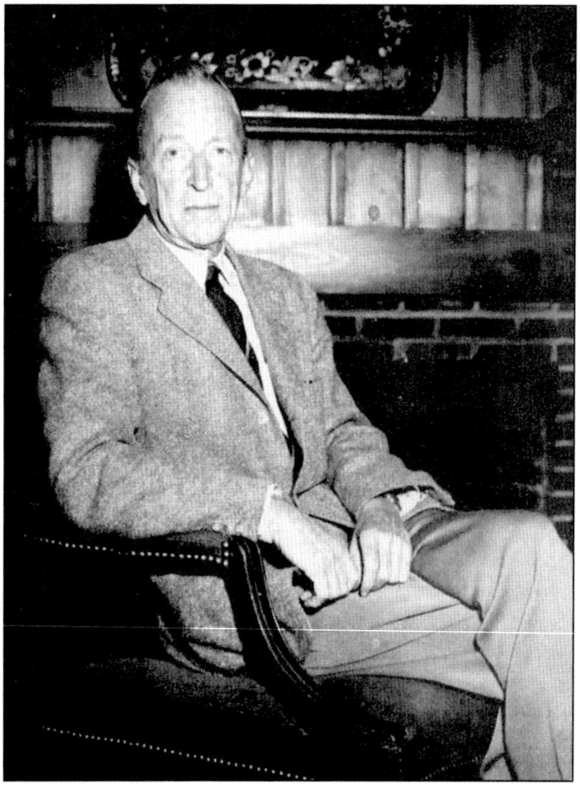

Stuart B. Foster. Dr. Stuart Foster (1891–1978) was considered the school's Mr. Chips. He taught from 1921 to 1957 and served as chairman of the Chemistry Department. He was also a member of the Framingham Choral Society. His daughter, Cynthia, was Class Baby of the Class of 1927.

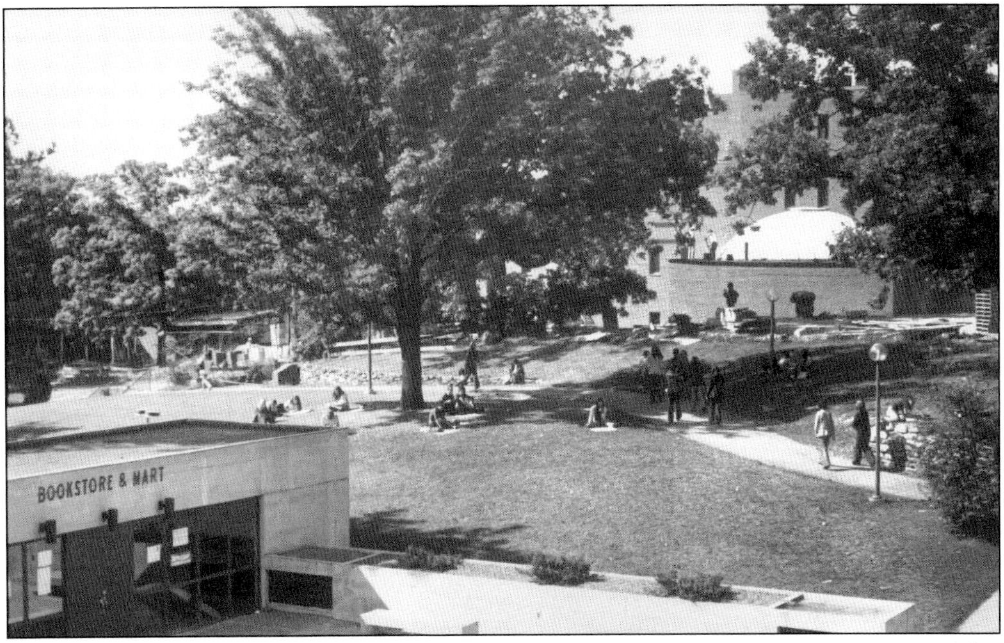

The Old Bookstore and Planetarium, c. 1976. On the left is the old Bookstore & Mart (1969–2001); on the right is the planetarium, attached to the Hemenway Hall annex. In 2002, the Arthur M. Doyle Technology Center replaced the bookstore, which moved to the new wing of Dwight Hall, the Athletic and Recreation Center. The Technology Center, named in honor of the late Arthur M. Doyle, a professor of physics and vice president of academic affairs, houses the offices of Information Technology Services.

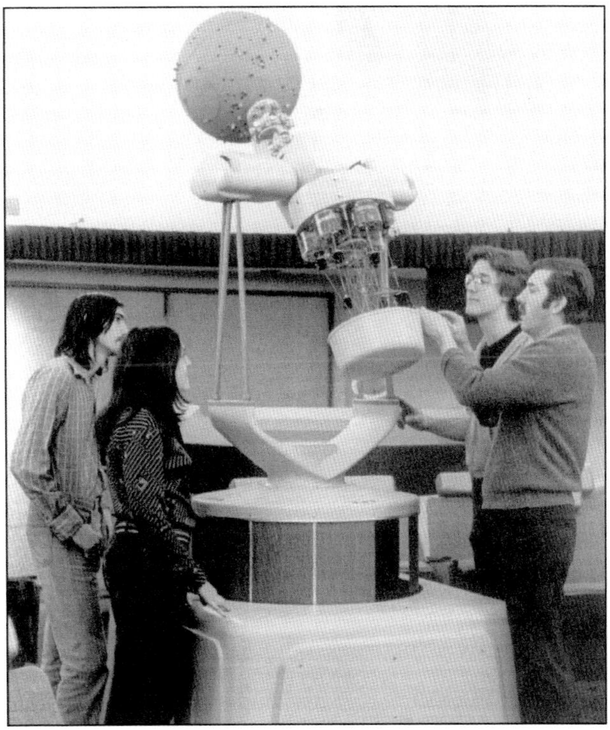

The Planetarium, March 19, 1975. Shown from left to right are Rick Fine ('77), Debbie DeCristoforo ('77), Marc Cedrone ('78), and John Murray, associate professor of physics, making minor adjustments to the equipment inside the new planetarium. The planetarium was completely renovated in 2003 to cater to both the college's population and the many middle school students who visit the McAuliffe Challenger Center.

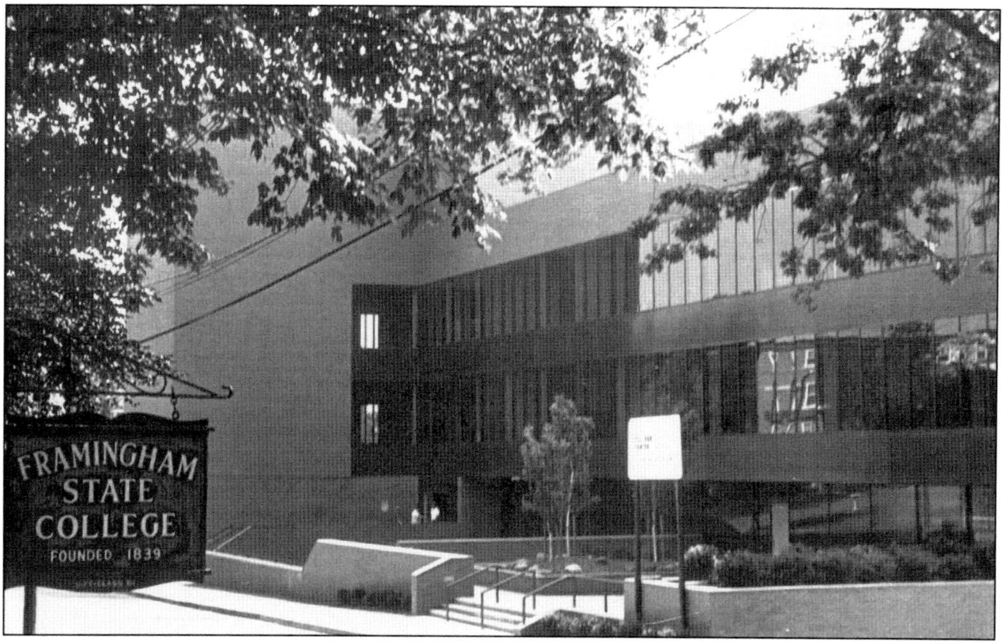

THE MCCARTHY COLLEGE CENTER. On April 1, 1976, the College Center opened. In 1985, it was named in honor of D. Justin McCarthy, the president of the college, who retired that year. The $4.25 million center was completed in 1975 but lacked the operational funds to open, due to a statewide 10 percent budget cut. A transfer of $80,000 from the state's reserve revenue account allowed the facility to finally open.

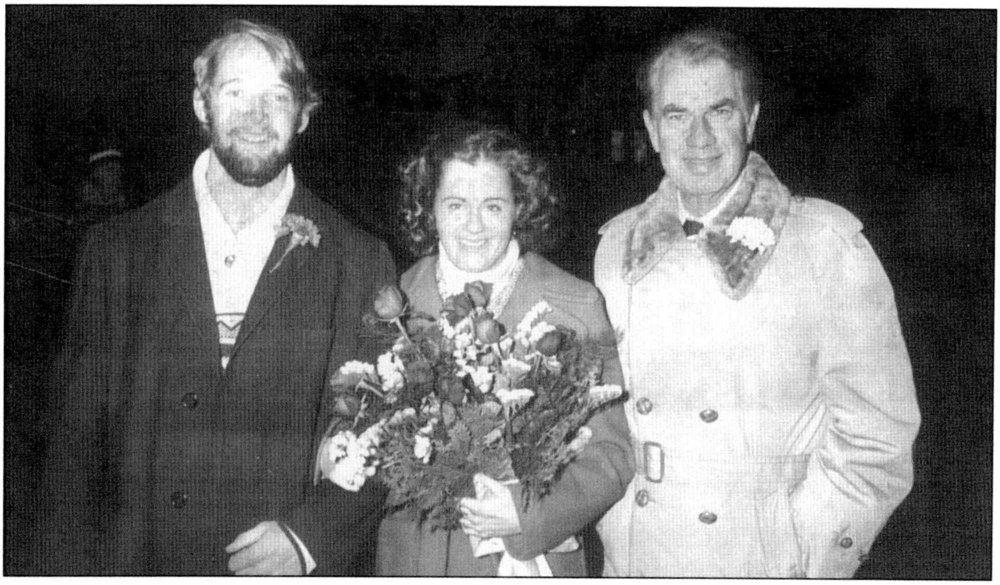

D. JUSTIN MCCARTHY, 1980. During halftime at the 1980 Homecoming football game, Dr. D. Justin McCarthy (right) stands with the Homecoming king and queen, junior Daniel Caulfield and senior Cary Alexander. Under McCarthy's leadership, 1961–1985, the college experienced its greatest growth: the student body increased 600 percent, the faculty tripled, numerous buildings were constructed, and the sports programs dramatically expanded. In 1981, the FSC Board of Trustees (the school's first) was established.

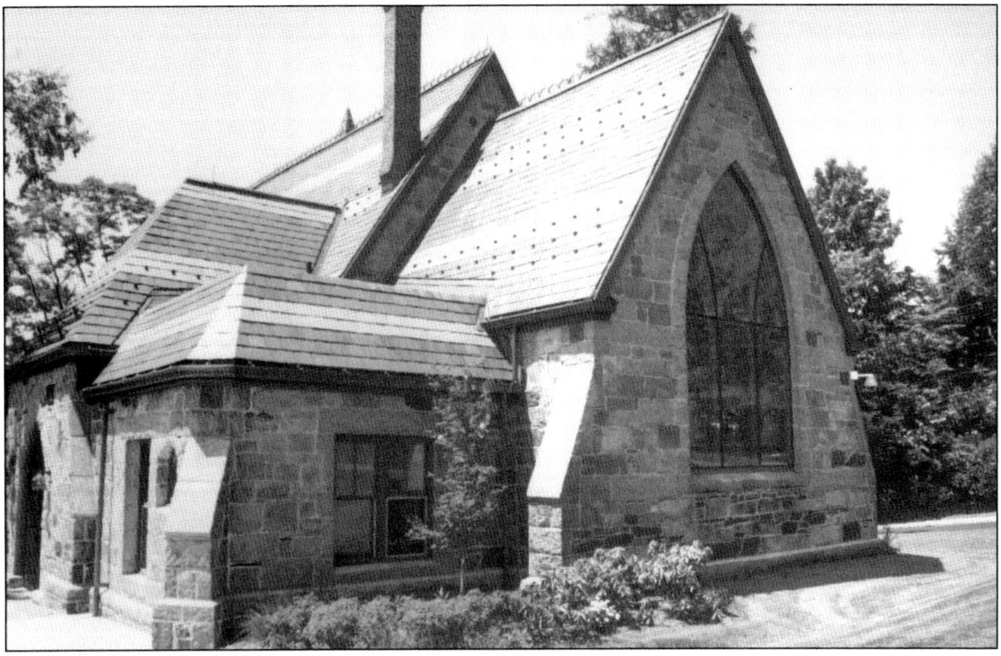

The Ecumenical and Cultural Center. The Ecumenical and Cultural Center reopened in 2000. Built in 1870 as St. John's Episcopal Church, it was sold in 1952 to the Seventh-Day Adventist Church of Natick as a meetinghouse. In 1969, it was sold to the college, which renamed it the Interdenominational Religious Center. Closed in 1985 due to structural deterioration, it was placed on the National Register of Historical Places in 1990. Through concerted efforts, it was restored and reopened in 2000.

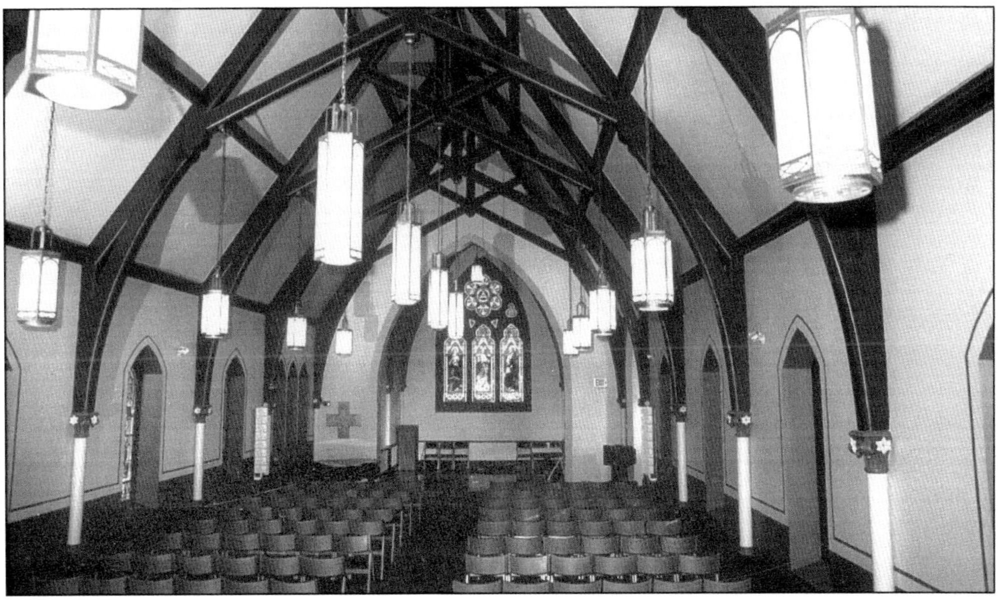

Inside the Ecumenical and Cultural Center. The center hosts religious and memorial services, as well as entertainment and educational events hosted by the Arts and Humanities Program. So significant was the role of religion in the institution, that until the 1950s, students were required to attend chapel services.

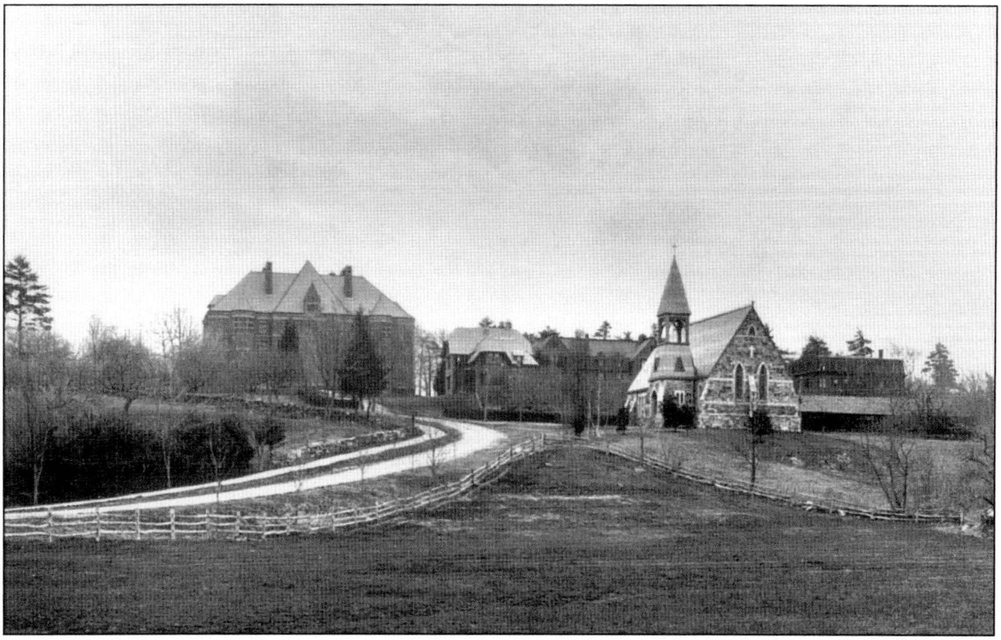

A View up Maynard Road, c. 1890. St. John's Episcopal Church stands in front of, from left to right, May, Crocker, and Normal Halls. Designed by Framingham architect Alexander Rice Esty, the church held its first service on Easter Sunday 1871. Now the Ecumenical and Cultural Center, it is one of only two buildings remaining in Framingham constructed of local granite.

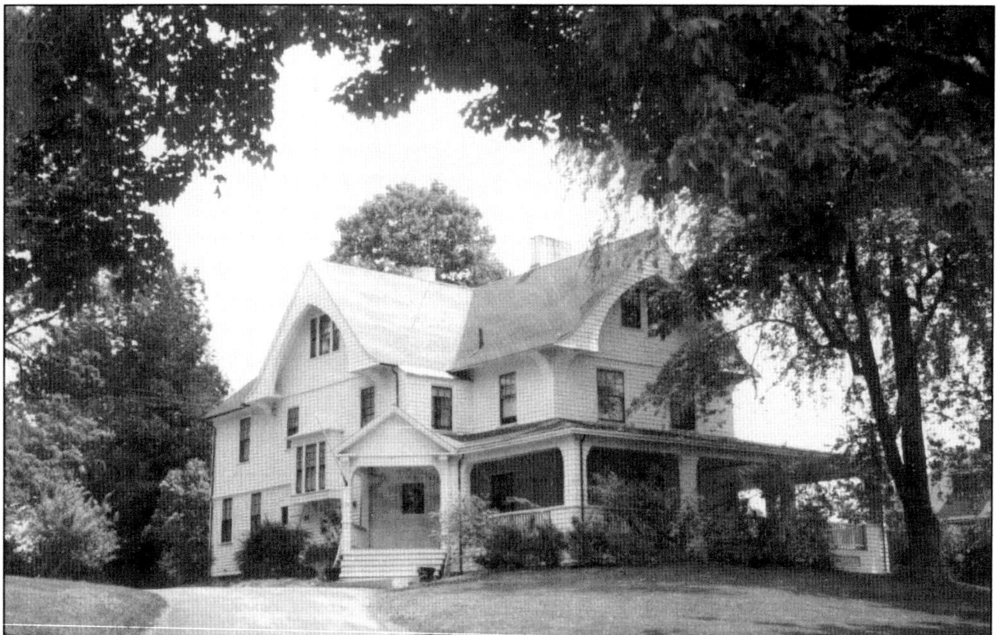

Bement House (the President's House). Former owner Henry Bement allowed this house to be used as a temporary dormitory for some students after the Hurricane of 1938. The school purchased it in 1958, initially using it as a small dormitory for seniors. It served as the president's house for approximately three decades. Currently, it is closed, awaiting repairs.

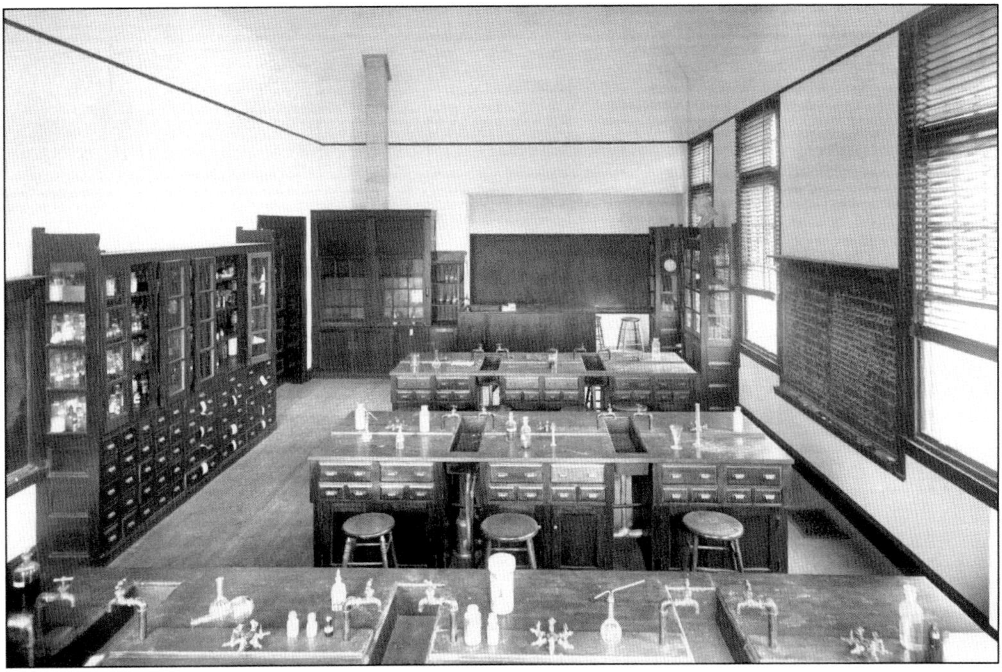

The Chemistry Lab, May Hall, c. 1890s. A century ago students were utilizing the latest techniques in the school's chemistry lab. At the time, they could barely envision the technology to which their grandchildren would have access.

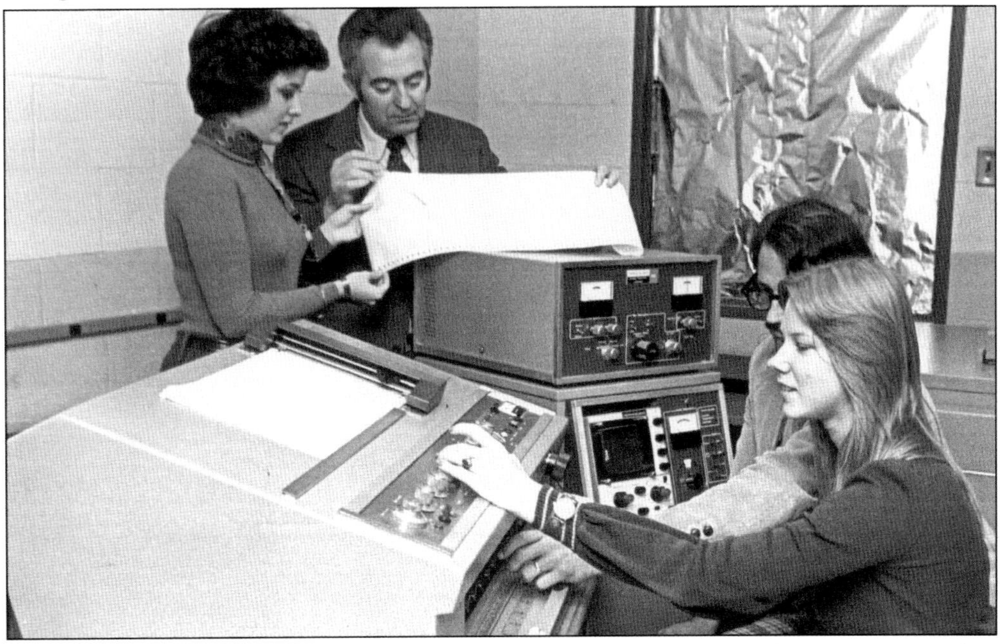

The Chemistry Lab, May Hall, 1974. Chemistry students use the Perkin-Elmer F12 B, a nuclear magnetic resonance spectrometer, which helps determine molecular structure. From left to right are Jean Bettencourt, Dr. Charles Zapsalis (chairman of the Chemistry Department), Dr. Larry Simonson, and Diane Hendrickson. Zapsalis, to whom the college awarded an honorary degree of doctor of laws in May 2001, died on January 29, 2003.

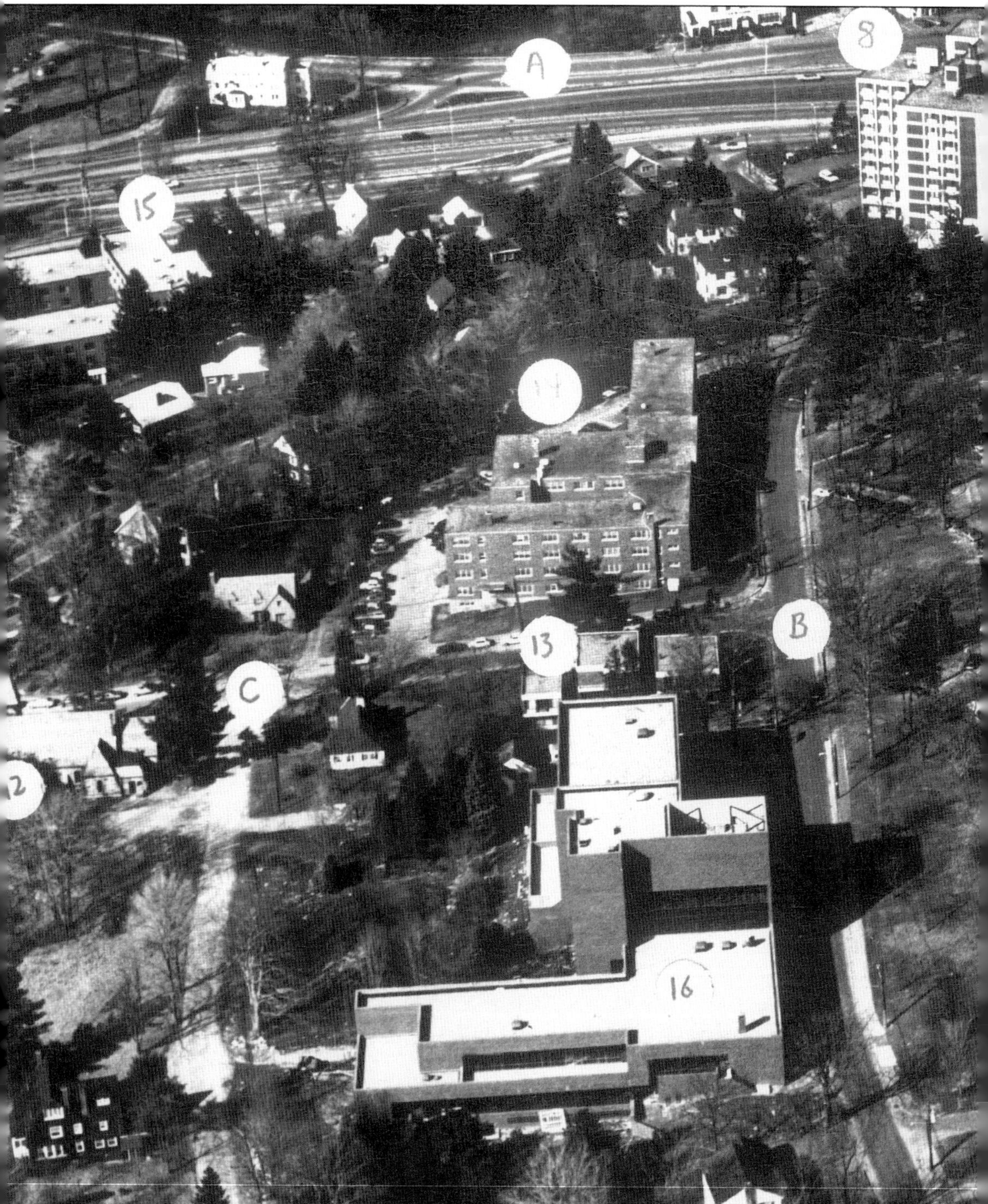

A Map of the Campus, c. 1976. Shown on this map are the following: 1. Dwight Hall; 2. Dwight Field (now the site of the Athletic Center and Bookstore); 3. Peirce Hall; 4. Horace Mann Hall; 5. Crocker Hall; 6. May Hall; 7. Hemenway Hall; 8. Corrine Hall Towers; 9. Larned Hall;

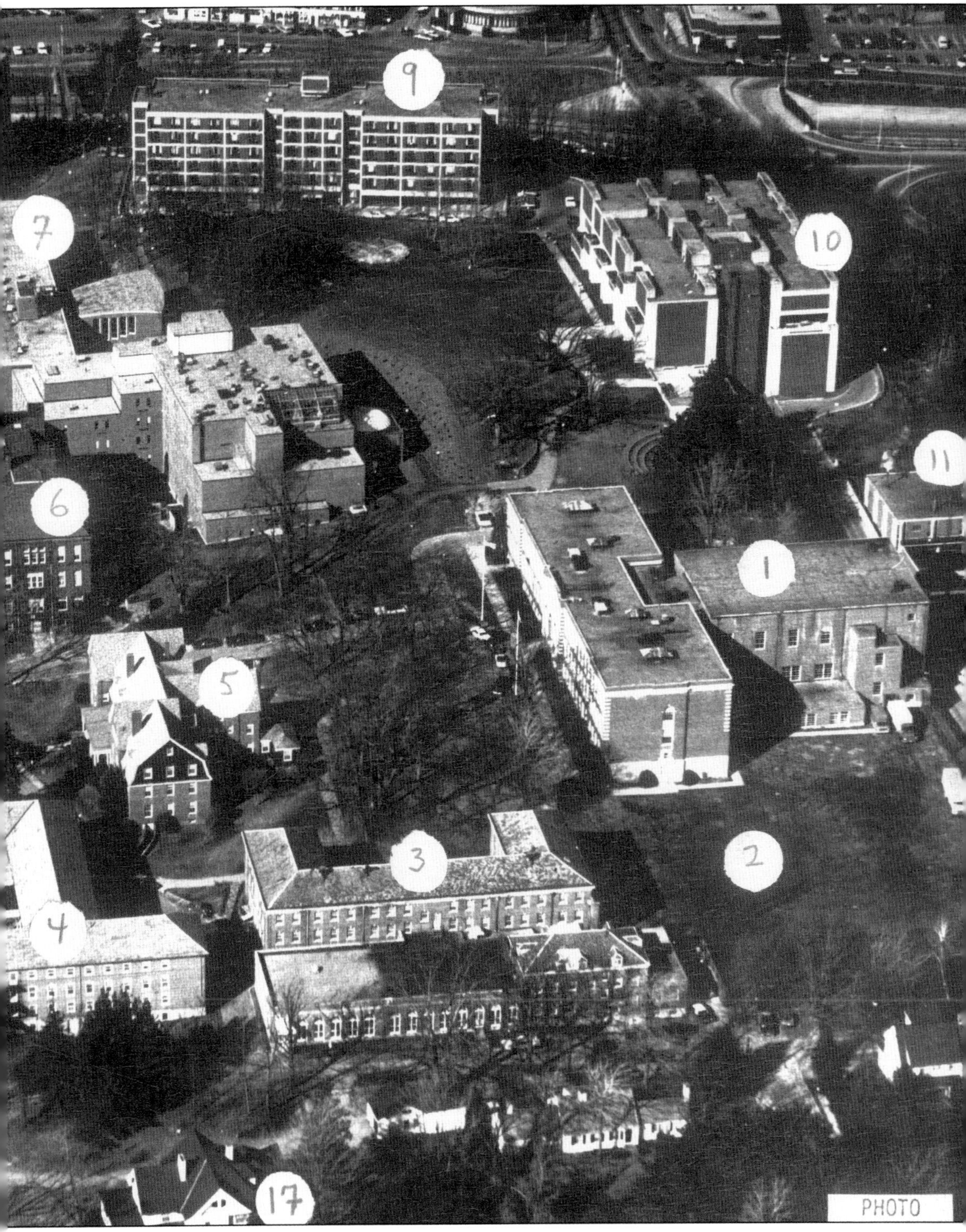

10. the Whittemore Library; 11. the power plant; 12. the Ecumenical Center; 13. Foster Hall; 14. O'Connor Hall (with the McAuliffe Center in the rear); 15. Linsley Hall; 16. the McCarthy Center; 17. Bement House (the president's house); A. Route 9; B. State Street; C. Maynard Road.

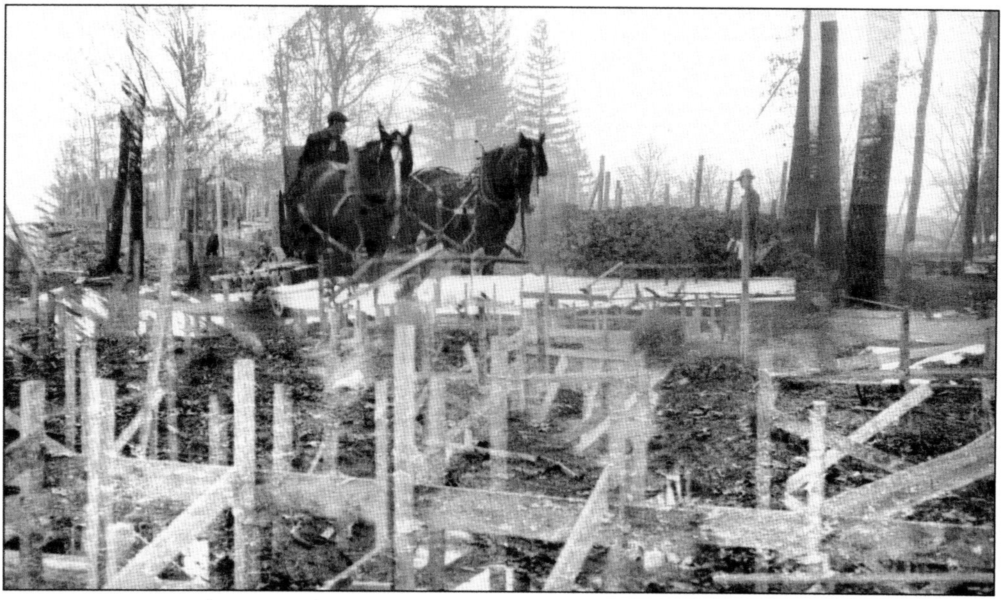

CONSTRUCTION, 1914. In 1914, in constructing Peirce Hall, a horse-drawn carriage delivers building materials to the job site. Back then, buildings were built with the brute strength of man and animal. Despite any disadvantages compared to the tools available in modern construction, Peirce Hall was finished in six months' time.

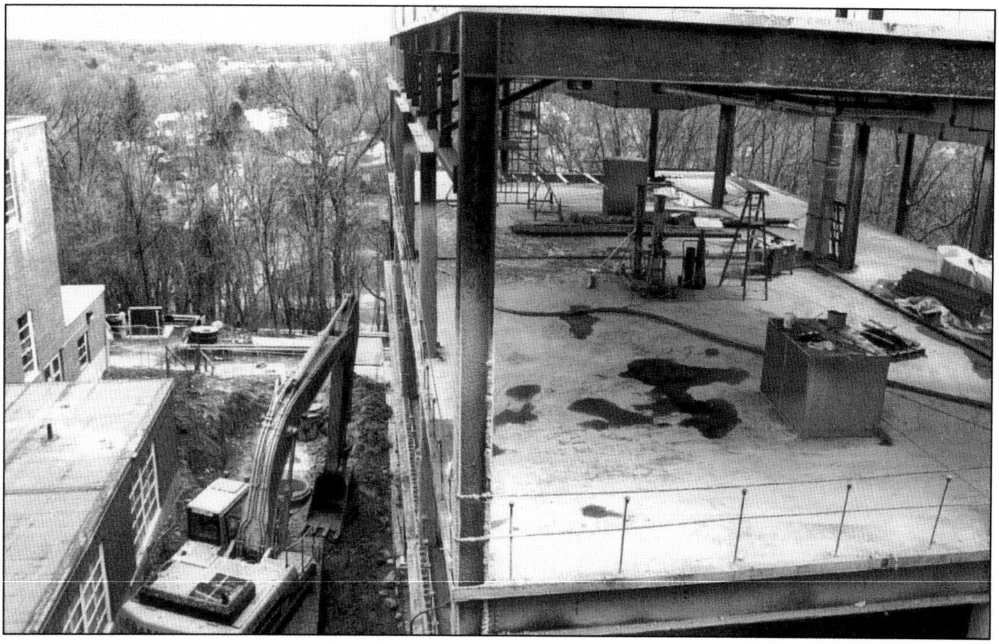

CONSTRUCTION, 2000. In 2000, the Athletic and Recreation Center was added to Dwight Hall. A bulldozer, standard fare in today's construction, has replaced the horse, and available technology has lessened the burden on modern construction workers—now both men and women.

Three

The Presidents

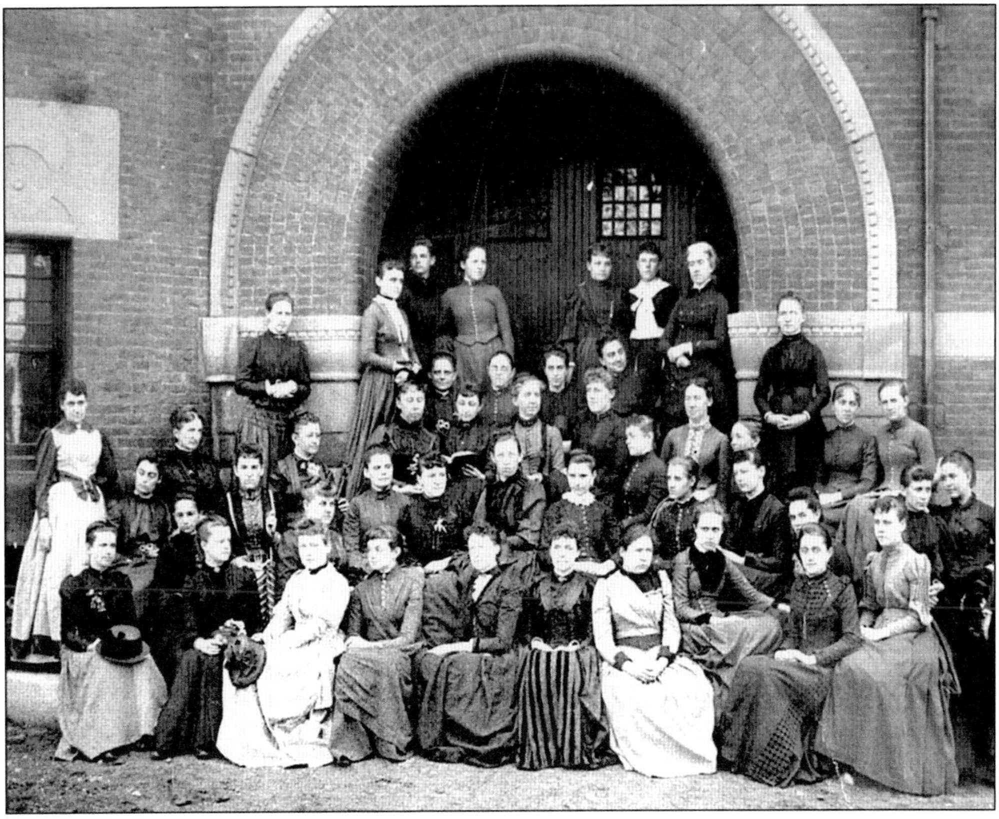

A Graduating Class, c. the 1890s. Ellen Hyde (back right) presided over a score of graduations during her leadership of the school, from 1875 to 1898. She is quoted as saying that she was "dumped into the hole left by [previous principal] Miss Johnson, and there wriggled about for 23 years." During her reign, the Normal School celebrated its semicentennial, in 1889. She was at the institution, as a teacher and principal, for a total of 35 years.

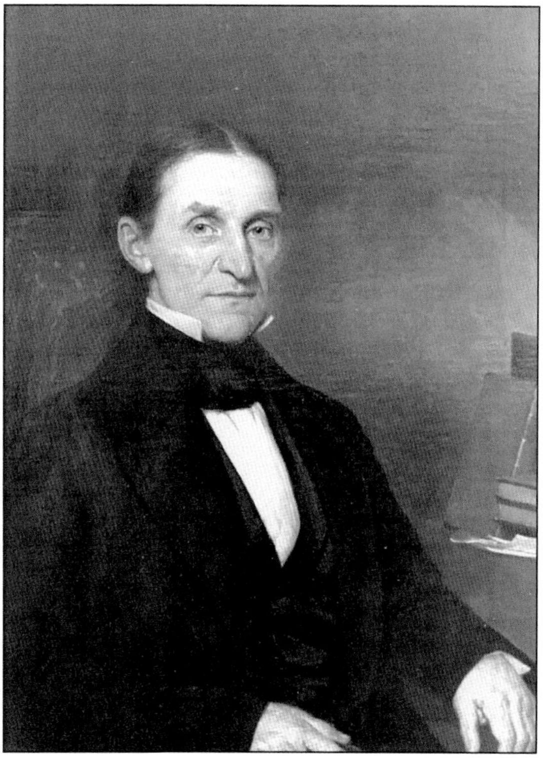

Cyrus Peirce, 1839–1842, 1844–1849. Cyrus Peirce (pronounced purse) graduated from Harvard College and its Divinity School, where he served as a pastor, teacher, and headmaster. At age 49, he left his job as headmaster of Nantucket High School to assume the challenging duties of creating the Normal School in Lexington. The new endeavor was so stressful that his health was affected, forcing him to resign. After two years, sufficiently recovered, he returned. At the end of each class day, he told his students to "Live to the Truth," a phrase that remains the school's motto to this day.

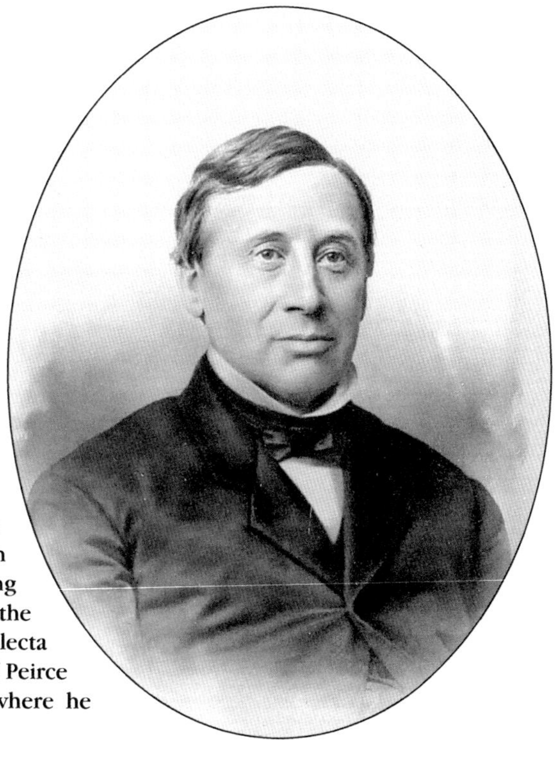

Samuel Joseph May, 1842–1844. Samuel May, an abolitionist and South Scituate Unitarian minister, was selected to replace the ailing Cyrus Peirce as principal. An expanding enrollment led to the relocation of the school to West Newton and the hiring of new faculty. The first graduate of the school to be appointed as a teacher was Electa Lincoln. May departed upon the return of Peirce as principal and relocated to Syracuse, where he worked in a church. He died in 1871.

Eben S. Stearns, 1849–1855. A stickler for excellence, Eben Stearns was selected to head the school at age 30. He introduced many changes: admission standards were tightened, school terms were increased from three to four, advanced graduate courses were created, and, in 1850, diplomas were awarded to graduates. During his tenure, the enrollment increased dramatically, necessitating another move, in 1853, from West Newton to the college's present location in Framingham. When Stearns left in 1855, many faculty members followed, resulting in the enrollment dropping dramatically from 154 to 30.

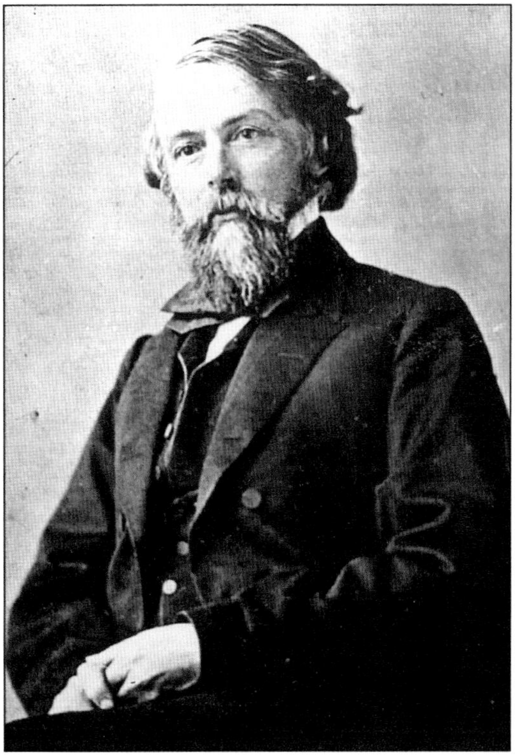

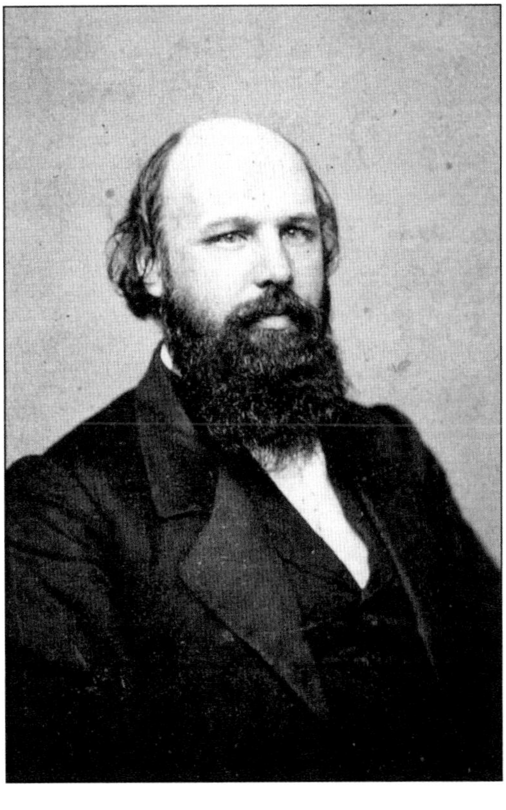

George B. Bigelow, 1855–1866. The first layman to head the school, George Bigelow added to and improved its curriculum in English literature, modern history, higher mathematics, and advanced foreign languages. School enrollment was stimulated by the Civil War, resulting in the need for female teachers. In 1864, 173 female students were being instructed by Bigelow and six teachers.

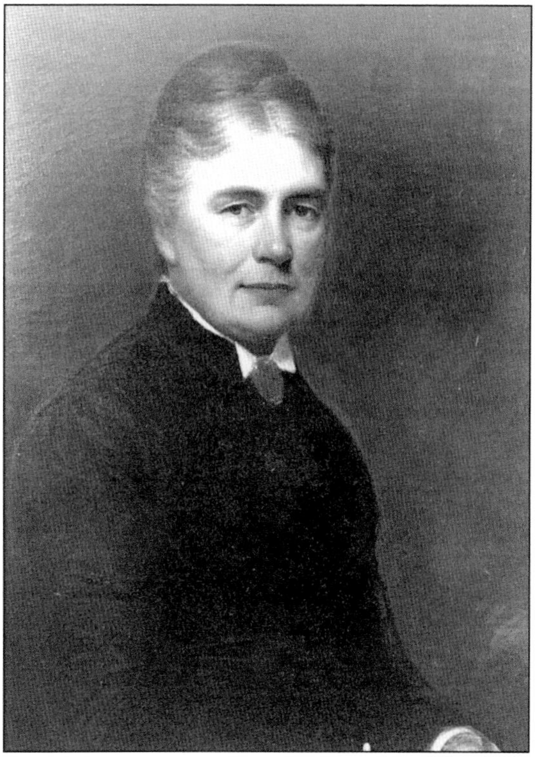

Annie Johnson, 1866–1875. The first female principal to head the school, Annie Johnson received her education at Bowdoin College. She started teaching at age 15 and taught every grade through high school prior to coming to the Normal School. Under her watch, the school building was renovated, steam heat was installed, a third-floor library was added, a two-room Model School was developed, and, most significantly, Normal Hall dormitory was built. In 1875, she accepted the position of principal at Bradford Academy.

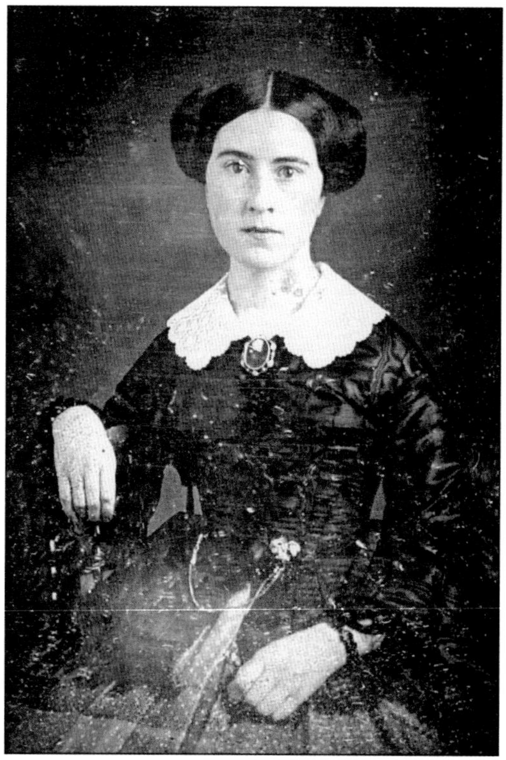

Ellen Hyde, Class of 1862. While many of the college's graduates have gone on to become presidents of other colleges, the talented Ellen Hyde has been the only graduate in the history of FSC to become its principal.

Ellen Hyde, 1875–1898. When Annie Johnson left, Ellen Hyde was named principal. Previously, Hyde had been an assistant to Johnson, just as Johnson had been to her predecessor. Hyde attended the Normal School, graduating in 1862. The school continued to expand under her guidance: the Model School became the Practice School and grew from two mixed-age rooms to nine grades; the Boston School of Household Arts relocated from Boston to Framingham; and the Glee Club formed. Also during Hyde's tenure, May and Crocker Halls were built.

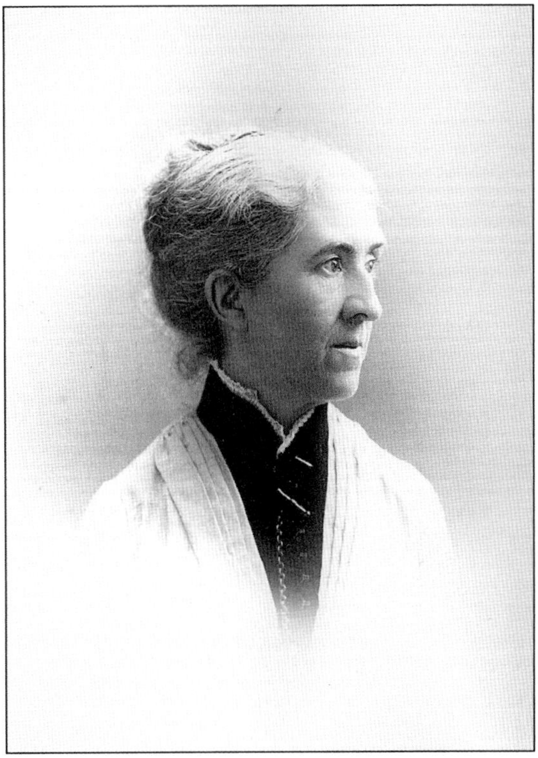

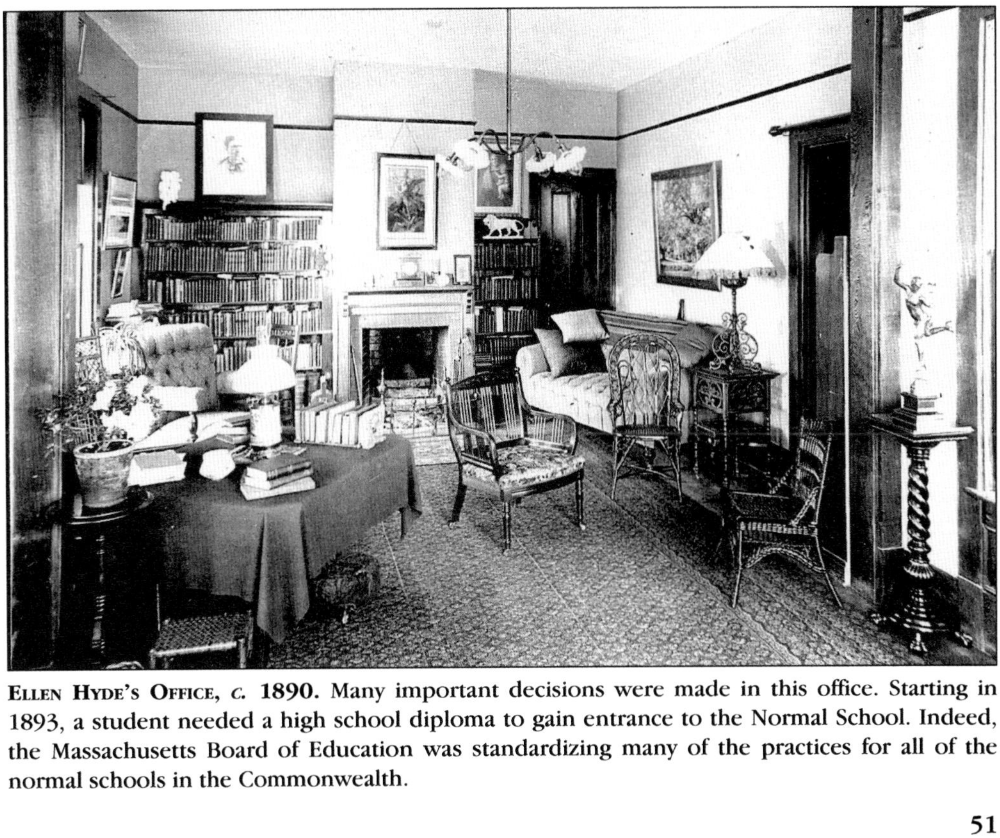

Ellen Hyde's Office, c. 1890. Many important decisions were made in this office. Starting in 1893, a student needed a high school diploma to gain entrance to the Normal School. Indeed, the Massachusetts Board of Education was standardizing many of the practices for all of the normal schools in the Commonwealth.

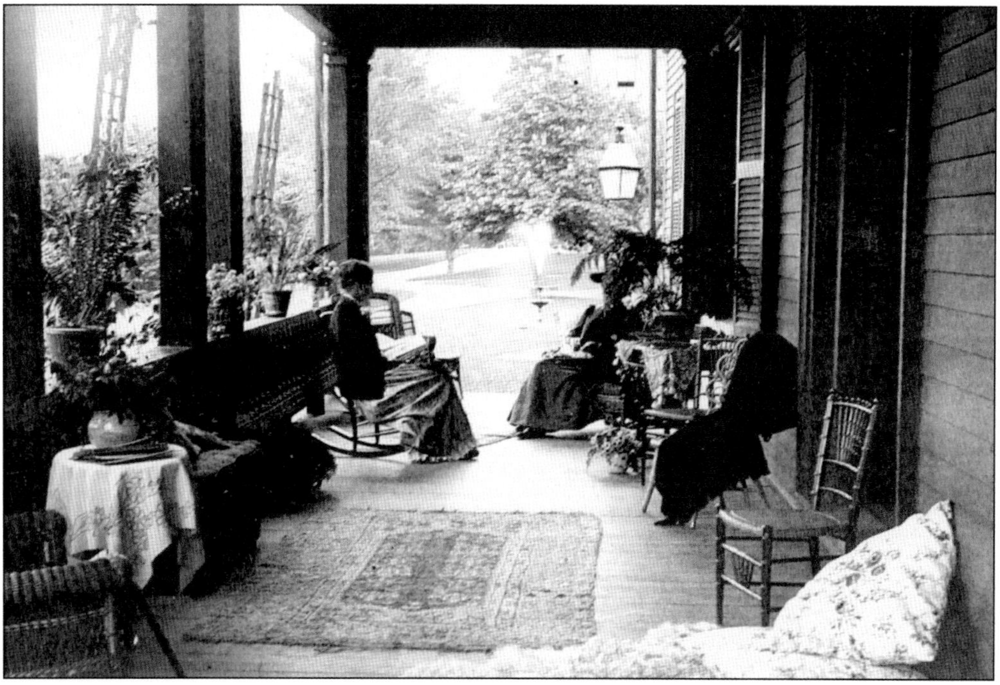

Ellen Hyde, on the Piazza, c. 1895. Ellen Hyde's younger cousin Elizabeth also attended the school, graduating in 1875. Like Hyde, Elizabeth also made her mark in higher education, teaching African American and Native American students in the Hampton Normal Institute (now Hampton University) in Virginia for more than three decades.

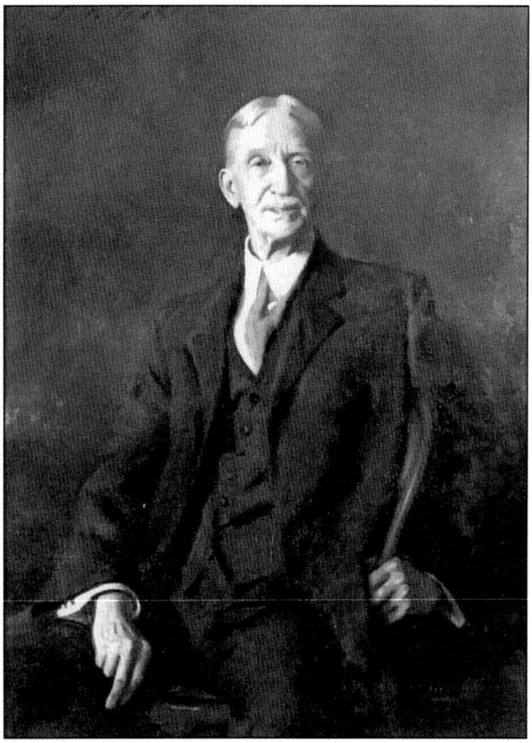

Henry Whittemore, 1898–1917. A Civil War veteran and graduate of Dartmouth, Henry Whittemore had taught in the public schools and was the superintendent of schools in Waltham prior to being named principal of the Normal School. Under his watch, Wells Hall and Peirce Hall were constructed, the Household Arts program was extended to three years, and an increased emphasis was placed on sports and physical fitness.

JAMES CHALMERS, PH.D., 1917–1930. A divinity graduate of Wheaton College in Illinois, James Chalmers he earned a Ph.D. from Eureka College. Prior to coming to the Normal School, he taught English at Ohio State and was president of the Wisconsin State Normal School and South Dakota State College, as well as superintendent of schools in Fitchburg. Horace Mann Hall was built during his tenure.

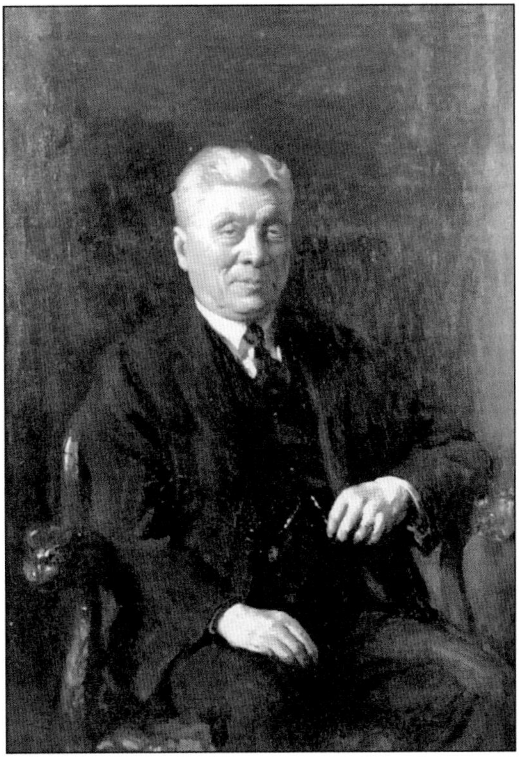

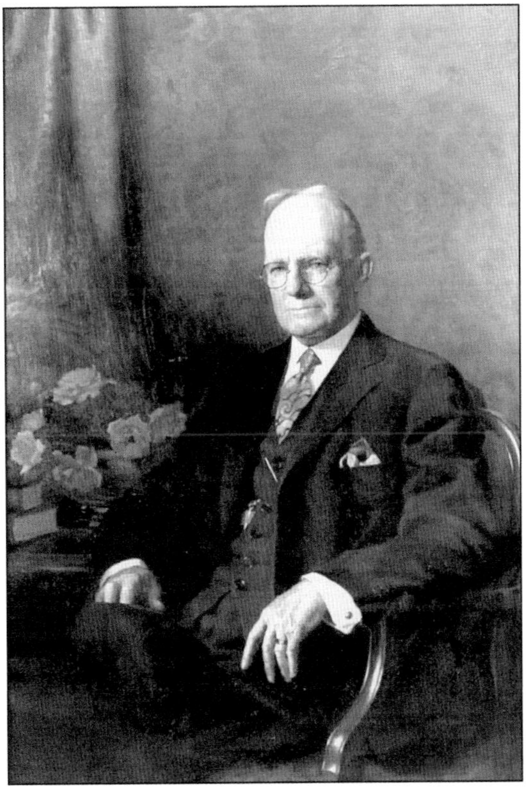

FRANCIS A. BAGNALL, 1930–1936. In 1932, the State Normal School at Framingham (also called the Framingham Normal School) became the State Teachers College at Framingham (also known as Framingham State Teachers College). Indeed, all of the state normal schools were now called state teachers colleges, and principals were now called presidents. Bagnall left the school and relocated to Washington, D.C., where he became an educational policy consultant.

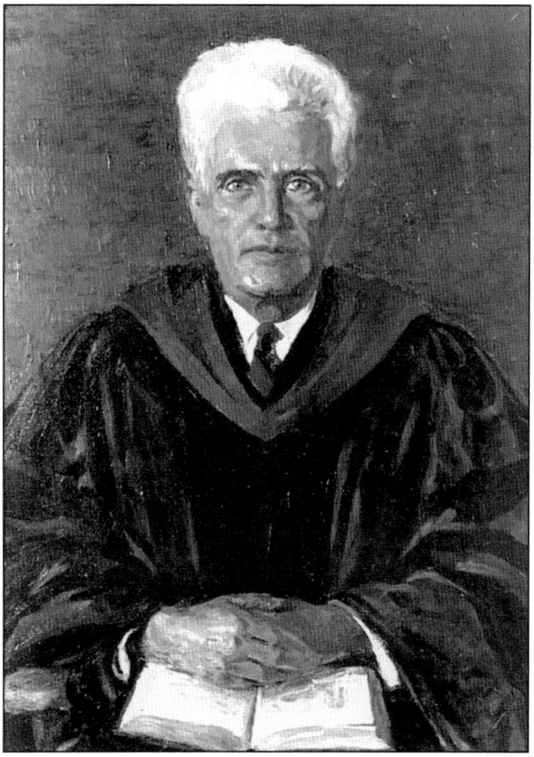

MARTIN F. O'CONNOR, ED.D., 1936–1961. President O'Connor graduated from Boston College and Harvard University. Dwight Hall opened during his tenure. Following World War II, the need for teachers greatly increased, necessitating the creation of the Intensive Teacher Preparation Program in 1955 to address the shortage of elementary school teachers. In 1959, the school was authorized to award a B.A. degree. A year later, the name of the school was changed, to the State College at Framingham.

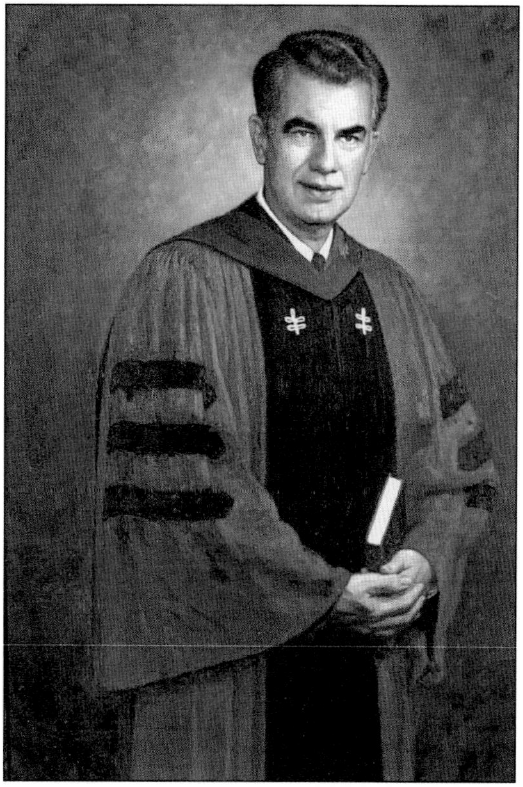

D. JUSTIN MCCARTHY, ED.D., 1961–1985. A graduate of Bridgewater State College and Harvard University, D. Justin McCarthy witnessed unparalleled growth at the school, which in 1968, formally became Framingham State College. During his 24 years in office, the school was authorized to grant a master's degree in education, men were admitted beginning in 1964, the number of majors grew to 27, enrollment increased from 632 to 3,200, the faculty increased from 45 to 140, and 10 buildings were constructed.

PAUL F. WELLER, PH.D., 1985–1996. Paul Weller received a B.S. from the University of Illinois and a Ph.D. in chemistry from Cornell University. After working in the private sector as a research chemist, he entered the field of higher education, serving as a vice president for academic affairs at the California State Polytechnic University at Pomona. At FSC, he strengthened the cultural and artistic programs, bringing a large number of renowned speakers to campus. The McAuliffe Challenger Center was established during his tenure.

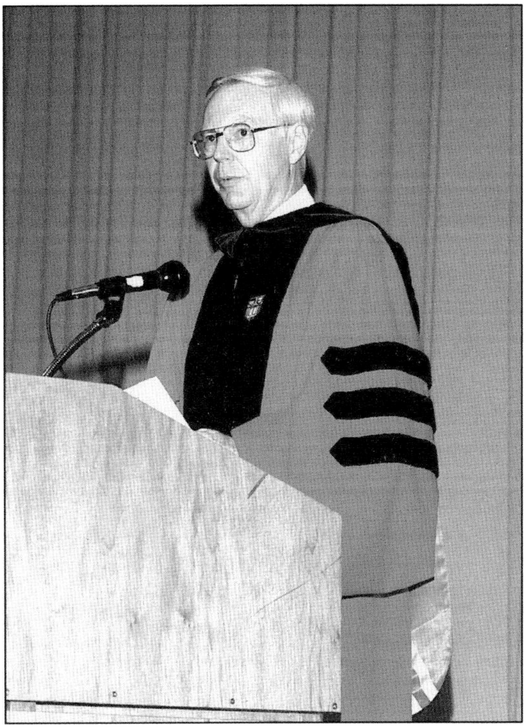

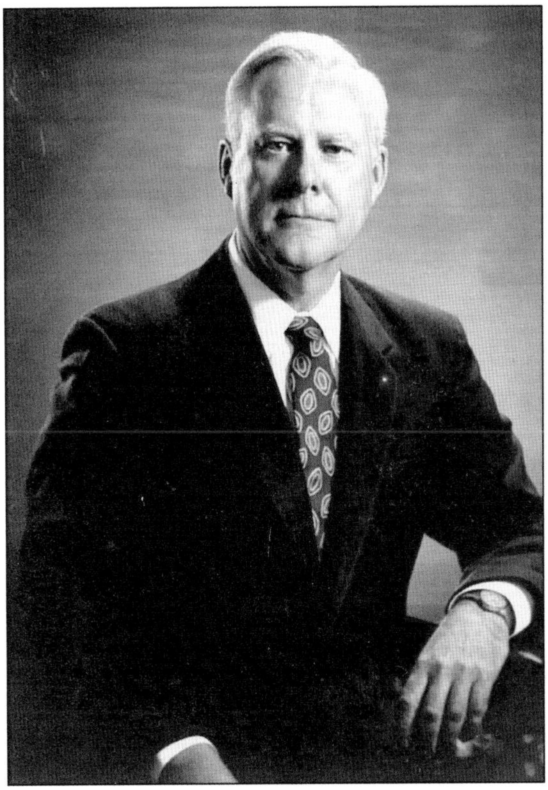

RAYMOND N. KIEFT, ED.D., 1996–1999. Raymond Kieft, a longtime resident of Colorado, served as president of Mesa State College before coming east. During his tenure at FSC, funds were authorized to construct the new athletic center and technology programs were started. After a relatively short stint as president, he returned to his home state and its board of higher education.

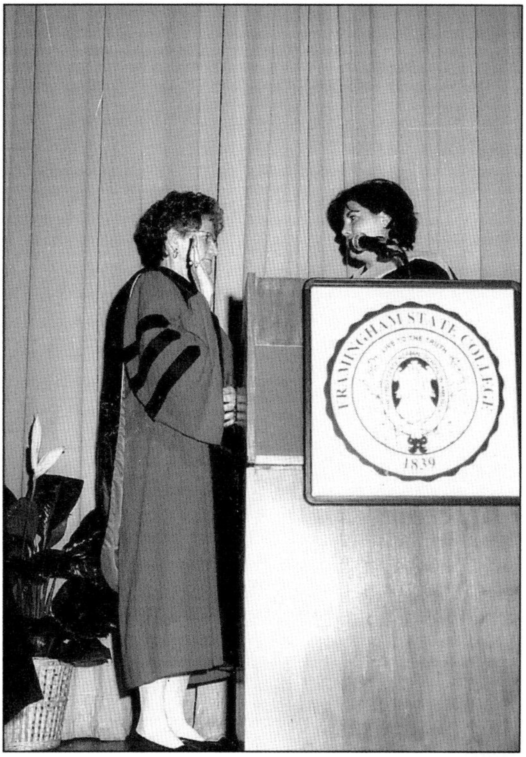

HELEN L. HEINEMAN, BEING SWORN IN. Lt. Gov. Jane Swift swears in Dr. Helen Heineman, the first woman and the first faculty member in the college's history to become president. Dr. Heineman rose through the ranks, starting in 1974 as a member of the English Department. From there, she became department chair, academic vice president, and provost.

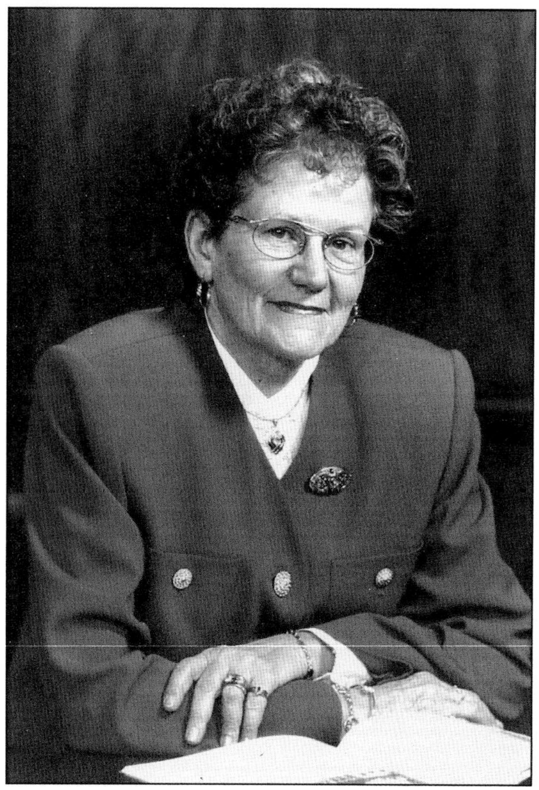

HELEN L. HEINEMAN, PH.D., 1999–PRESENT. Dr. Heineman graduated from Queens College in 1958 as class valedictorian. She earned a degree in English literature. She received her M.A. from Columbia University, also in English, and a Ph.D. in the same subject from Cornell. She is the author of several books on Victorian literature, the first of which was *Mrs. Trollope: The Triumphant Feminine in the Nineteenth Century*.

Four

THE GAY NINETIES TO THE ROARING TWENTIES

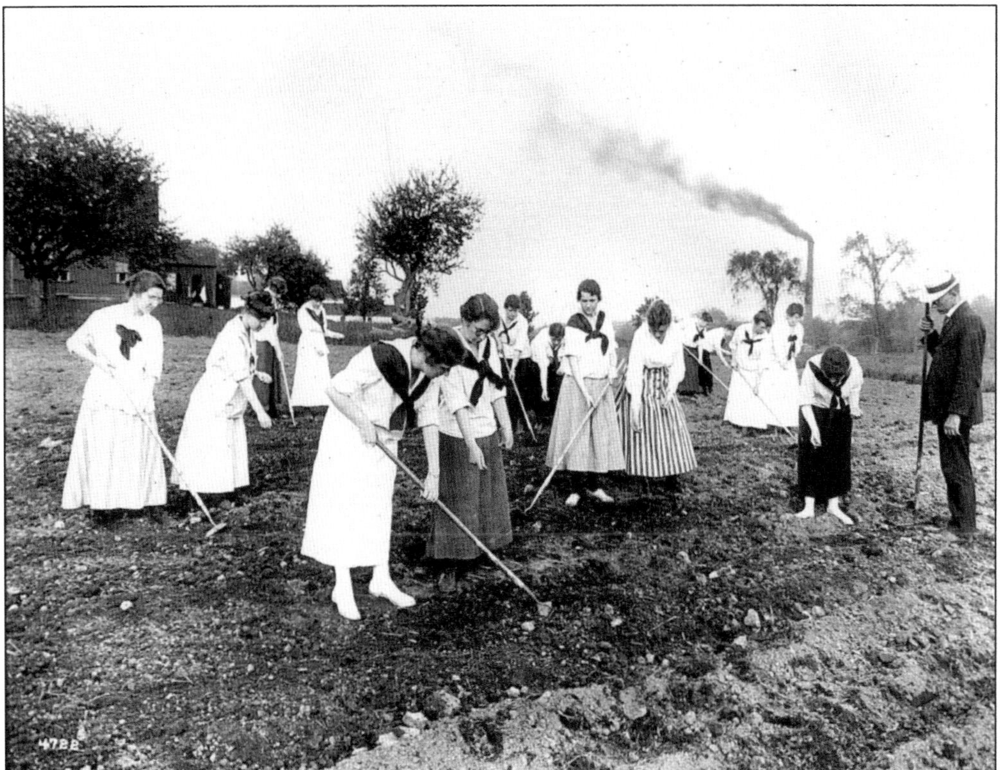

TILLING THE SOIL *c.* **1910–1915.** Framingham State College was always a hands-on institution, stressing practicality as well as theory. To that end, students were required to put their learning to the test, as shown in this garden outside of Crocker Hall.

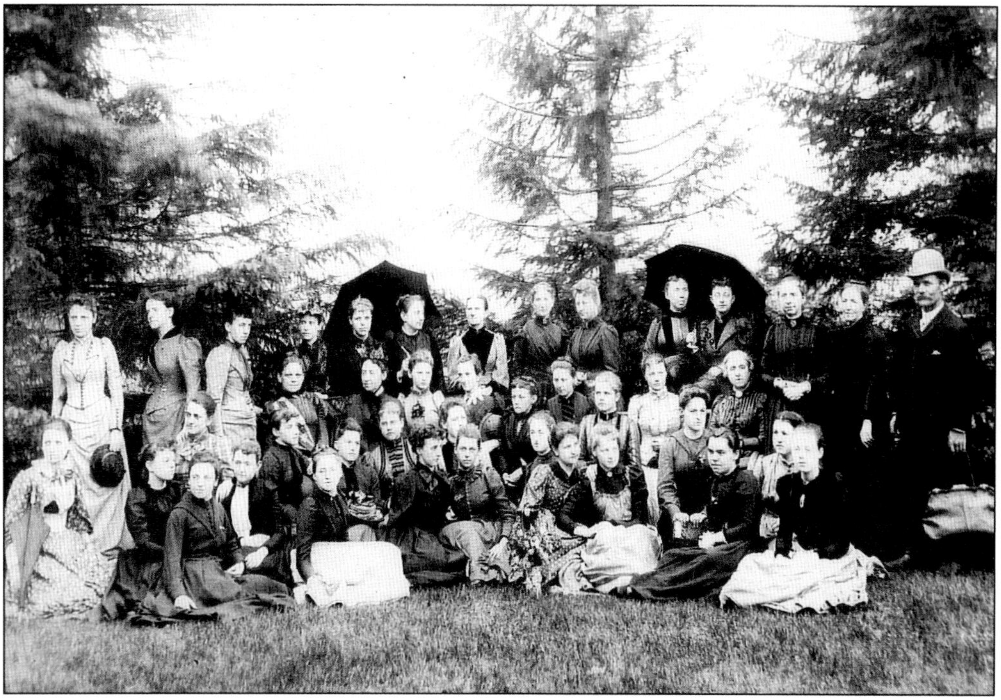

The Class of 1877. With the opening of the Normal School's first dormitory in 1869, many students now lived on campus. Prior to the construction of Normal Hall, many of the students either commuted to the school (they were called "train girls") or lived near the school, boarding in the homes of private citizens.

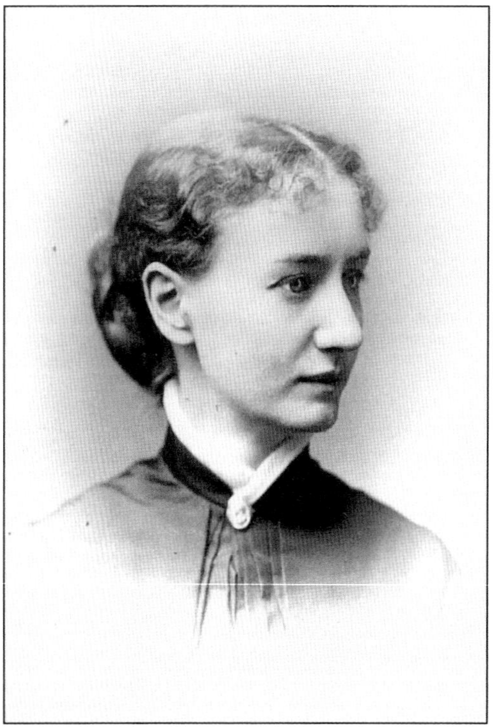

Jeanette W. Williams, Class of 1874. By the 1880s, admission standards were starting to rise. At the start of 1880, only one-third of the Normal School students had graduated from high school. By the end of the decade, this number had markedly increased. Initially, the feeling was that raising the standards would lead to a decrease in the number of applicants; in fact, the opposite occurred.

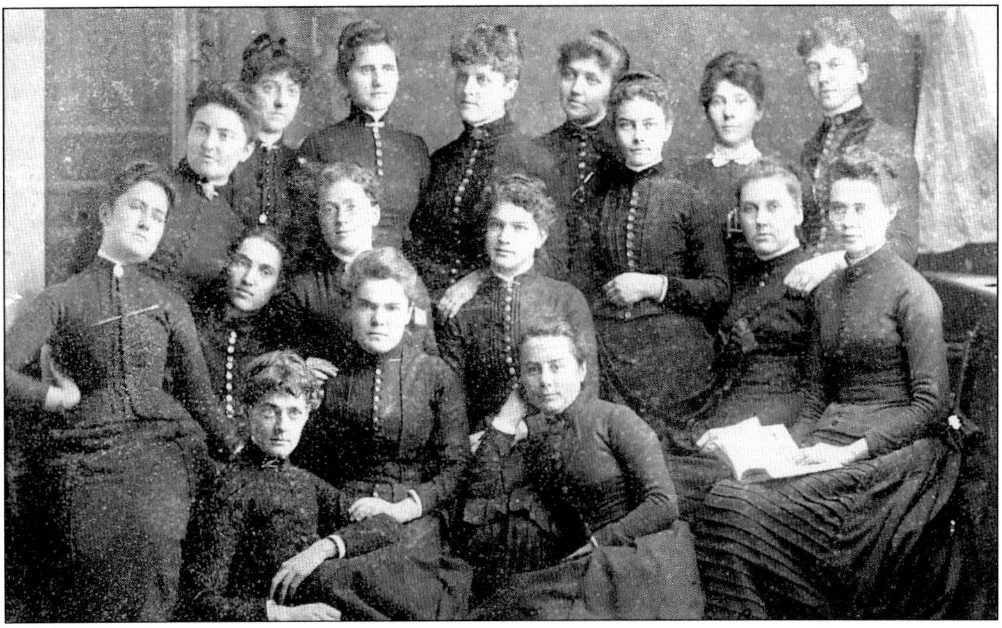

The Class of 1887. The Normal School was a leader in practical education. It created the Model School, soon retitled the Practice School and then the Training School, where college students, supervised by their instructors, taught elementary school. The system, a precursor to student teaching, was even more involved as the practice teachers actually ran the elementary school.

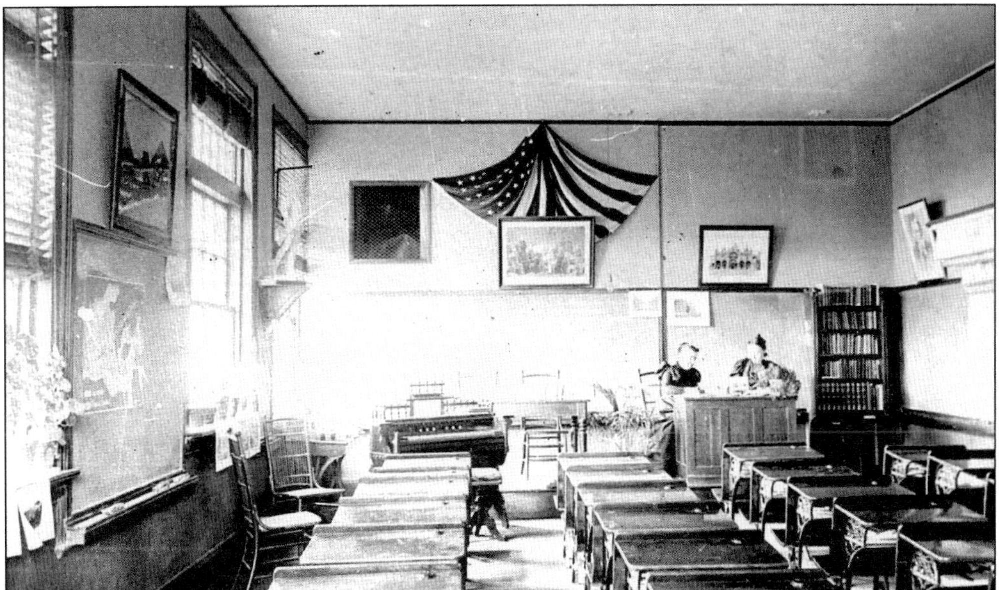

Preparing for Class. By 1890, classes started at 8:45 a.m. and ended by 1:45 p.m., Tuesday through Saturday. The day began with readings from the Scripture, singing, and prayer. Classes were divided into 55-minute segments, and exercise was stressed both during the day and after. Following dinner, at 5:30 p.m., students were expected to study for two hours, with the day ending at 10:00 p.m.

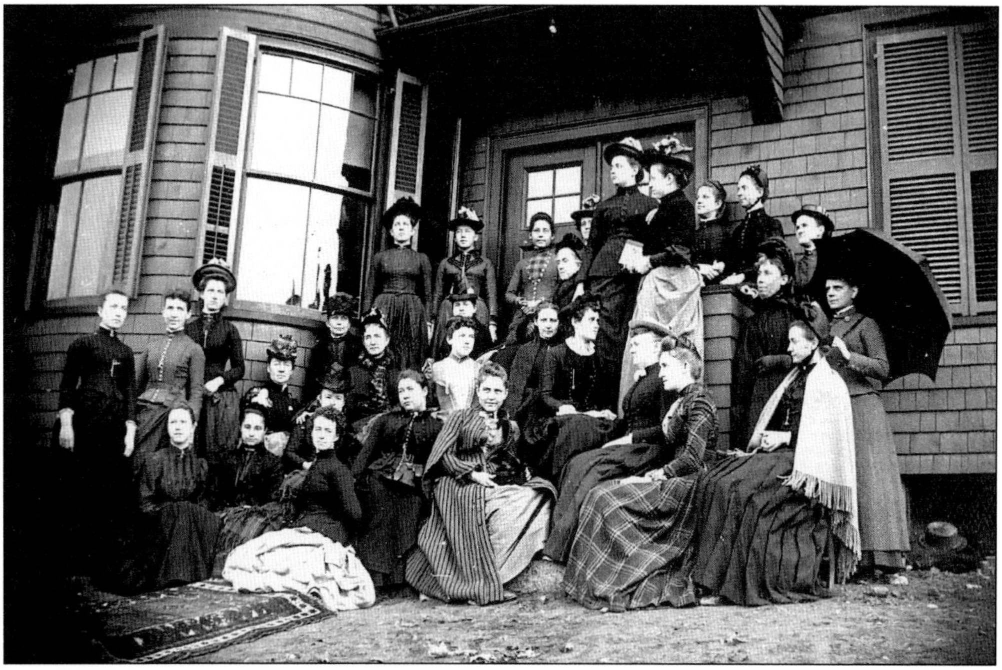

Ellen Hyde and the Class of 1890. Ellen Hyde, principal of the Normal School from 1875 to 1898, sits in the back center, just below the students standing at the door to Crocker Hall. She was the first, and so far only, graduate of the school to be its chief administrator.

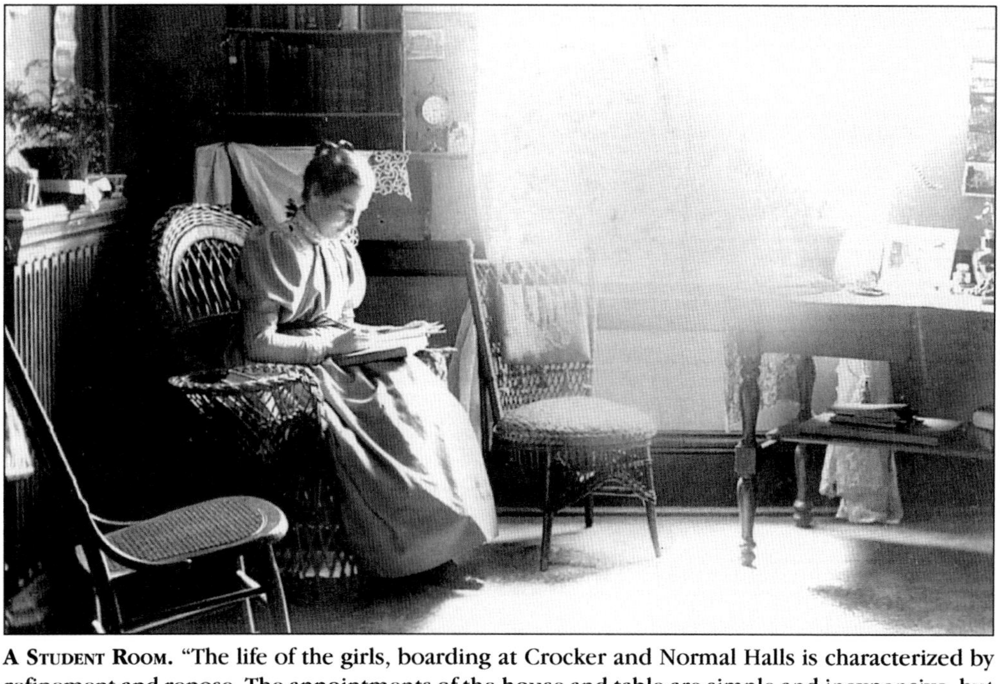

A Student Room. "The life of the girls, boarding at Crocker and Normal Halls is characterized by refinement and repose. The appointments of the house and table are simple and inexpensive, but all in good taste. The boarders are expected to be ladies as well as students. Such expectations will find their fulfillment in the demands which our pupils will in turn make upon their future scholars."—Kate Gannett Wells.

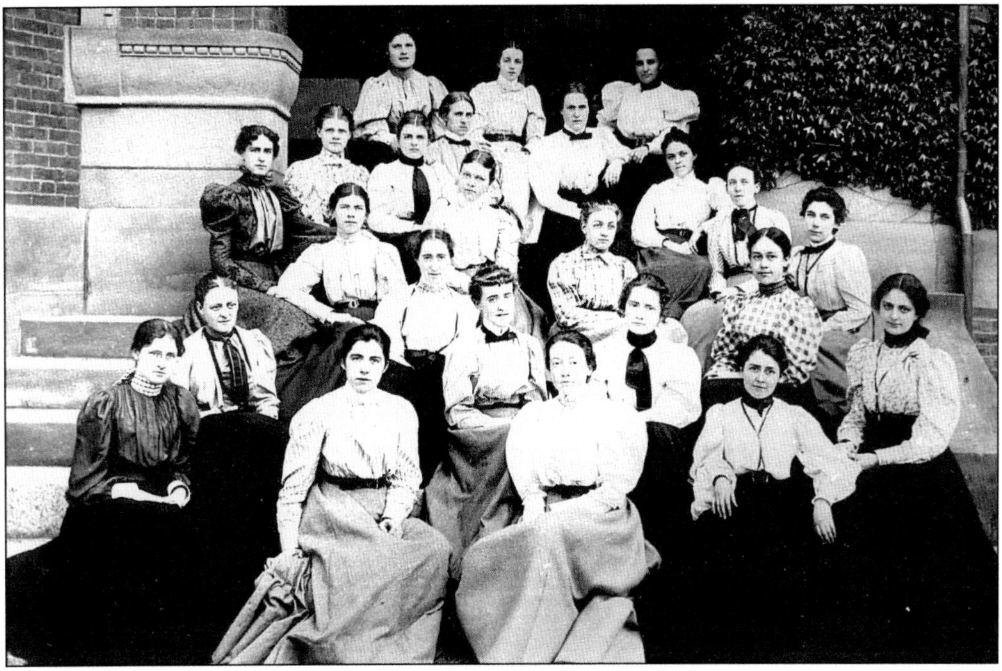

The Class of 1898. The year 1898 marked the end of Ellen Hyde's term as principal, which started in 1875. Henry Whittemore succeeded, with a term in office that would be nearly as long as Hyde's, ending in 1917. Both are acknowledged to be among the school's greatest leaders.

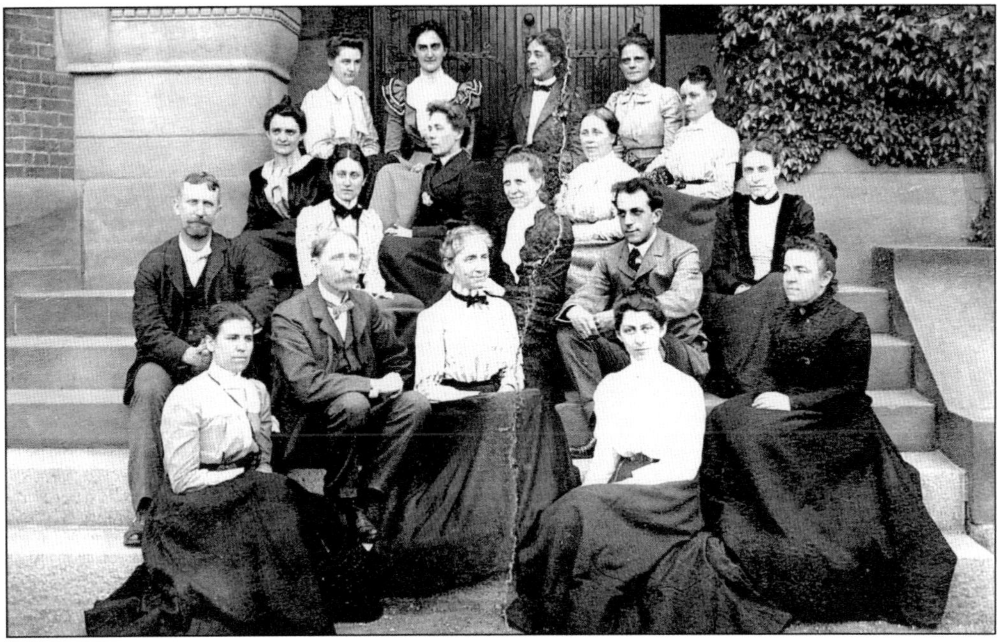

The Faculty, on the Steps of May Hall, *c.* 1900. From left to right are the following: (first row) Phebe Beard, Henry Whittemore (principal), Amelia Davis, Anna Claflin, and Susan Emerson; (second row) Frederic Archibald, Anna Clark, Louisa Nicholass, Frederic Howe, and Nellie Dale; (third row) Alice Winslow, Mary Stevens, Mary Moore, and Elizabeth Holbrook; (fourth row) Lillian Ordway, Antoinette Roof, Elizabeth Malloy, and Jane Ireson.

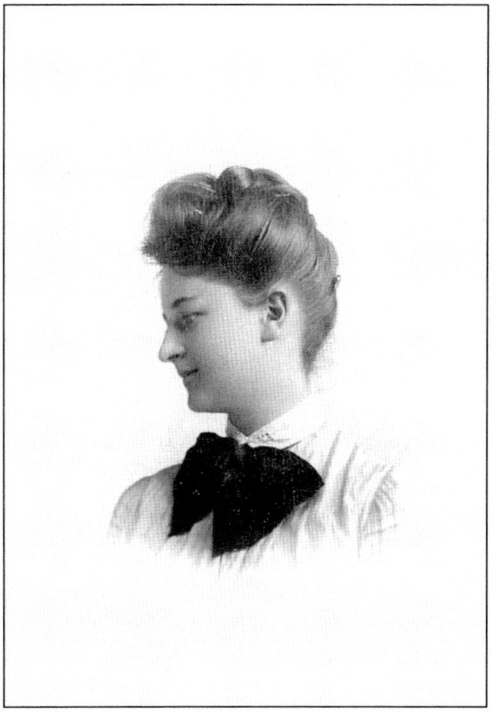

JANE DUNLAP, CLASS OF 1904, FROM WESTBOROUGH. Principal Henry Whittemore informed his students of the benefits they would receive from their campus room and board fee of $3.75: "lodging with heat, light, excellent food, well-prepared and served, laundry and service." He also warned them not to expect as much from the local families "who open their doors to them."

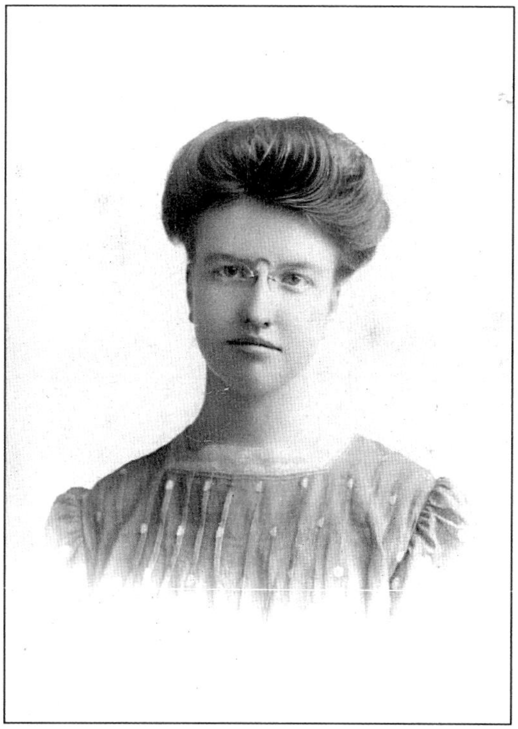

FLORENCE HAYDEN, CLASS OF 1905. This Household Arts graduate became an instructor of therapeutic cookery at New England Baptist Hospital in Roxbury. By 1905, she and her fellow students were enjoying many modern conveniences: heat, hot water, electricity, and paved sidewalks. They were also able to participate in debates such as the role of education on society. "Are the schools to be blamed if the perfect society has not yet arrived?" asked the Massachusetts Board of Education's 1903 report.

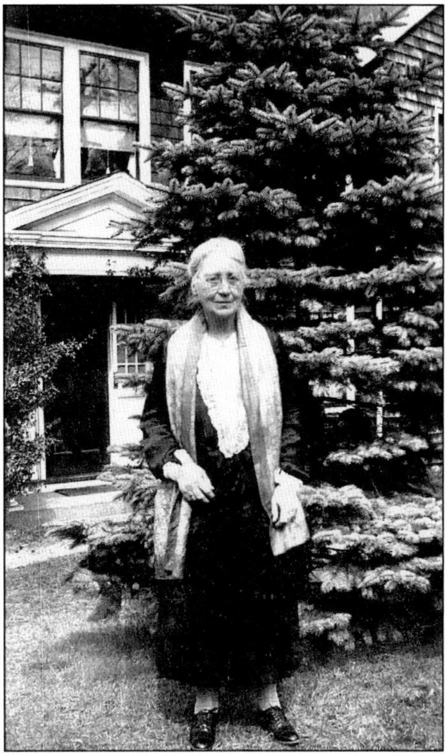

MARY MOORE, ENGLISH TEACHER, 1893–1917. Booker T. Washington continued to visit the school even after the death of his wife, Olivia Davidson Washington, in 1889. Olivia Davidson (see page 80) was a member of the Class of 1881. The Washingtons' daughter Portia in 1896 attended the Practice School and lived under the tutelage of Mary Moore, an alumna of the Class of 1873. Portia Washington continued her relationship with the school, visiting until the 1930s.

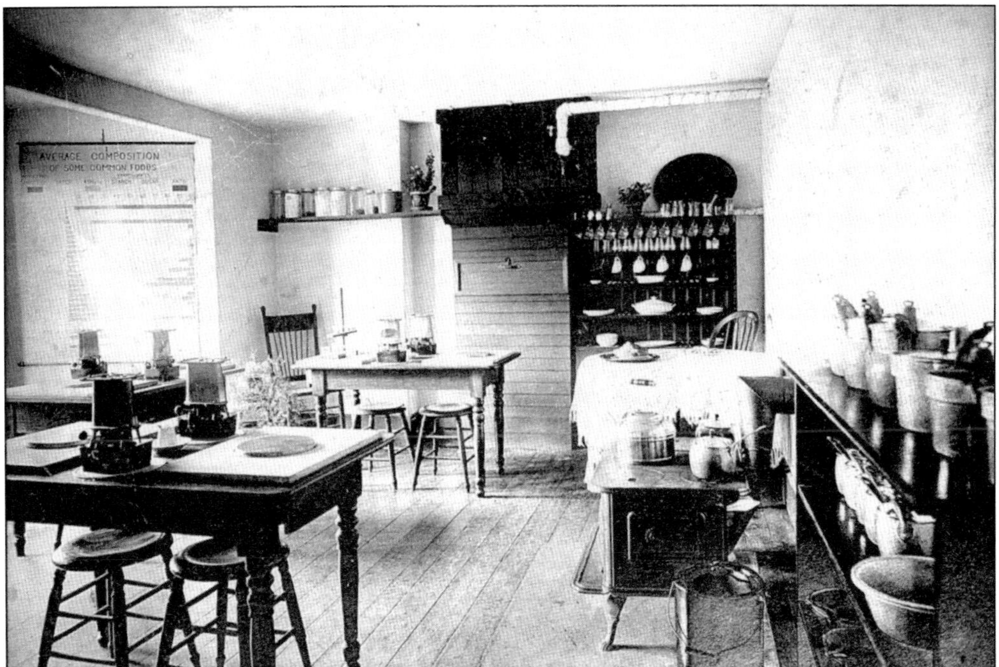

THE KITCHEN, 1905. Handwritten information on the back of this photograph indicates that this kitchen was located in the basement of May Hall. It was used as a commuter lunchroom, established by Edith Savage, dean of women.

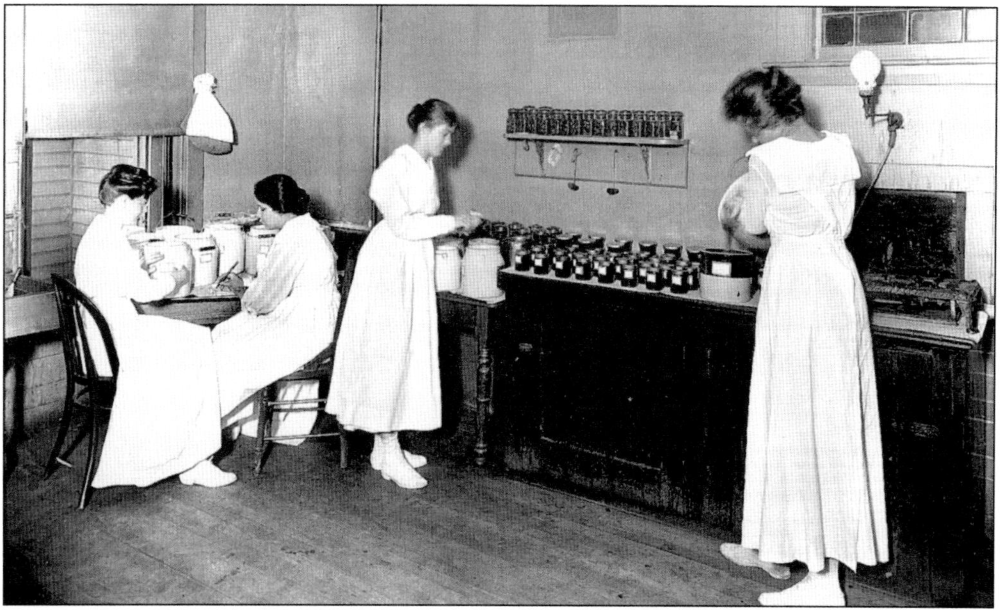

HOUSEHOLD ARTS, THE EARLY 1900s. The two-year course of study for these students required classes in the sciences, including chemistry, physics, and biology, as well as dietetics, laundering, and cooking, canning and preserving. The cooking program was so well received that organizations often scheduled meetings at the college to take advantage of the refreshments it prepared and served.

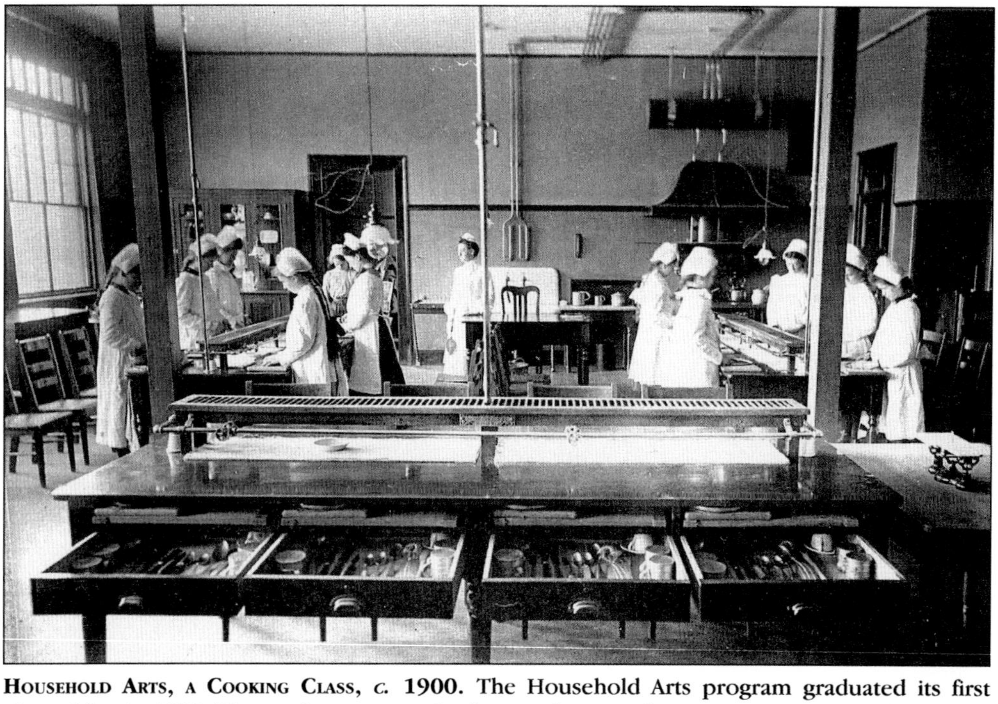

HOUSEHOLD ARTS, A COOKING CLASS, *c.* 1900. The Household Arts program graduated its first class of five in 1899. The graduates were the first students in the nation to receive a diploma in Household Arts. This course of study became so popular that at one time the school considered abolishing its elementary education program; fortunately, the college decided against the move.

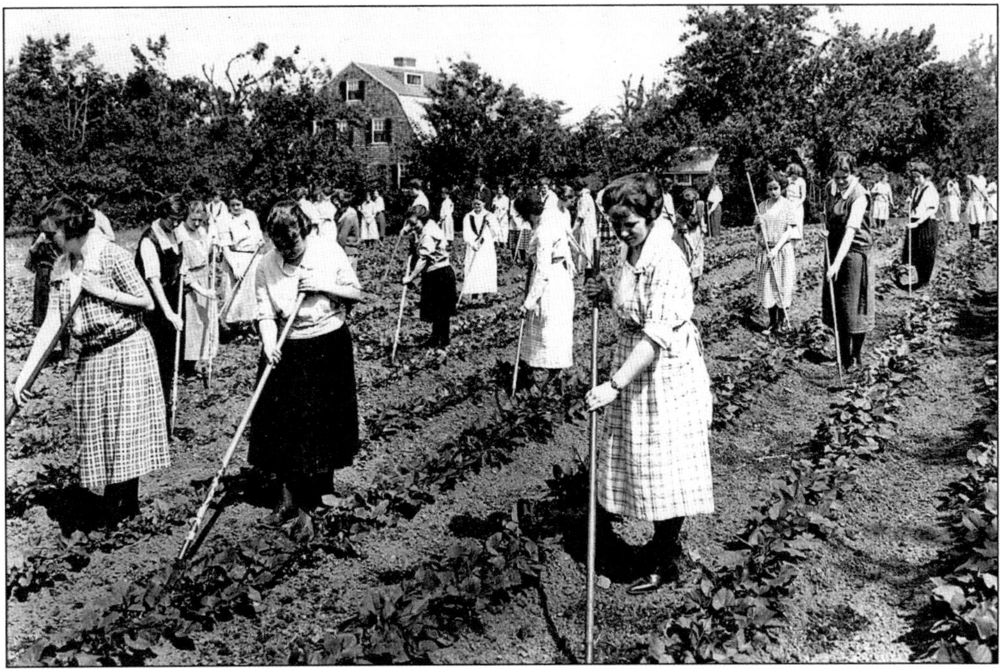

Working the Field, c. 1910–1915. Physical exertion was the rule rather than the exception, and the fact that these were women, not men, made no difference. Hard work was a daily part of life, and when students were finished in the field, they were expected to engage in recreational exercise.

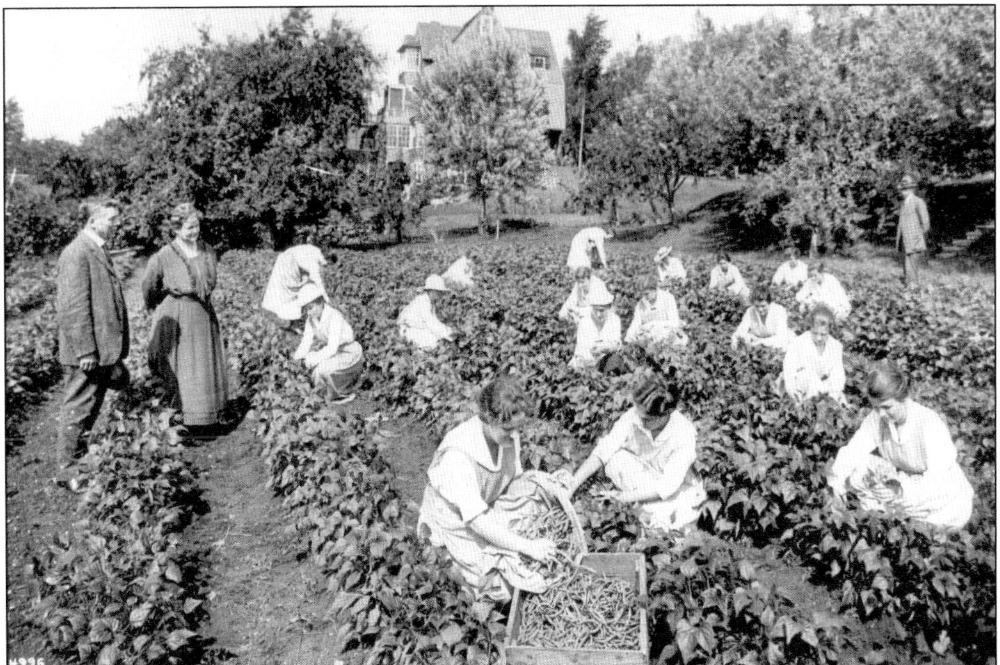

Growing Green Beans. In addition to working outside, activities included classroom lessons and recreation. Daily exercise offered choices of tennis, baseball, basketball, volleyball, and even golf. Attire for gym class often consisted of blouses with black bloomers.

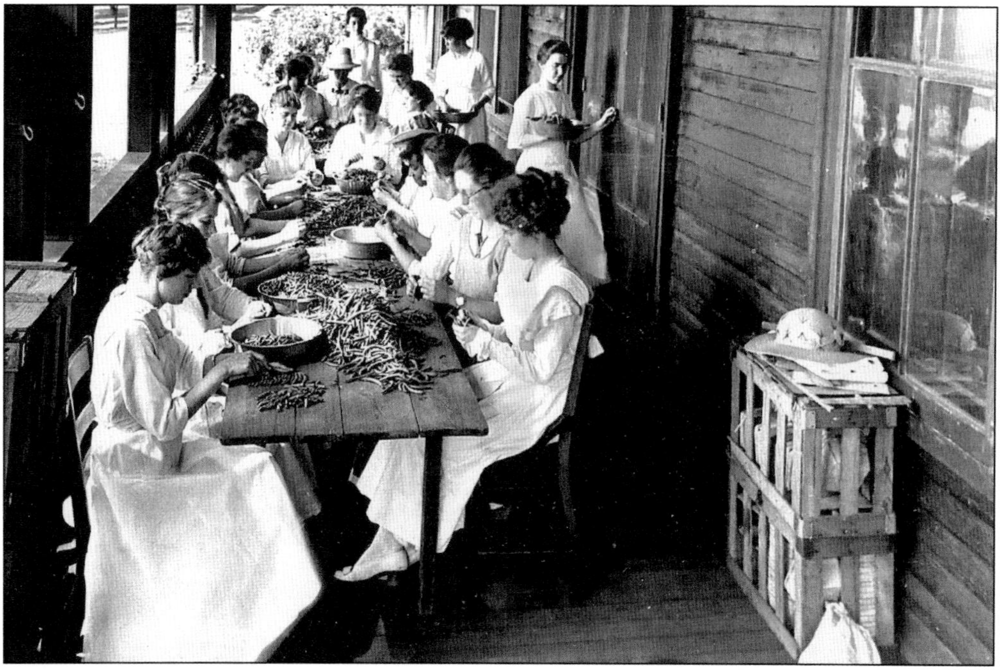

Preparing the Food. As part of the Household Arts program, a practice house for home management was established. A faculty member and seven seniors rented a nearby house, in which they lived and worked. When the owner sold the house, the program was forced to relocate.

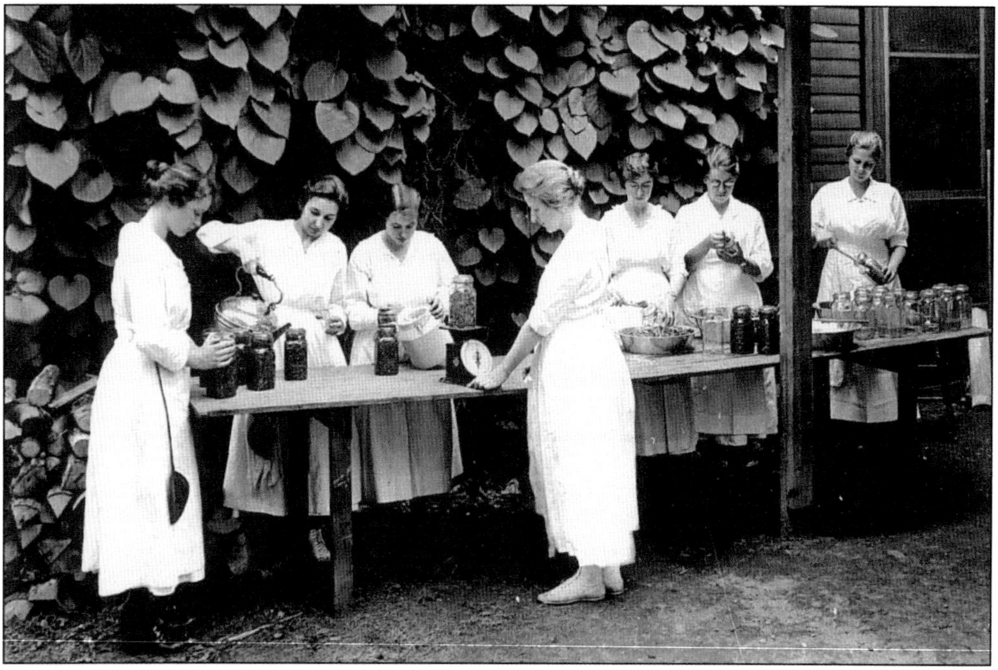

Canning, outside Crocker Hall, *c.* 1914. Canning was one of the courses in the Household Arts curriculum. When federal legislation called for the instruction of agriculture and home economics, funds were provided for the school to prepare its graduates to provide training in canning and food preservation. Principal Henry Whittemore eagerly accepted the challenge.

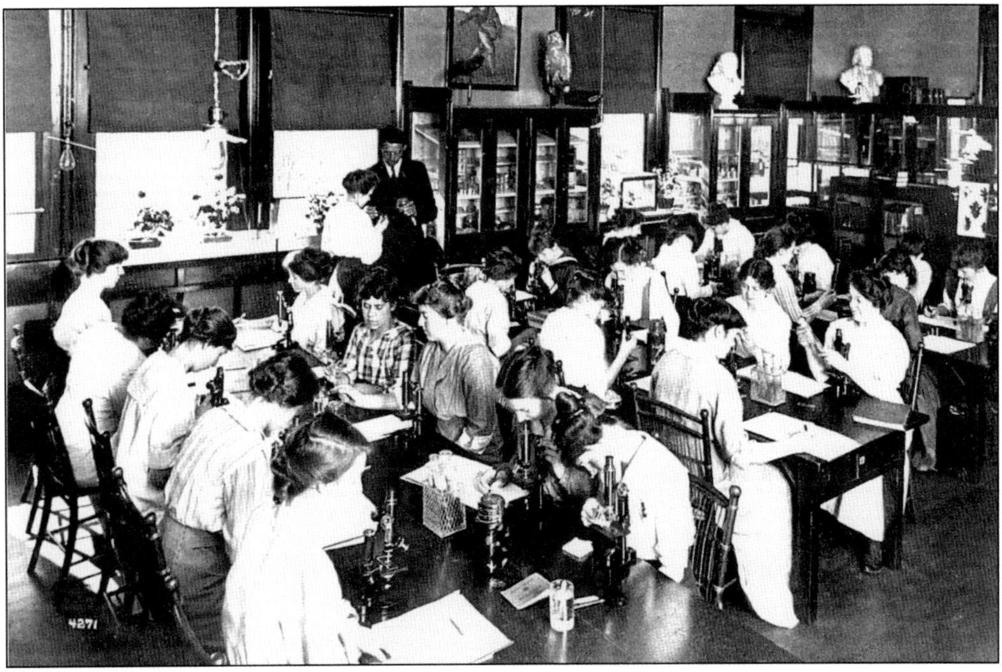

Science Class. Regardless of one's major, whether Household Arts or education, science was a basic requirement. Students were expected to be well rounded, not one-dimensional. It was assumed that they would be able to discuss the subtleties of the universe as effortlessly as world events.

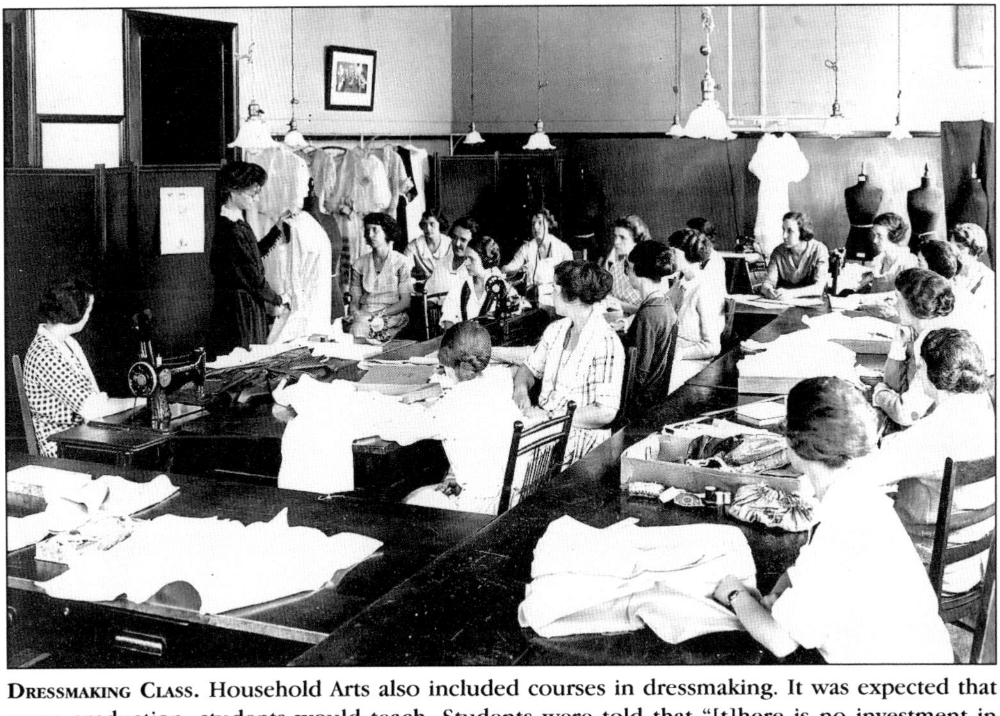

Dressmaking Class. Household Arts also included courses in dressmaking. It was expected that upon graduation, students would teach. Students were told that "[t]here is no investment in life-work more satisfying, more secure, more remunerative, more correct, none more honorable than that of a consecrated teacher."

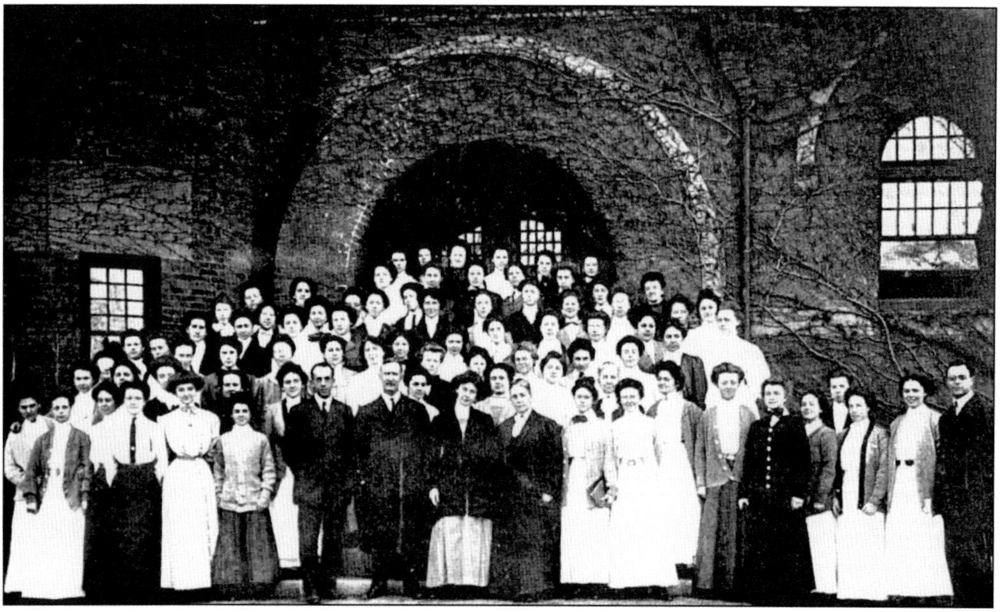

The Class of 1910. There were now 10 normal schools in Massachusetts, all of which had an elementary education component. The Household Arts program was unique to Framingham, as were a secondary education program in Bridgewater and a commercial program in Salem.

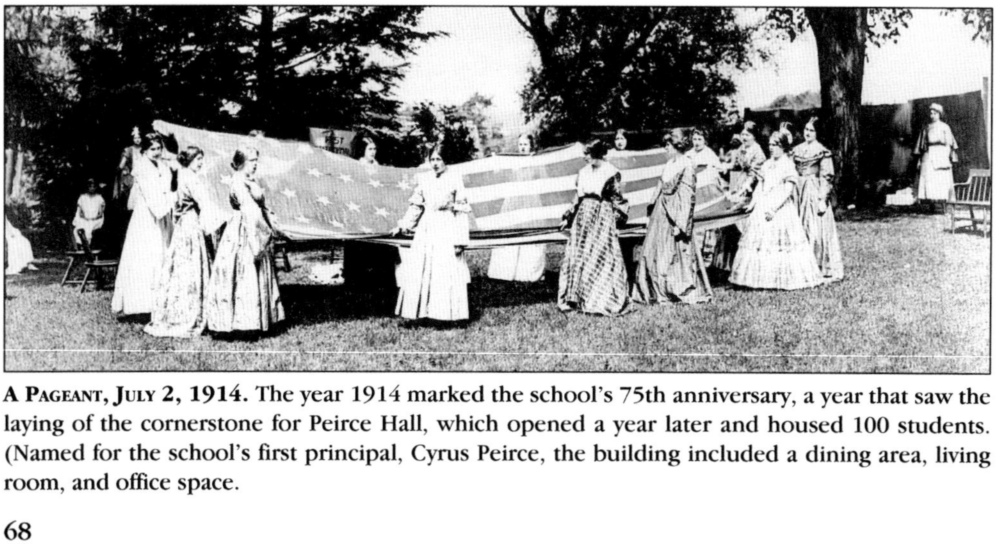

A Pageant, July 2, 1914. The year 1914 marked the school's 75th anniversary, a year that saw the laying of the cornerstone for Peirce Hall, which opened a year later and housed 100 students. (Named for the school's first principal, Cyrus Peirce, the building included a dining area, living room, and office space.

THE ROLL OF HONOR, WORLD WAR I. As in the past, to meet the needs of the nation, the students of Framingham rose to the challenge. Working with the Red Cross, clothing classes made bandages, surgical dressing pads, sweaters, caps, and scarves. Food classes, adhering to the slogan "Food Will Win the War," worked on rationing techniques. Some made an even greater sacrifice, serving in the war itself.

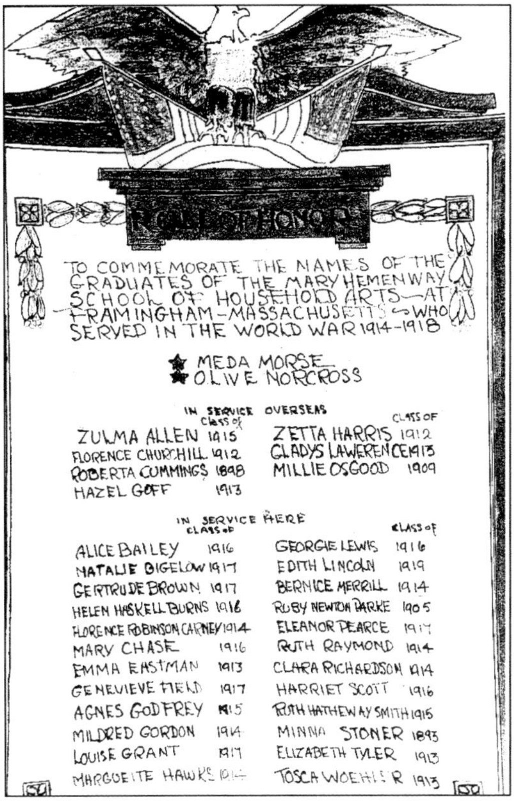

ROLL OF HONOR

TO COMMEMORATE THE NAMES OF THE GRADUATES OF THE MARY HEMENWAY SCHOOL OF HOUSEHOLD ARTS—AT FRAMINGHAM-MASSACHUSETTS—WHO SERVED IN THE WORLD WAR 1914-1918

★ MEDA MORSE
★ OLIVE NORCROSS

IN SERVICE OVERSEAS

	Class of		Class of
ZULMA ALLEN	1915	ZETTA HARRIS	1912
FLORENCE CHURCHILL	1912	GLADYS LAWERENCE	1913
ROBERTA CUMMINGS	1898	MILLIE OSGOOD	1909
HAZEL GOFF	1913		

IN SERVICE HERE

	Class of		Class of
ALICE BAILEY	1916	GEORGIE LEWIS	1916
NATALIE BIGELOW	1917	EDITH LINCOLN	1919
GERTRUDE BROWN	1917	BERNICE MERRILL	1914
HELEN HASKELL BURNS	1916	RUBY NEWTON PARKE	1905
FLORENCE ROBINSON CARNEY	1914	ELEANOR PEARCE	1917
MARY CHASE	1916	RUTH RAYMOND	1914
EMMA EASTMAN	1913	CLARA RICHARDSON	1914
GENEVIEVE FIELD	1917	HARRIET SCOTT	1916
AGNES GODFREY	1915	RUTH HATHEWAY SMITH	1915
MILDRED GORDON	1914	MINNA STONER	1893
LOUISE GRANT	1917	ELIZABETH TYLER	1913
MARGUERITE HAWKS	1914	TOSCA WOEHLER	1913

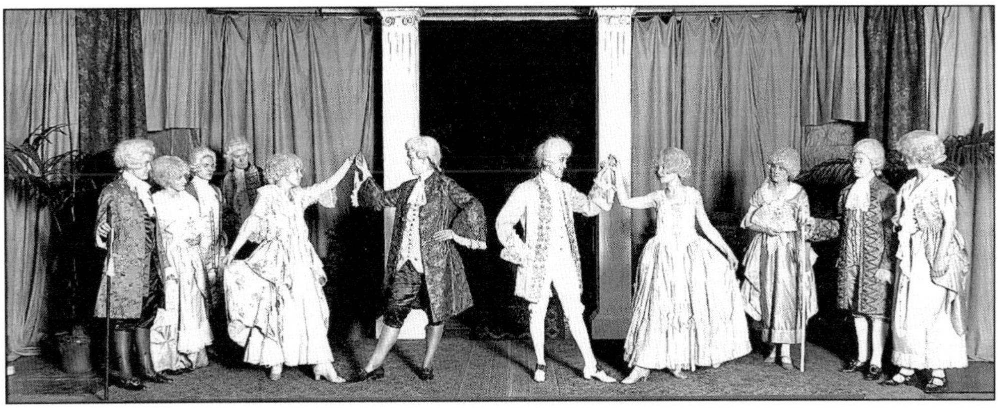

***MONSIEUR BEAUCAIRE*, 1925.** An aspect of student life, in addition to study and athletics, was social, whether singing in the Glee Club or acting in a school play. Making things more difficult was the lack of male actors. Like any difficulty encountered by one attending the school, this, too, was overcome rather easily.

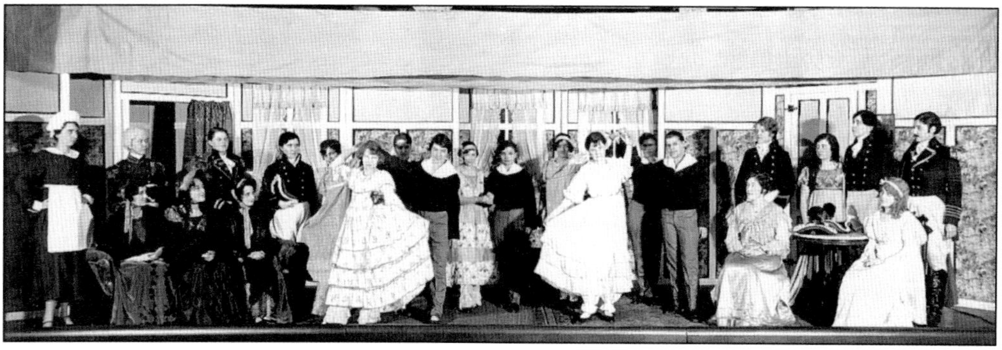

Quality Street, **1929.** Until the Great Depression, enrollment was increasing, reaching approximately 500 by the end of the 1920s. Severe economic times reversed the trend, which lasted the entire decade of the 1930s. While tuition was free to Massachusetts' residents, a student still had to pay room and board ($325) and fees ($25 per term), a significant sum in those days.

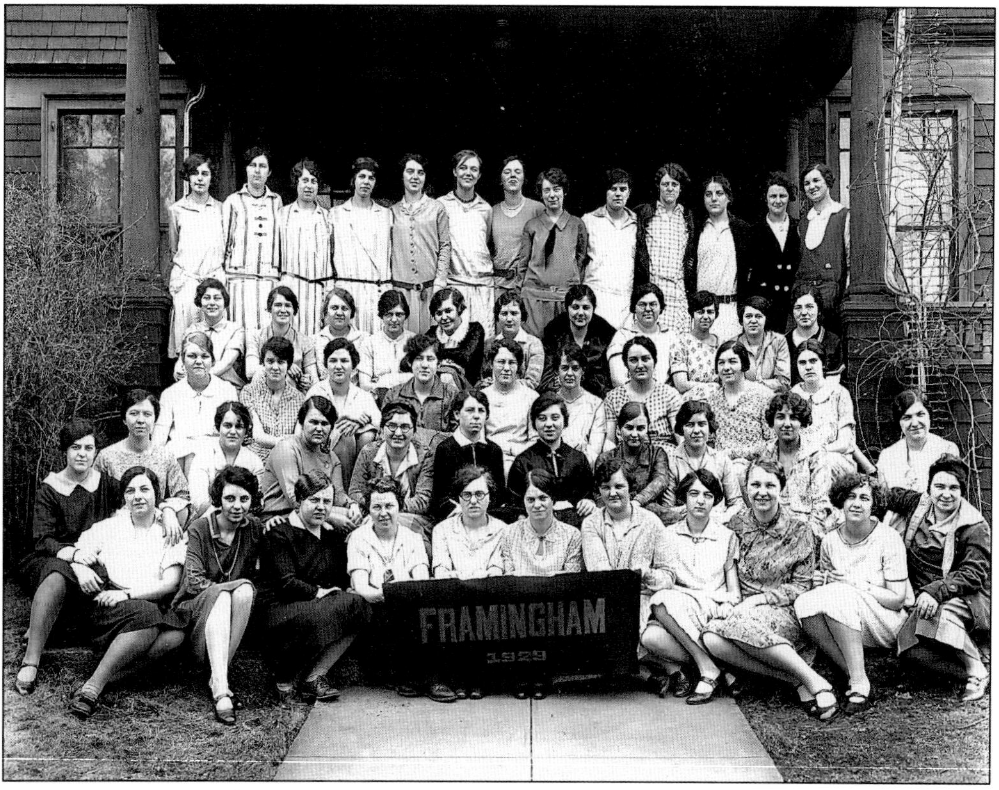

The Class of 1929. The Roaring Twenties were typified by flappers; those who possessed a liberated attitude and awareness, who challenged and provoked. Needless to say, none, at least openly, attended the Normal School, which insisted that its women carry themselves with quiet and understated dignity and respect.

Five

THE DEPRESSION AND WAR YEARS

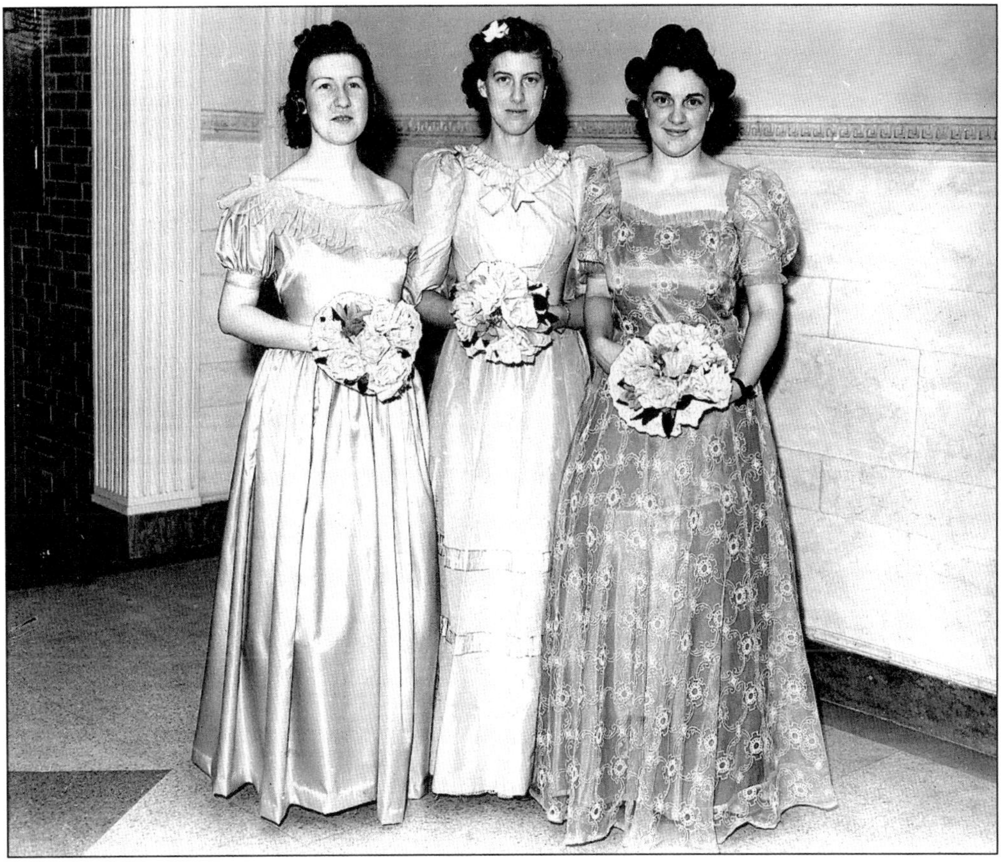

THE CENTENNIAL BALL, APRIL 13, 1939. Dressed in clothing of the early-19th-century, from left to right, are Mabel Ricker, Eleanor Pike, and Beatrice Ammidown. They were chairs of the ball commemorating the school's 100th birthday. In 1939, the Fine Arts Club, rather than presenting its annual play, sponsored a ball in which all came dressed as they would have in 1839. It was the hope of the 1939 club that the ball would be duplicated in 2039, the school's 200th anniversary.

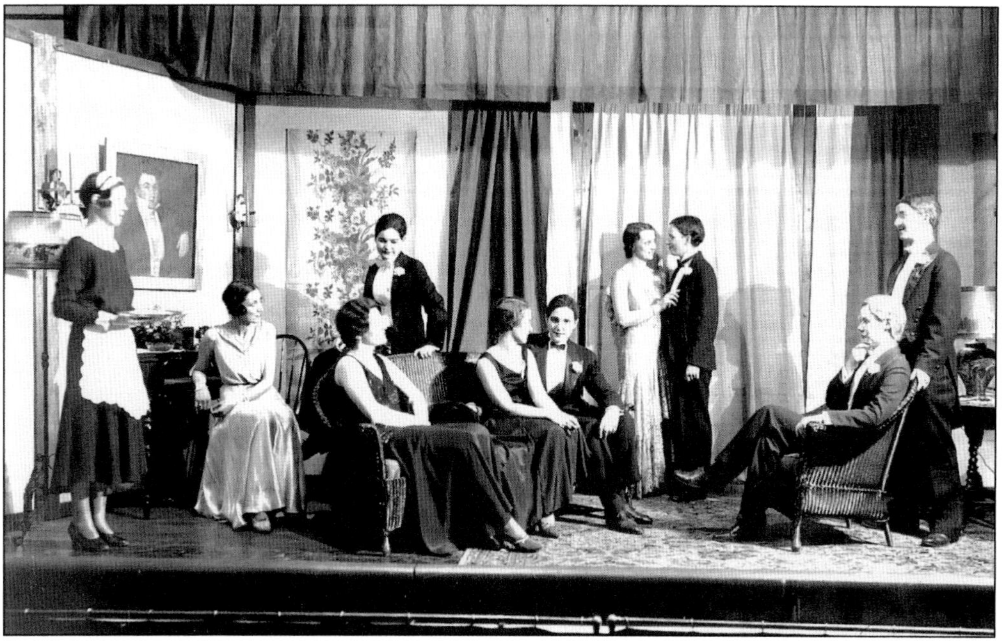

Holiday, **1931.** Music and entertainment have been a campus staple for many years. A Glee Club was active by the end of the 19th century. Frederic Archibald (see page 61) came to the school in 1898 to teach music. Through his encouragement, the students took advantage of the many musical events in nearby Boston.

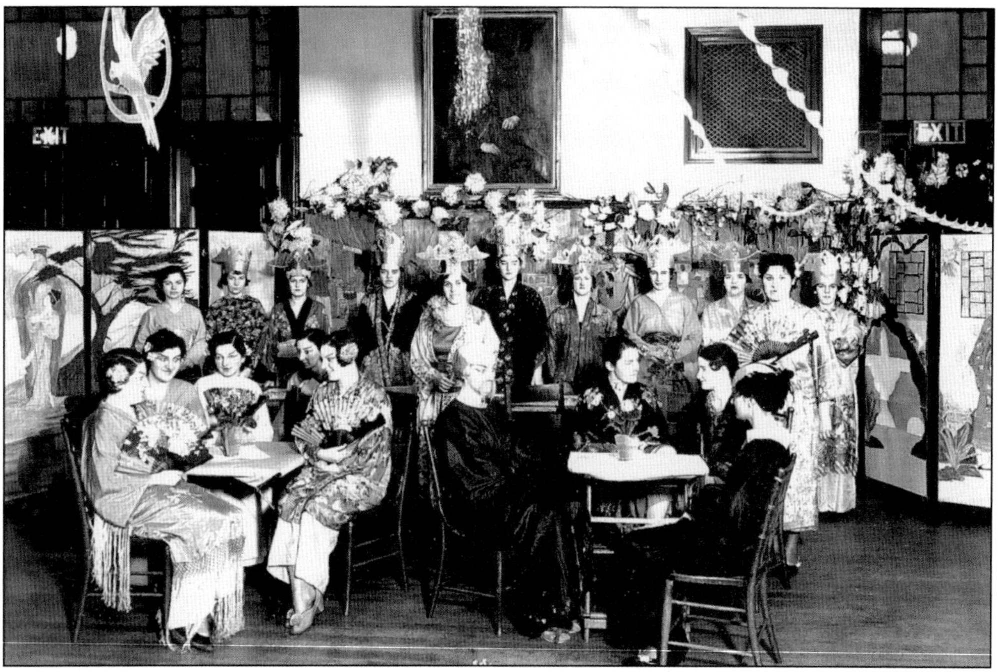

Mousmé of the Toy Shop, **1933.** The Commuter Club, which performed this play, was one of many student organizations. Some others included the yearbook, formerly the *Quill,* renamed the *Dia*l in 1915), and the school newspaper, the *Gatepost*, which was originally known as the *Hilltop News*. The paper's first editor was Marie Blakie, Class of 1933.

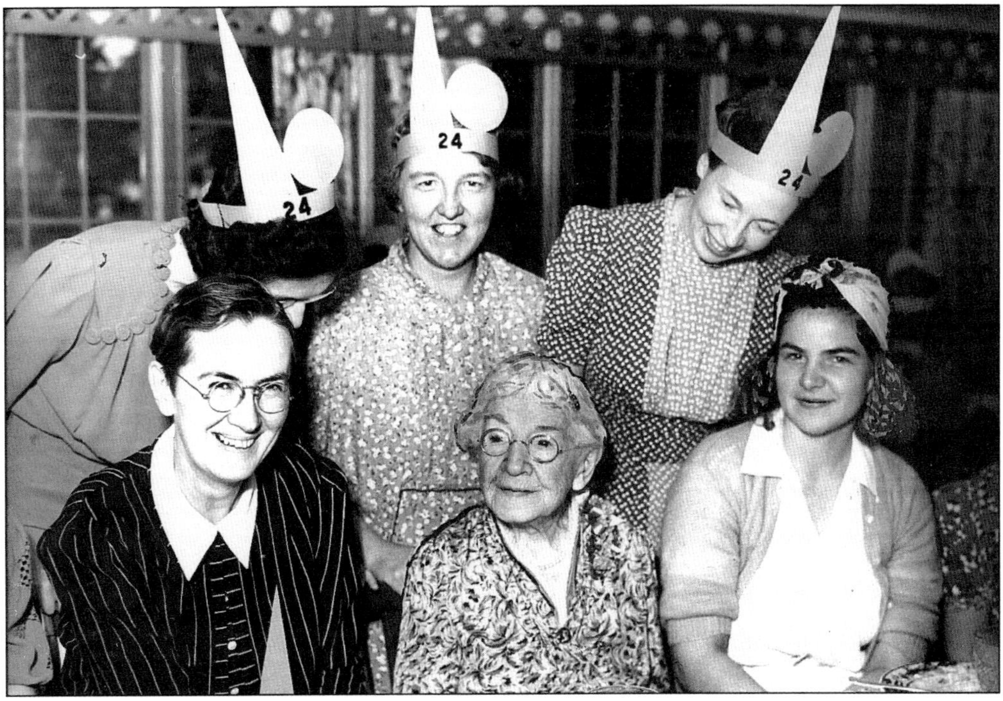

The Alumnae Reunion, June 10, 1939. At the age of 95, Eliza Porter (front center) was the oldest graduate to attend the alumnae celebration of the school's 100th anniversary. An 1864 graduate, she is accompanied by, from left to right, the following: (front row) faculty member Ruth Carter and Carol Porter, Eliza Porter's 18-year-old granddaughter; (back row) 1924 graduates Henderson Gaskill, Sybil Daniels, and Helen F. McKenna.

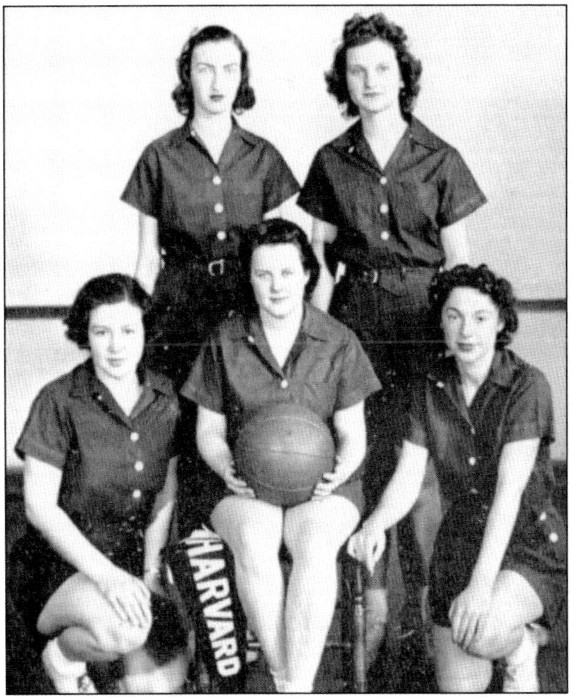

Harvard-Yale, 1940. The annual Harvard-Yale Weekend started in the early 1900s and coincided with the fall Harvard-Yale football games. It was a gala weekend for the campus, with intramural athletic competitions, including field hockey, basketball, and volleyball. By the early 1960s, it was renamed the Black and Gold Weekend. Pictured, from left to right, are the following: (front row) Cora Webb ('41), Catherine Carney ('40) (captain), and Dorothy Dacey ('41); (back row) Mary O'Donnell ('40) and Helen Maxwell ('41).

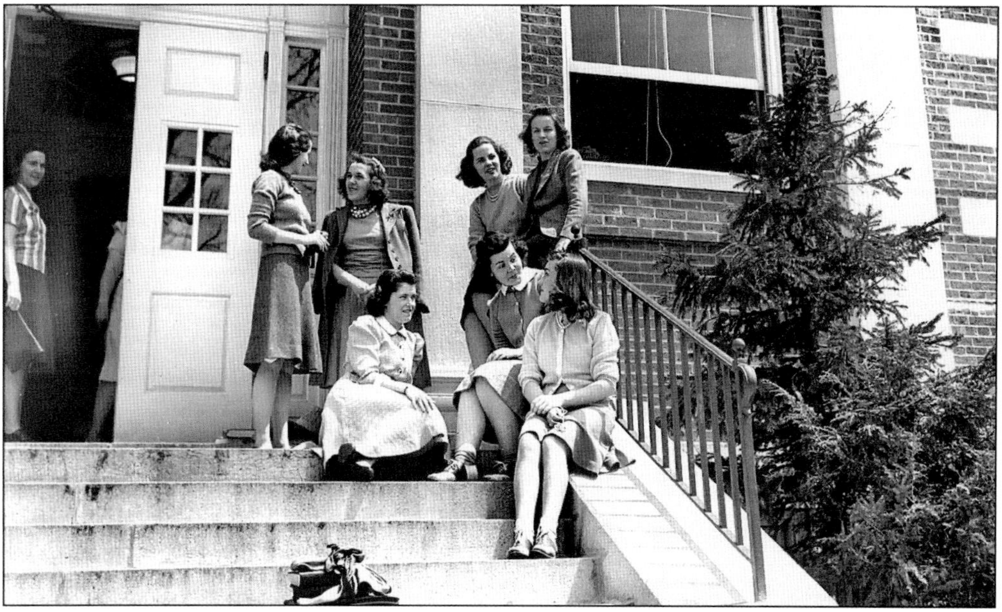

STUDENTS LOUNGING, MAY, 1940. On a warm spring day, seven students gather on the steps of Dwight Hall to catch up on the news of the day. In 1940, the school was entering its second century and Europe was at war—a war which the United States would enter in 1941.

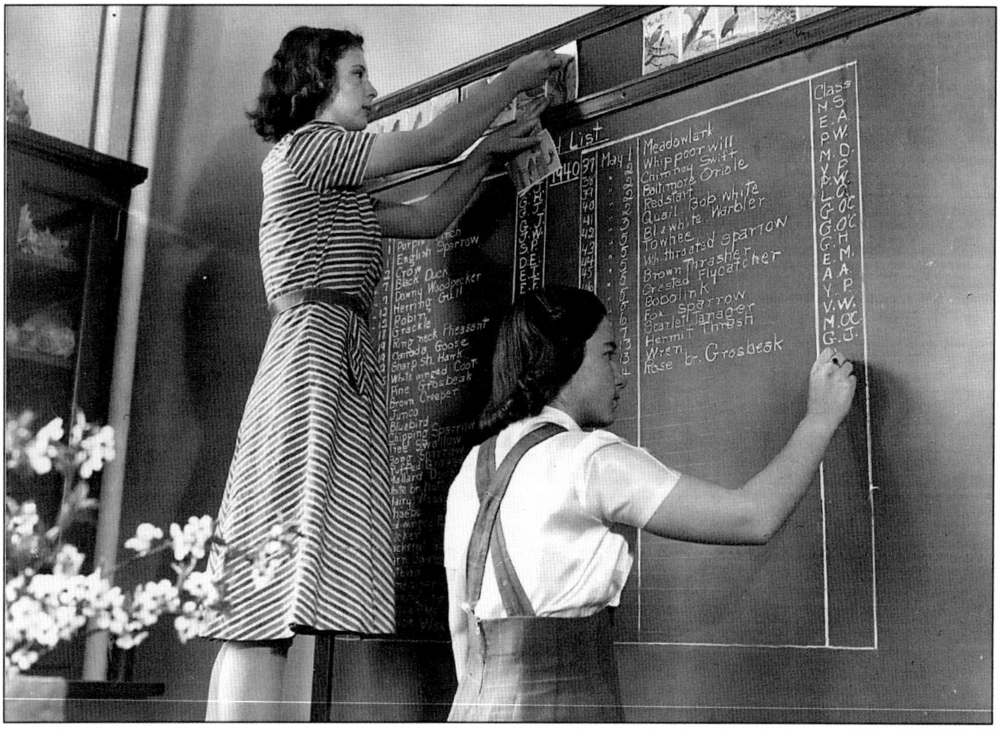

A BIRD LIST, MAY 15, 1940. Two students prepare a bird list and data for use in biology class. Students at the time were confined to their rooms from 7:30 p.m. to 9:30 p.m., and they were expected to study. Starting at 9:30 p.m., students prepared for bedtime, which came at 10:00 p.m. Upper-class students were allowed to be out until 11:00 p.m. one evening during the week.

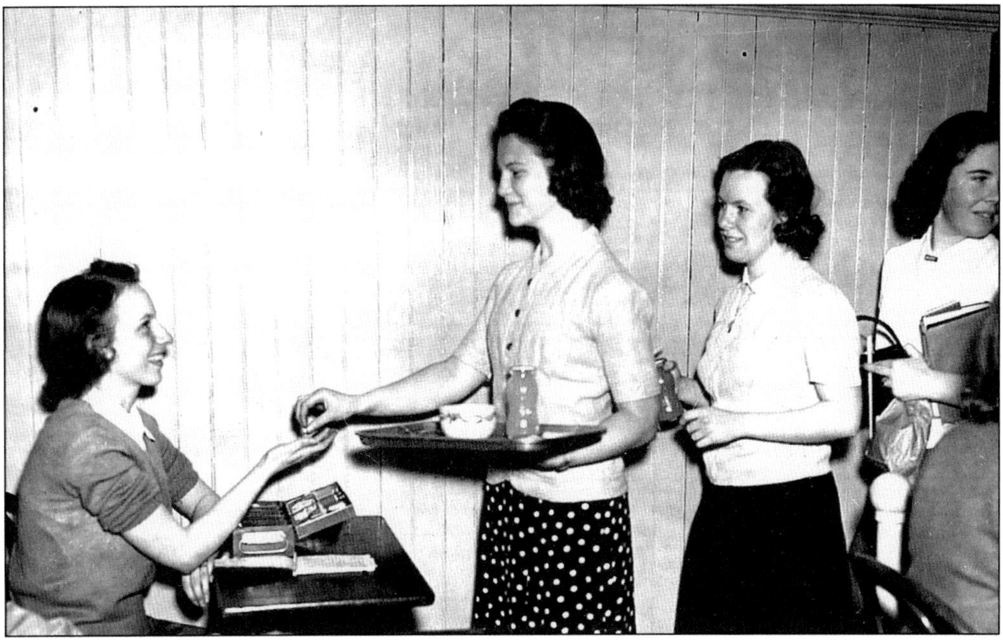

Lunch, May 1940. Smoking had been generally prohibited until 1939, when a new policy was adopted allowing it in certain areas. However, students were still forbidden from smoking in public in the town of Framingham. A student who violated the prohibition faced stern punishment, including expulsion.

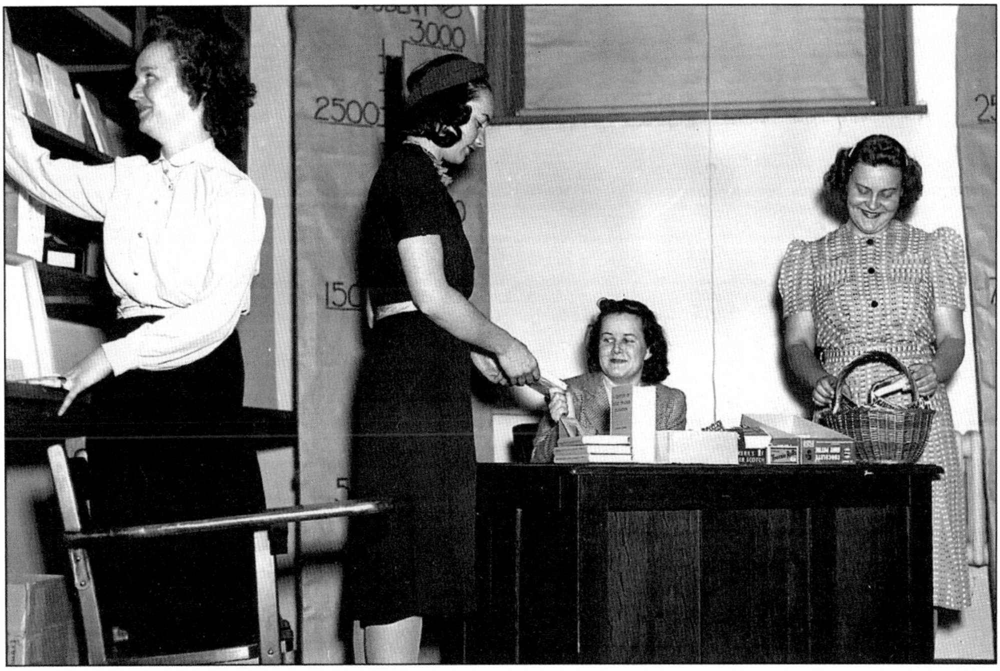

Student Market, 1940. Students working diligently were a common sight. The student handbook indicated a strong belief in the "high standard of scholarship, intellectual integrity, and thoroughness in all our undertakings; in making diligent search through our contacts with other people and books after the best that life has to offer."

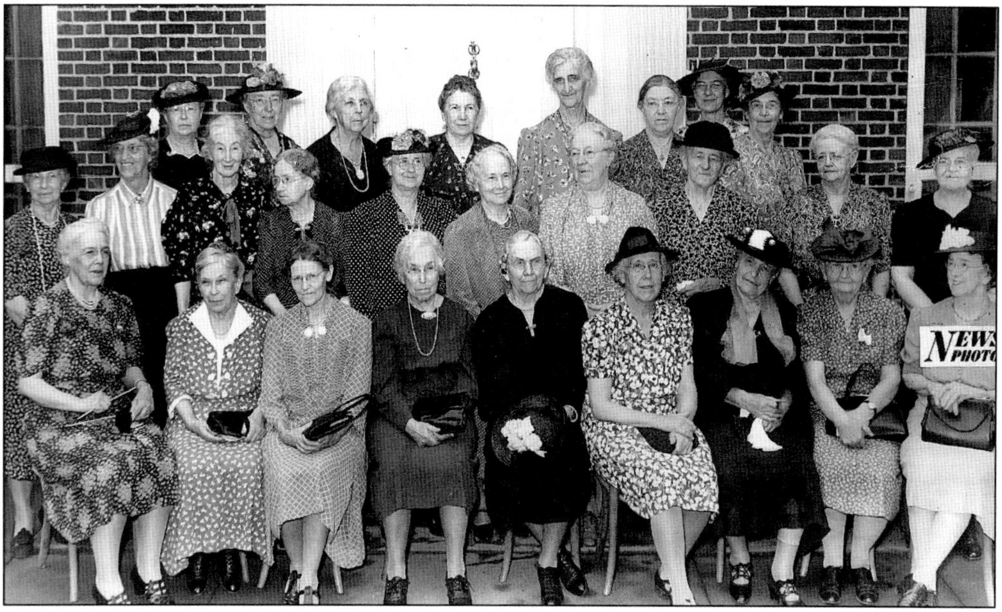

The Oldest Graduates, June 1941. A noteworthy feature of the college is the loyalty of many of its graduates, who keep in touch with both classmates and the institution long after they have graduated. Six months after this photograph was taken, Pearl Harbor was attacked, and during the ensuing war, the school provided more dietitians to the armed services than any other school except Iowa State.

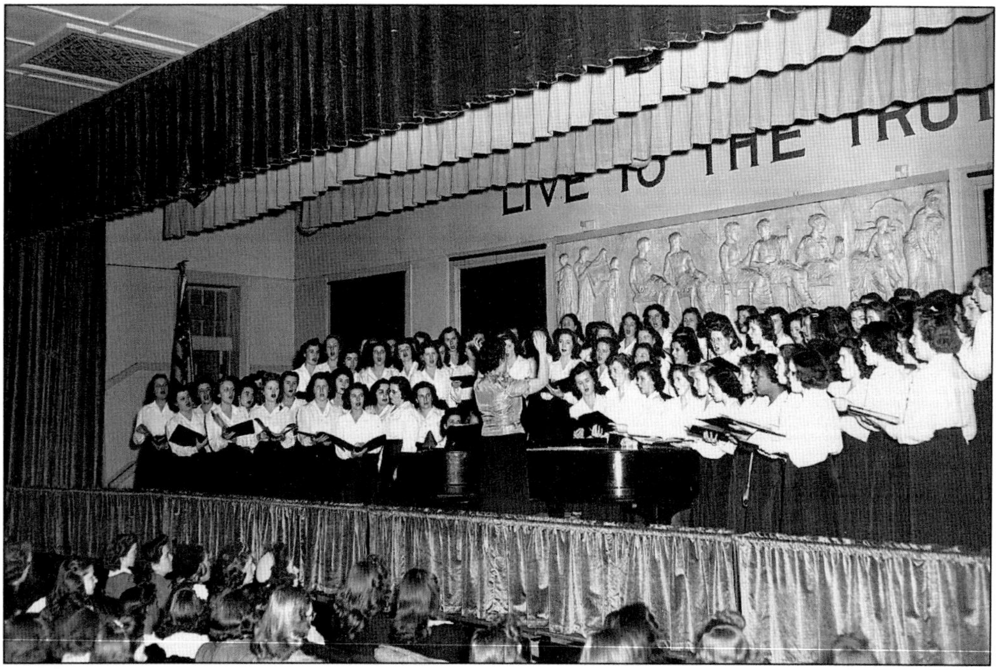

The Glee Club, 1943. The Glee Club formed during the administration of Ellen Hyde. Student activities were an essential aspect of the institution. The student handbook stressed loyalty, sportsmanship, courtesy, integrity, scholarship, and involvement in all aspects of life. The school's motto to this day is "Live to the Truth."

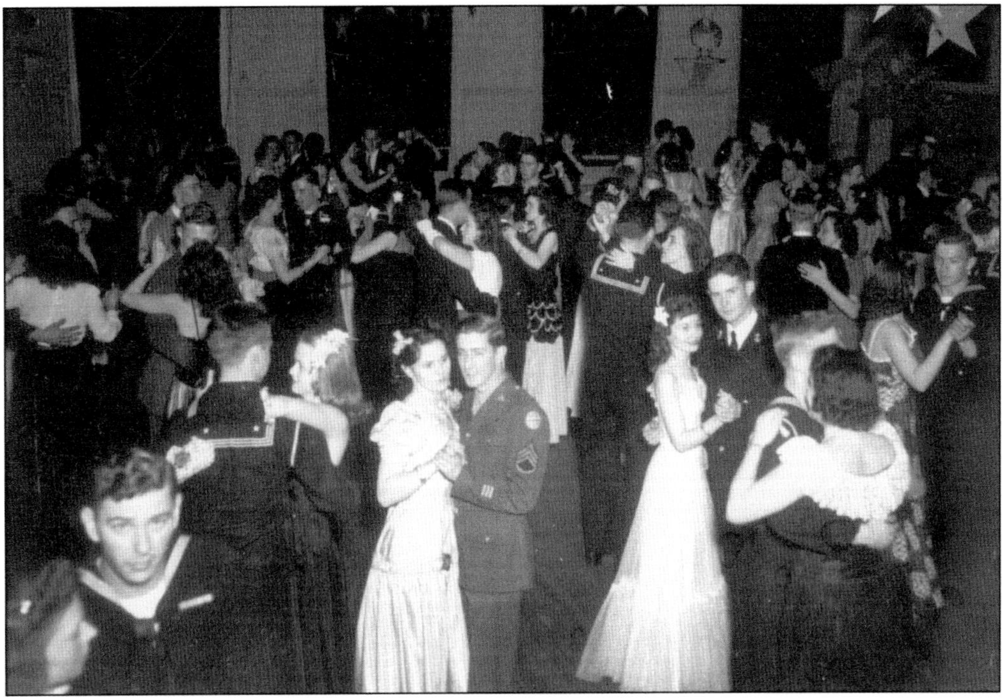

A School Dance. At these dances, the women of the college entertained servicemen on leave. During the war years, breakfast and lunch cost approximately 35¢ each, while dinner was a whopping 50¢. In 1954, the costs were similar, still 35¢ for breakfast, 50¢ for lunch, and 90¢ for dinner.

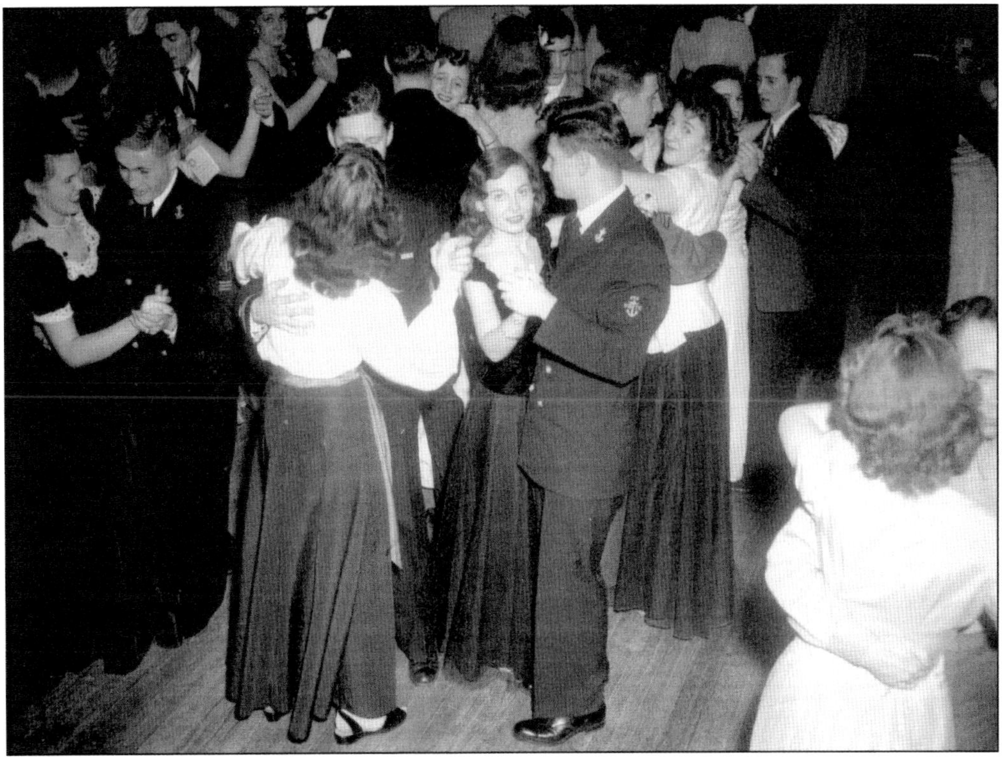

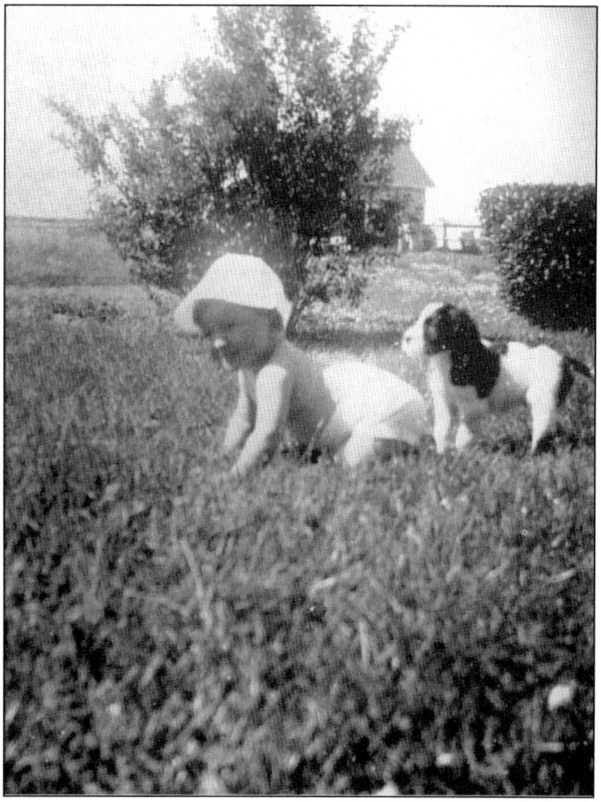

Class Baby, c. late 1930s. Often a recent alumna or faculty member who was a new mother had the honor of having her child designated Class Baby. Students, however, were not so recognized. Indeed, until 1949, a student who was married and/or had a child was dismissed. Pictured is William Paul Hoadley, son of Paul and Mary (Stevens) Hoadley, Class of 1939, Household Arts.

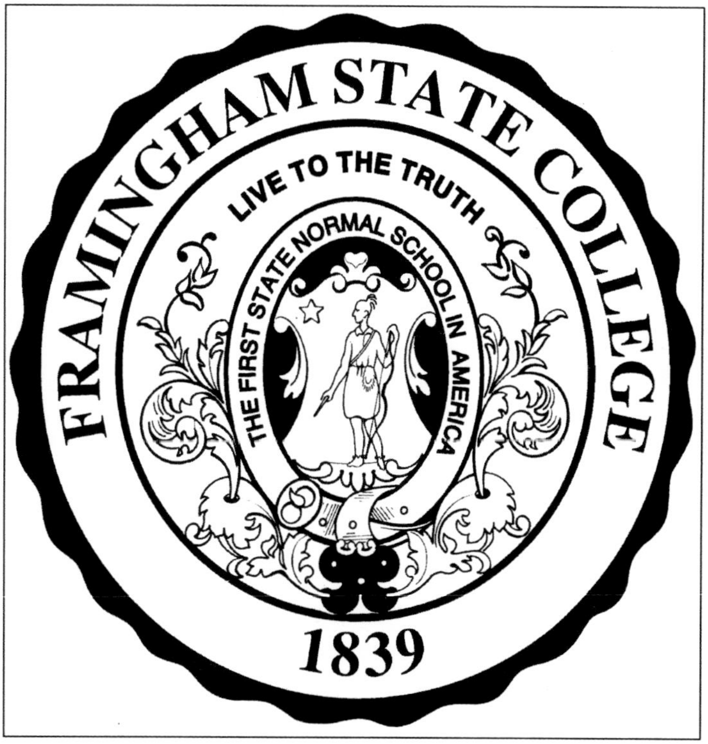

The College Seal. The college seal bears the school motto, "Live to the Truth," a phrase coined by the school's first principal, Cyrus Peirce.

Six

THOSE WHO MADE A DIFFERENCE

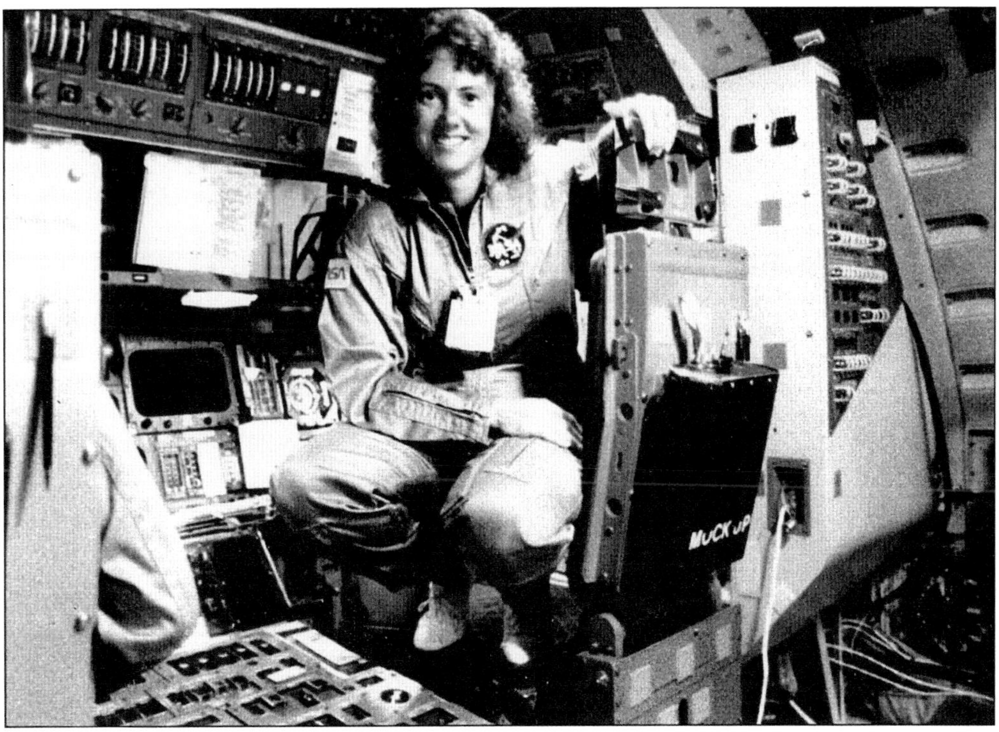

CHRISTA MCAULIFFE. Perhaps the most famous FSC alumna, Christa Corrigan McAuliffe graduated in 1970 and moved to New Hampshire, where she became a teacher. Selected by the National Aeronautics and Space Administration (NASA) to be the first teacher in space, she was a member of the ill-fated *Challenger* crew when the space shuttle exploded in 1986.

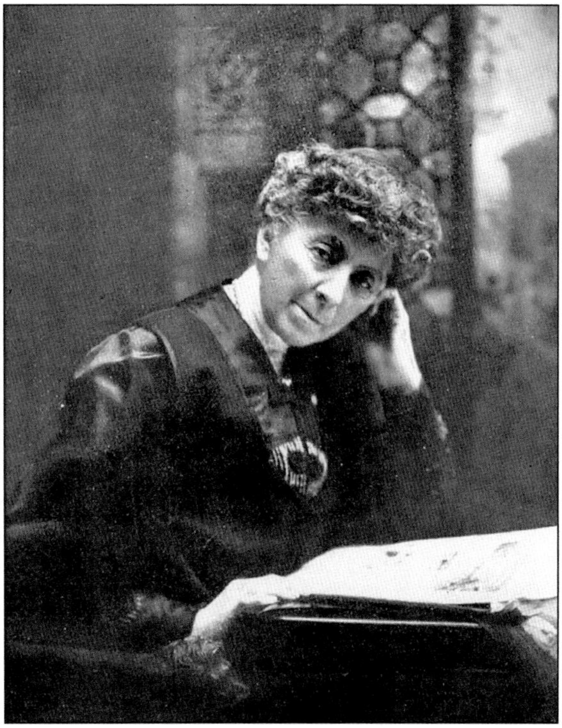

Jennie E. Howard. Jennie Howard (1866), Elizabeth B. Coolidge (1864), and Edith Howe (1867) formed a pioneering group of women educators who founded normal schools in Argentina, starting in 1883, at the request of Argentinean educator Domingo Sarmiento. Howard died in Buenos Aires in 1930. Her memoir, *In Distant Climes and Other Years,* was published posthumously in 1931.

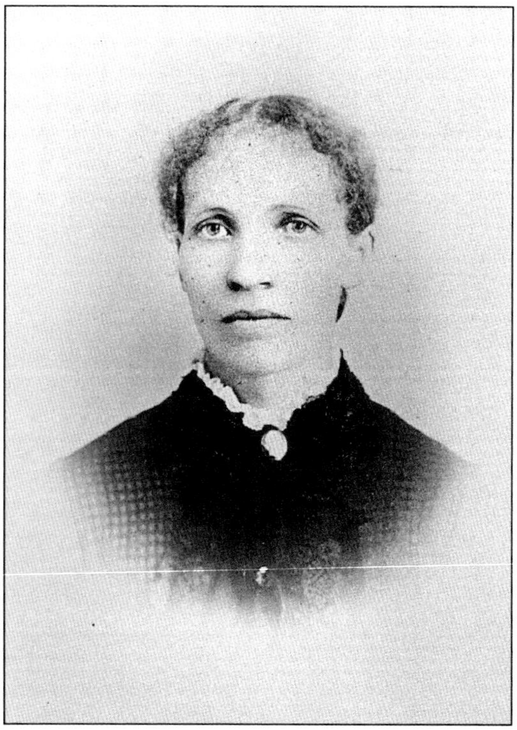

Olivia Davidson. An 1881 African American graduate of the school, Olivia Davidson married Booker T. Washington and helped him found the Tuskegee Institute, where a building has been named in her honor. A true pioneer throughout her life, she lived and worked in various areas of the country, including Virginia, Ohio, Mississippi, Alabama, Tennessee, and Massachusetts, until she died of tuberculosis in 1889.

Annie Dawson, Class of 1889. An Arikara Indian from the Dakota Territory, Annie Dawson became an Indian service agent, serving at Fort Berthold in North Dakota. Her attendance and graduation is further evidence of the college's historic commitment to diversity.

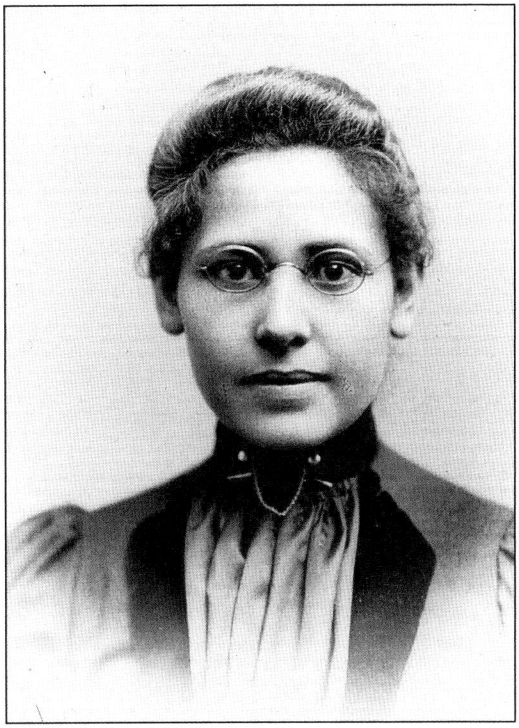

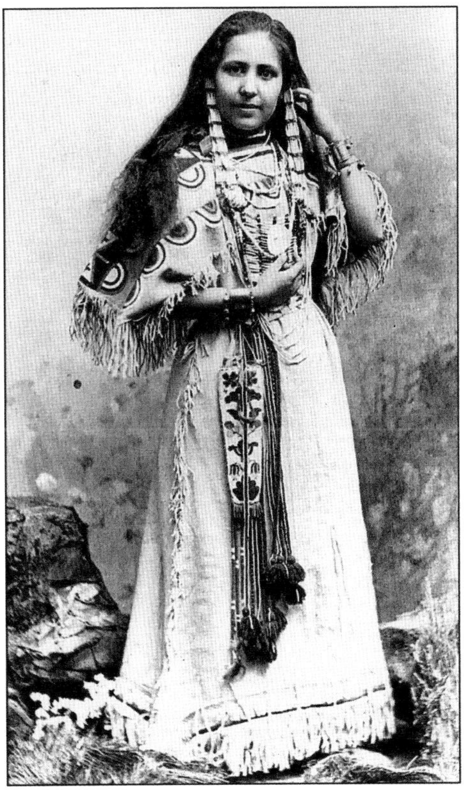

Annie Dawson, in Native American Dress. The school was at the forefront of advancing the rights of women and minorities. The nation's first African American female graduate from a teachers college was Mary E. Miles, Class of 1843. After graduation, she taught and became involved in the abolition movement. She eventually married Henry Bibb, an escaped slave, and together, they moved to Ontario, Canada. There, they cofounded the influential Underground Railroad newspaper *Voice of the Fugitive*. After Bibb's death in 1854, she remarried and founded schools for black children in Ontario.

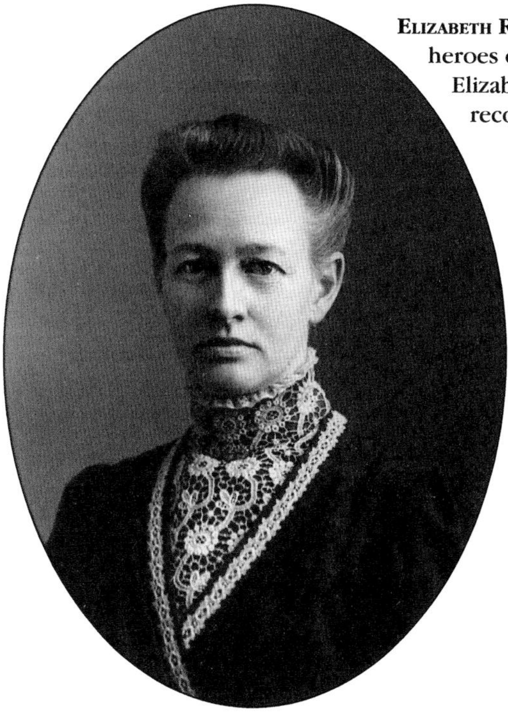

Elizabeth Robbins, 1892. This graduate typifies the unsung heroes of the Normal School. After graduation in 1894, Elizabeth Robbins taught at the internationally recognized Perkins Institute for the Blind.

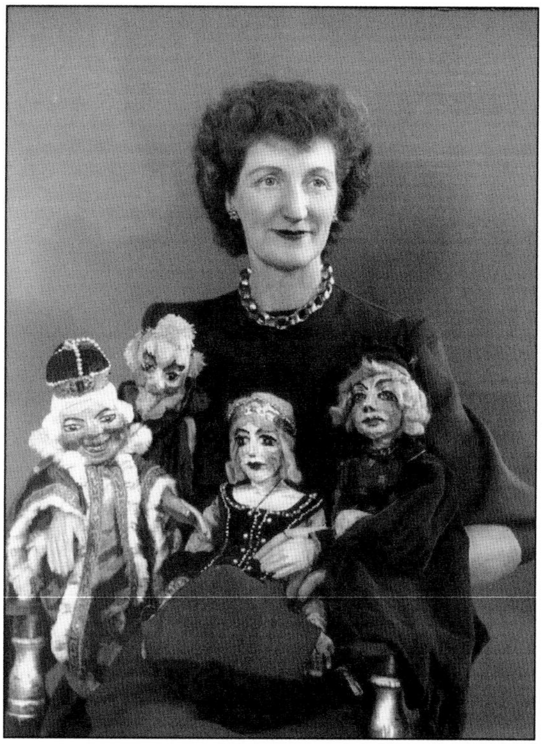

Louise Kingman, 1947. This Class of 1917 alumna returned to the college as a faculty member for 30 years. Louise Kingman taught subjects speech, drama, and physical education (including tennis and golf). She created puppets and marionettes as a teaching aid for children and eventually donated them to the college. A movie buff, she shot films depicting campus life during the 1930s and 1940s, which created a lasting, unique, and valuable record of the college's past.

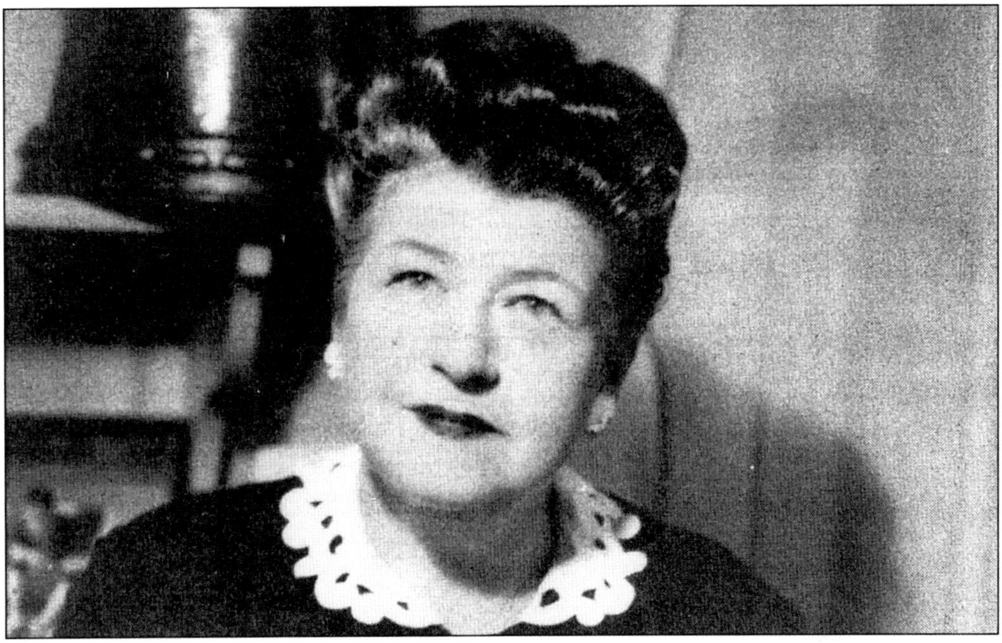

Ruth Graves Wakefield, Inventor of the Chocolate Chip Cookie. After graduating from the Normal School's Department of Household Arts in 1924, Ruth Graves Wakefield worked as a dietitian and food lecturer. In 1930, she published *Ruth Wakefield's Recipes: Tried and True*, which went through 39 printings. One of her recipes was for the tollhouse chocolate crunch cookie, named for the Toll House Inn, a restaurant she owned with her husband, Ken Wakefield. To this day, Nestlé prints both her recipe and the Toll House story on the back of its chocolate chip packages. In 1969, she donated her cookbook collection to the college.

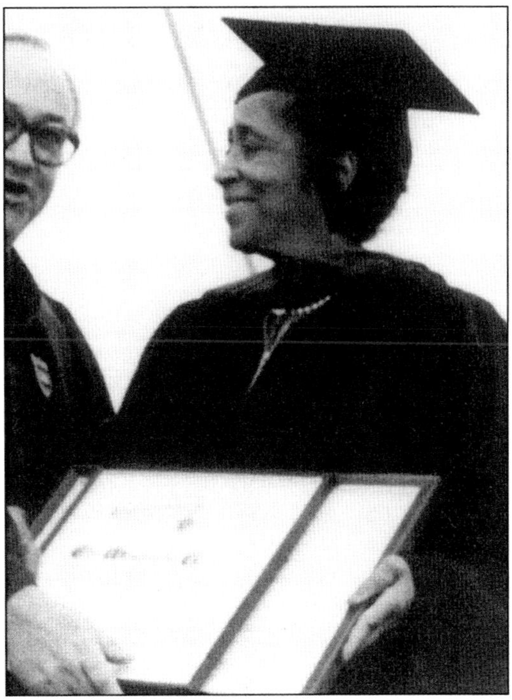

Ella Washington Griffin, Class of 1939. For nearly half a century, Ella Griffin was a worldwide advocate for literacy and education as she worked with both the U.S. government and the United Nations. With the latter she was head of the adult education section of UNESCO (the United Nations Educational Scientific Cultural Organization), retiring in 1965. Even after retirement, she continued to fight illiteracy. She was awarded an honorary doctorate from FSC in 1985.

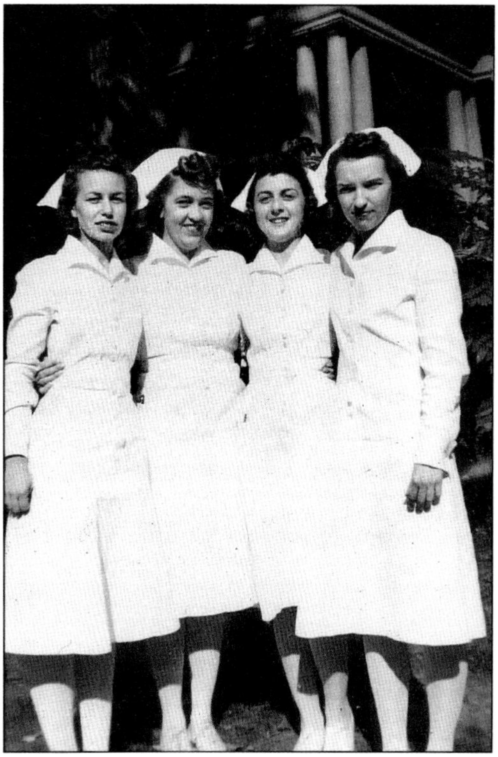

Connie Jordan, Class of 1941. Student, educator, and college administrator, Connie Jordan (left) has been a staunch supporter of the school throughout her life (see page 118 for a later picture of her). This photograph was taken in August 1942 at her graduation from a dietetic internship in Hartford, Connecticut. With her, from left to right, are Betty Totilis Davis ('41), Betty Shafran Horne ('41), and intern Rhoda Chase.

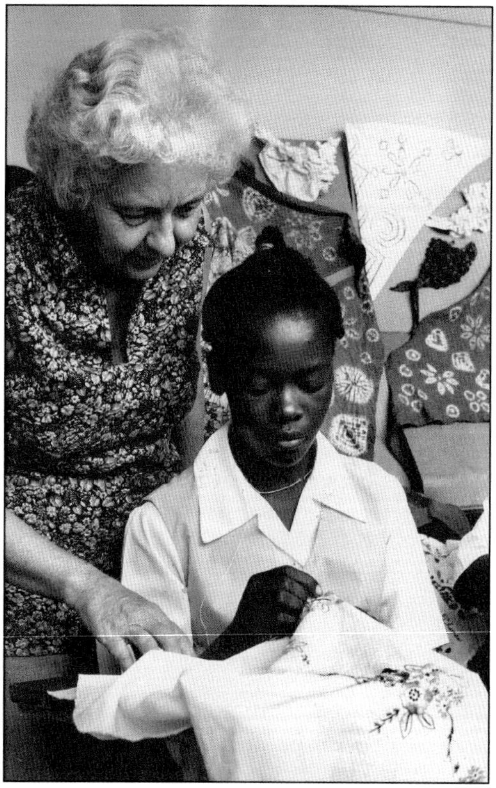

Beverly Allen, Class of 1976, Peace Corps Volunteer. Soon after her graduation at the age of 52, Beverly Allen, of the town of Dartmouth, volunteered for the Peace Corps. Assigned to Kingston, Jamaica, she taught sewing and embroidery to young students at a school sponsored by the YWCA. A graduate of the Clothing and Textiles program, she observed, "I love my job and these fantastic kids who have not had a good learning experience in life."

SHARON CHRISTA CORRIGAN, CLASS OF 1970. The future Christa McAuliffe was born on September 2, 1948, to Ed and Grace Corrigan. In 1966, she graduated from Marian High School in Framingham. Four years later, in 1970, she graduated from FSC, majoring in history and education. That same year, she married Steve McAuliffe. Their son, Scott, was born in 1976, and daughter, Caroline, in 1979.

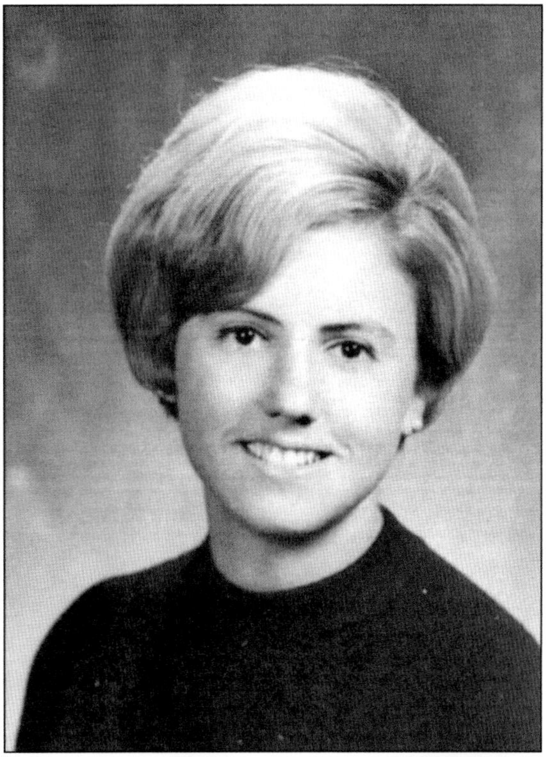

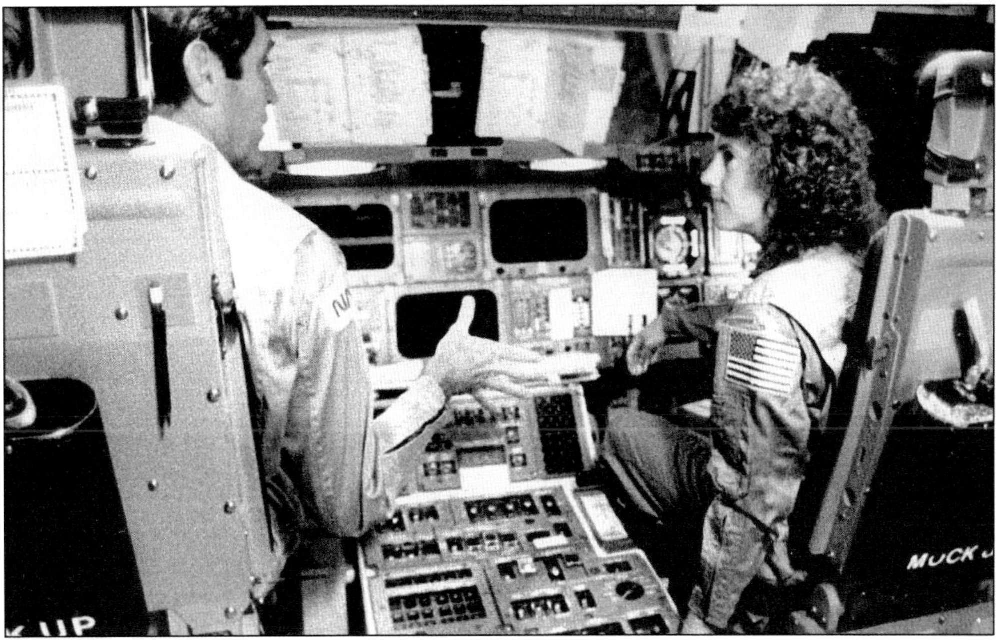

CHRISTA MCAULIFFE AT THE CONTROL PANEL. In 1984, after Pres. Ronald Reagan announced that "one of America's finest: a teacher" would become NASA's first citizen in space, 11,000 teachers applied. In 1985, the pool was reduced to 10 finalists, who were flown to Houston for interviews and tests. On July 11, Vice Pres. Bush announced that Christa McAuliffe had been selected as the first teacher in space.

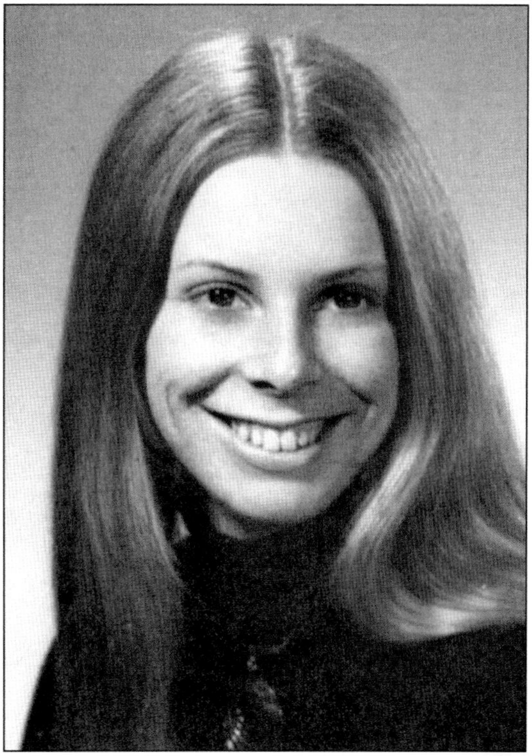

Paula Rooney, Class of 1973, College President. After receiving a degree in elementary education, Paula Rooney received a master's and Ph.D. from Indiana University. She held various college and university positions before being named president of Dean College, in the town of Franklin, in 1995.

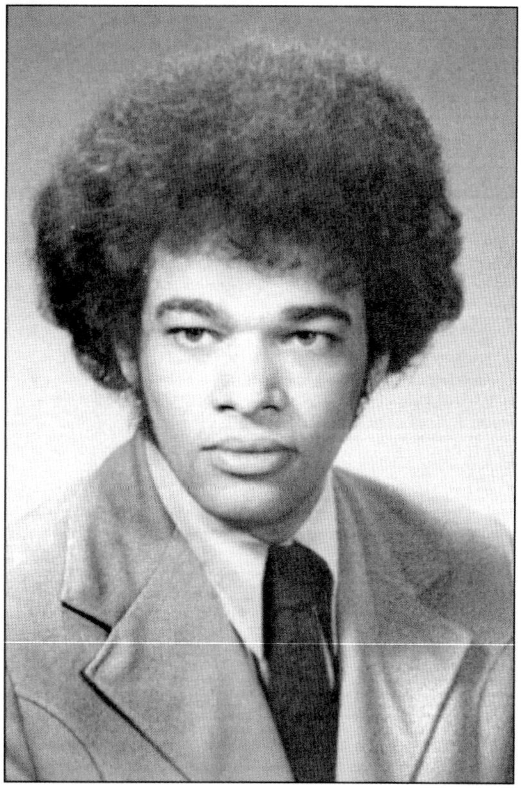

Jeff Stetson, Class of 1973, Playwright. A psychology major at FSC, Jeff Stetson earned a master's degree from Boston University. His first play, *The Meeting,* was originally produced in 1987. It relates a fictional meeting between Malcolm X and Martin Luther King. The play was chosen for several awards and was televised nationally on PBS's *American Playhouse* in 1989. It has been produced in many countries around the world. He was awarded an honorary doctorate by FSC in 1993. He currently lives in California, writing for both the stage and television.

Paul LeBlanc, Class of 1980, College President. After graduating from FSC with a major in English, Paul LeBlanc received a master's in English from Boston College and a Ph.D. from the University of Massachusetts at Amherst, with a discipline in composition theory and technology. A noted scholar and writer in the area of educational technology, he became vice president of Houghton Mifflin, where he was instrumental in creating the company's higher education technology group. He served as president of Marlboro College until June 2003, at which time he left to become president of the University of Southern New Hampshire.

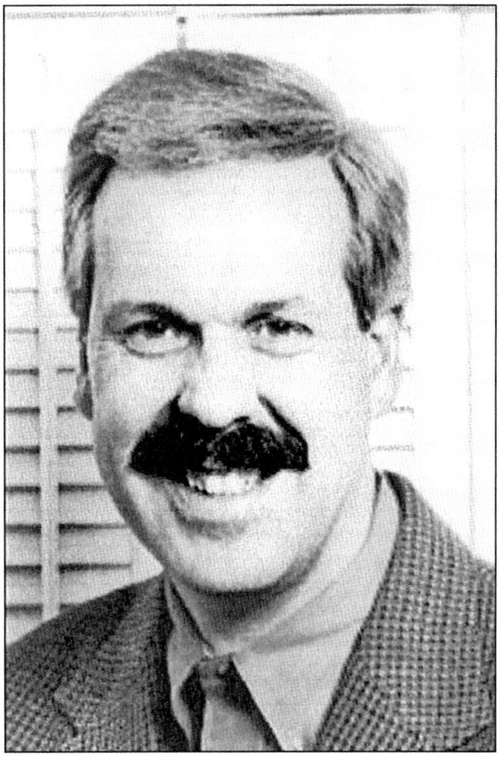

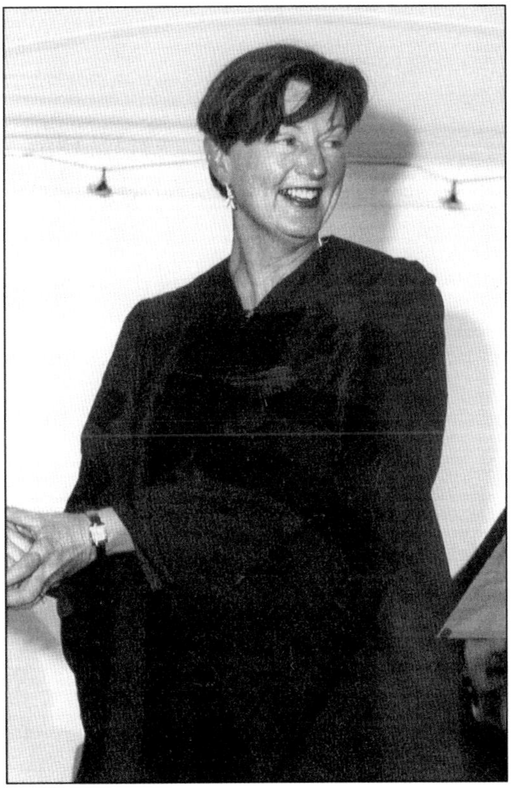

Barbara Gardner, Class of 1982, State Representative. After serving in the Massachusetts House of Representatives from 1986 through 2000, Barbara Gardner left to become the associate commissioner of school readiness at the Massachusetts Department of Education. As a state representative, she held many leadership positions, including first assistant majority leader and majority whip. Throughout her distinguished career, she has championed numerous educational issues. She is shown receiving an honorary degree in 2001. One year later, she was named to the FSC Board of Trustees.

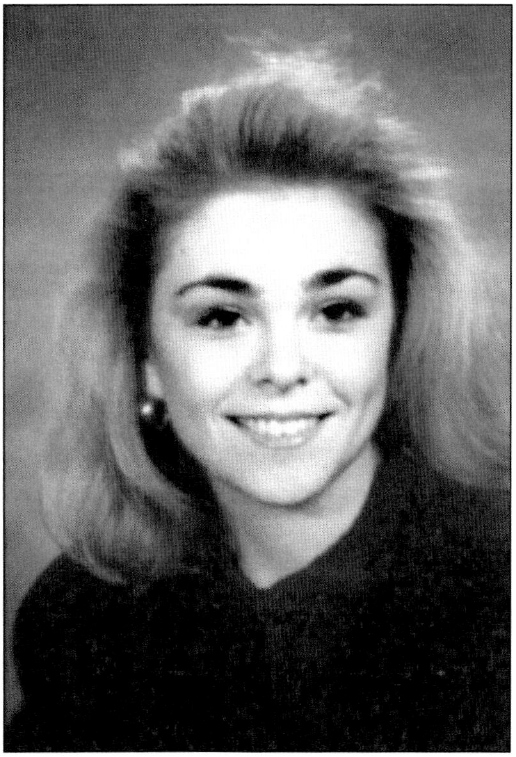

COMMUNICATIONS NOW—KRISTEN DALY, CLASS OF 1992. A communication arts major at FSC, Kristen has worked for several Boston-area television stations, including WBZ-TV, Channel 4, and WABU-TV, Channel 68, in news research, writing, reporting, and production. Currently, she is a news reporter and a frequent anchor for the *Ten O'Clock News* on WLVI-TV, Channel 56.

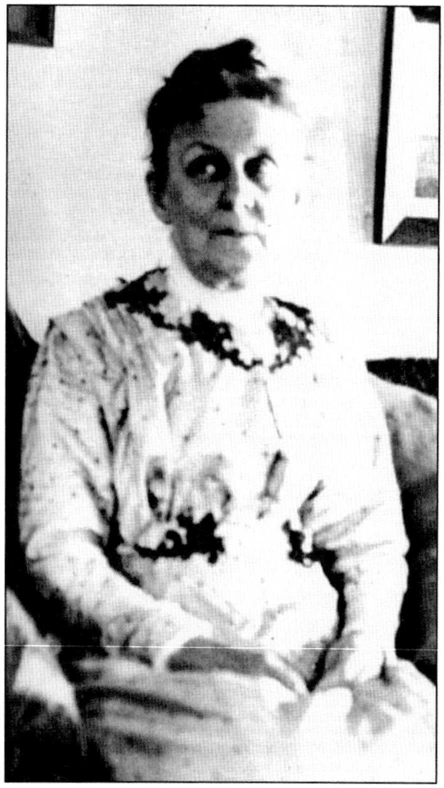

COMMUNICATIONS THEN—CHARLOTTE STEARNS, CLASS OF 1861. Regarded as the poetess of her class, Charlotte Stearns taught at the Normal School, as well as at Antioch College in Ohio. She passed her writing skills on to her son, T.S. (Thomas Stearns) Eliot, one of the preeminent literary figures of the 20th century.

Seven

From World War II to Vietnam

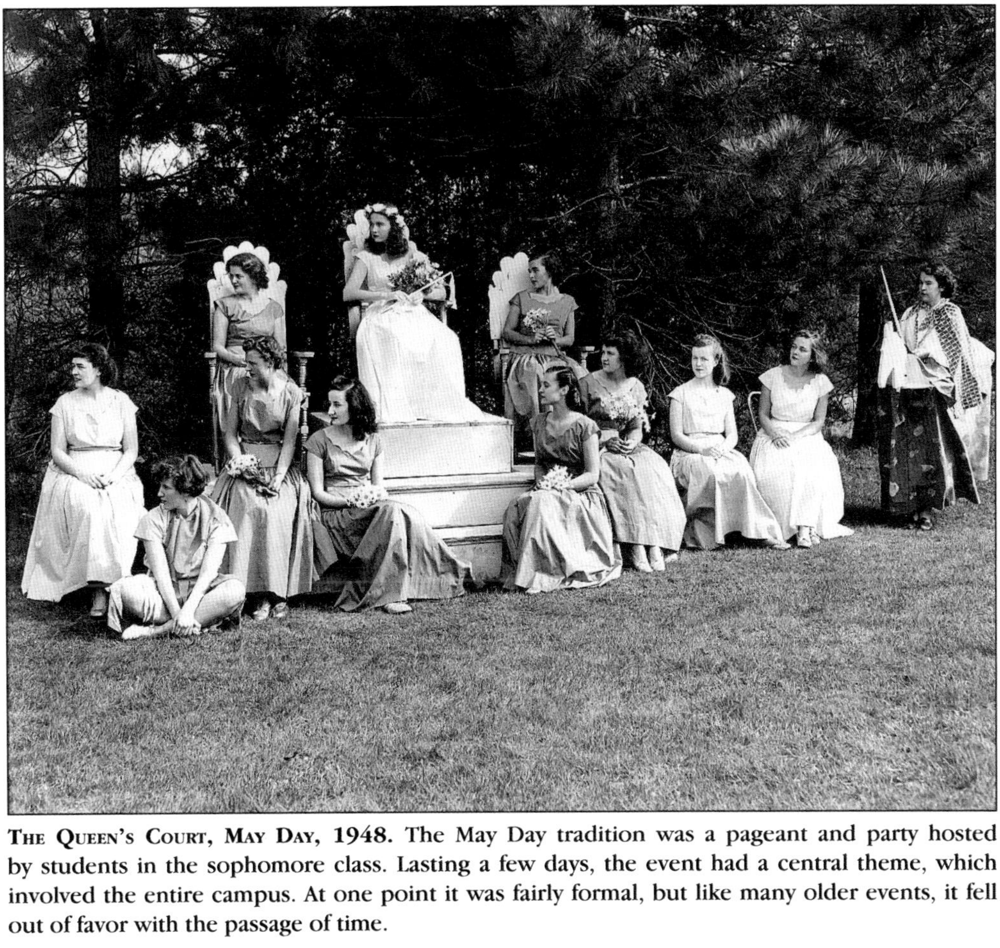

The Queen's Court, May Day, 1948. The May Day tradition was a pageant and party hosted by students in the sophomore class. Lasting a few days, the event had a central theme, which involved the entire campus. At one point it was fairly formal, but like many older events, it fell out of favor with the passage of time.

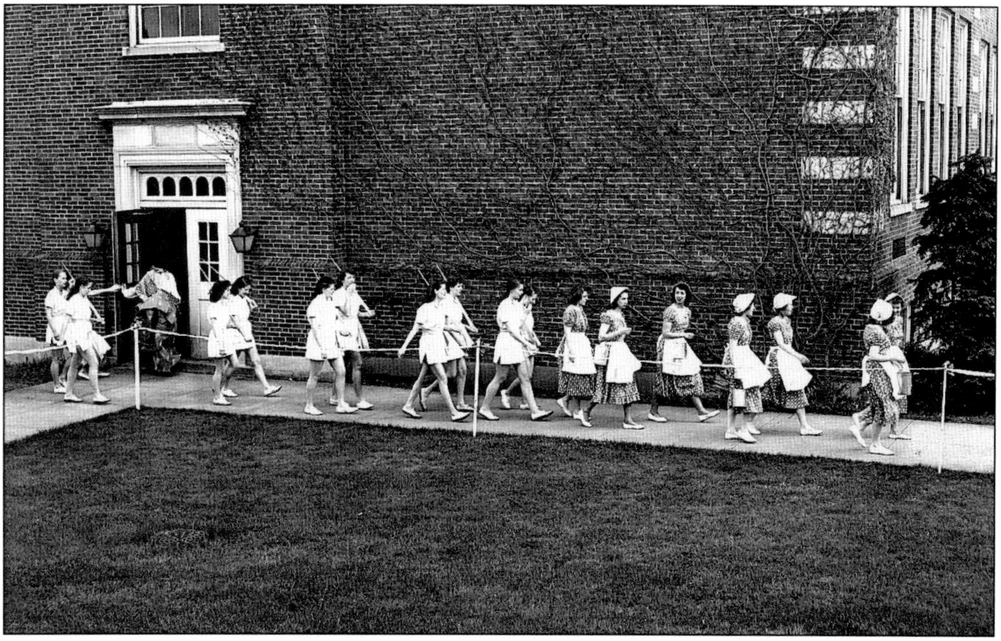

WOMEN MARCHING, MAY DAY, 1948. May Day queens promised to return in the future to attend the yearly event. In the early days, the festivities started with a chapel service. After prayers, members of the sophomore class, wearing their finest outfits, paraded down a predetermined route, followed by the May Day queen and her attendants.

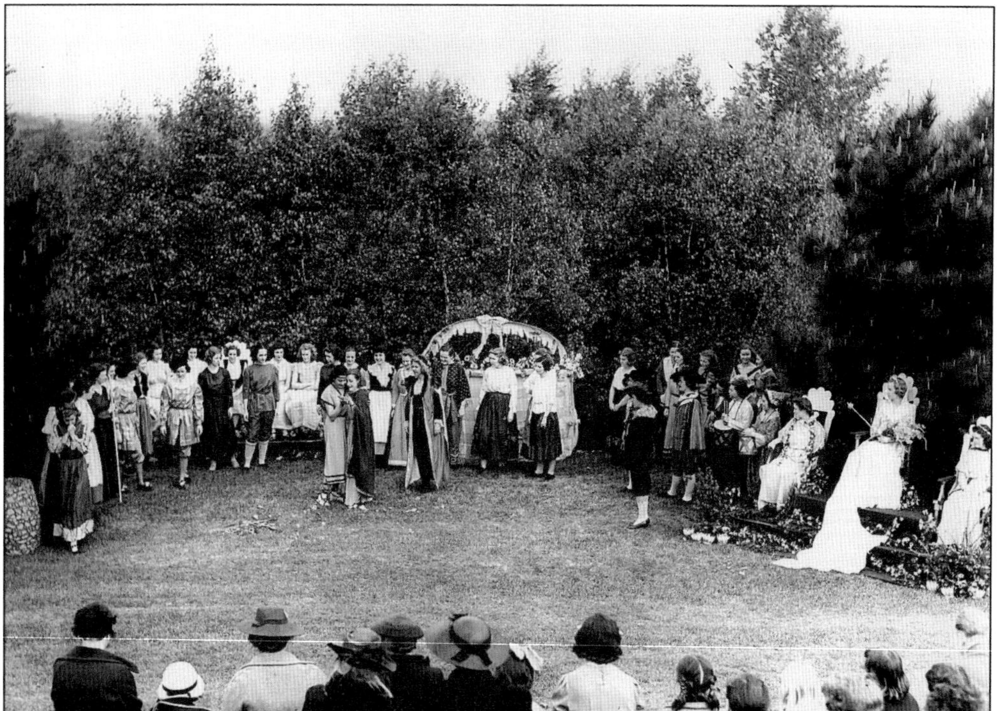

THE PAGEANT, MAY DAY, 1950. The May queen and her court preside over these popular festivities, with an audience made up of students, alumnae, and families of the participants.

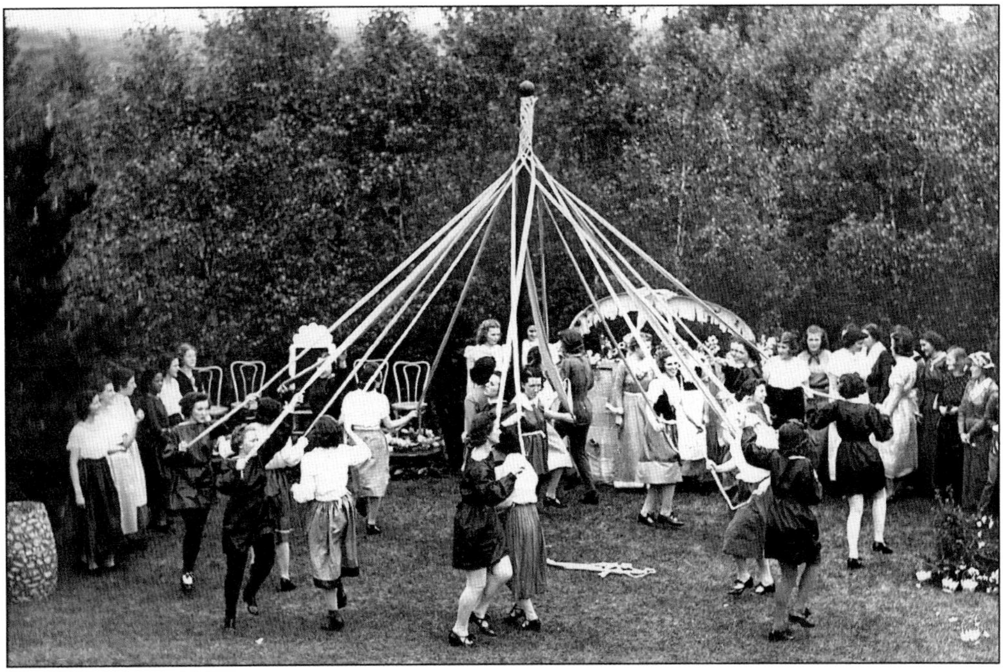

The Pole Dance, May Day, 1948. In the pole dance, students hold a lengthy ribbonlike cloth and march in opposite directions, winding the ribbon around the pole. Given the changing mores of modern times, the pole dance is no longer performed. Students in later years preferred activities such as attending a Red Sox game or the beach or some other activity. Indeed, the term May Day is no longer in use, having given way to the Sand Box.

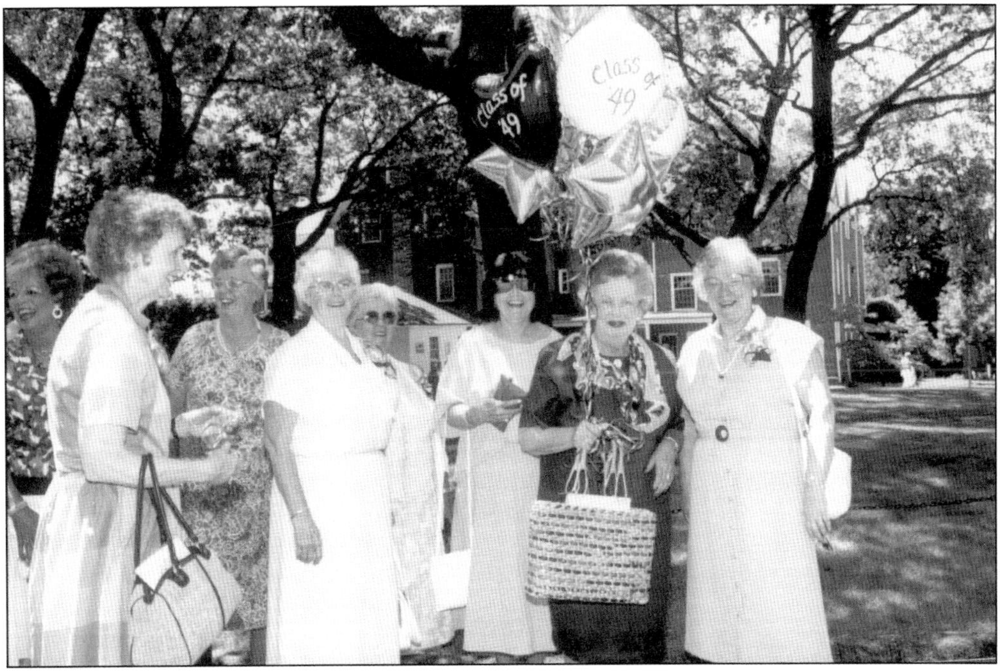

The Class of 1949. Alumnae of the Class of 1949 gather to celebrate decades of friendship and fond memories. The college prepared them well for their life endeavors.

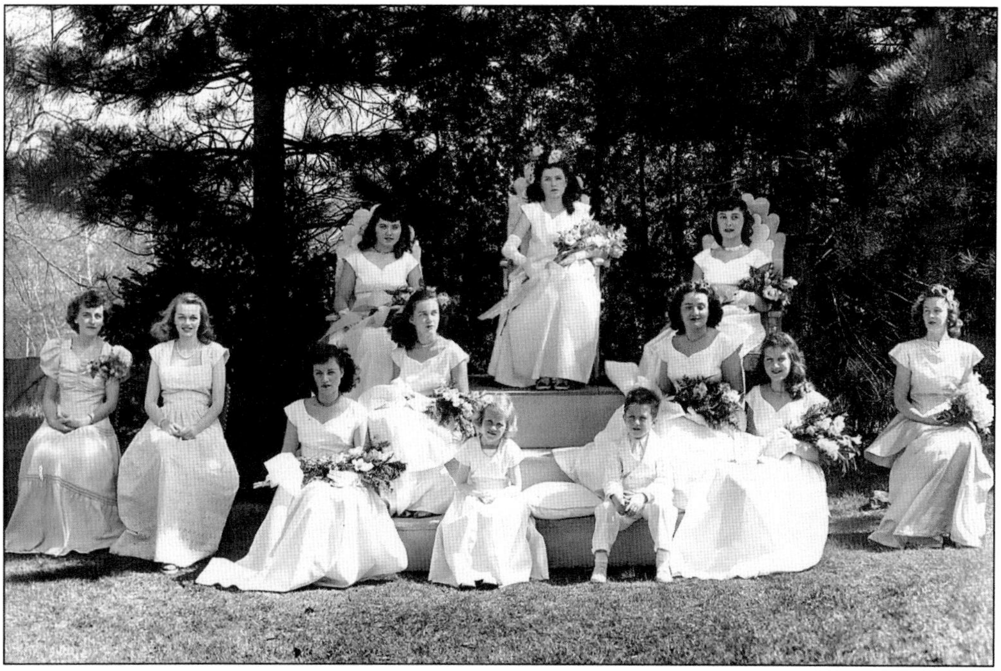

THE MAY DAY QUEEN, 1950. Times were more formal in 1950 than they are today, when it is hard to imagine students dressing so formally for a school function. Until the 1960s, skirts and dresses were standard outfits. One can only imagine the changes 50 years from now.

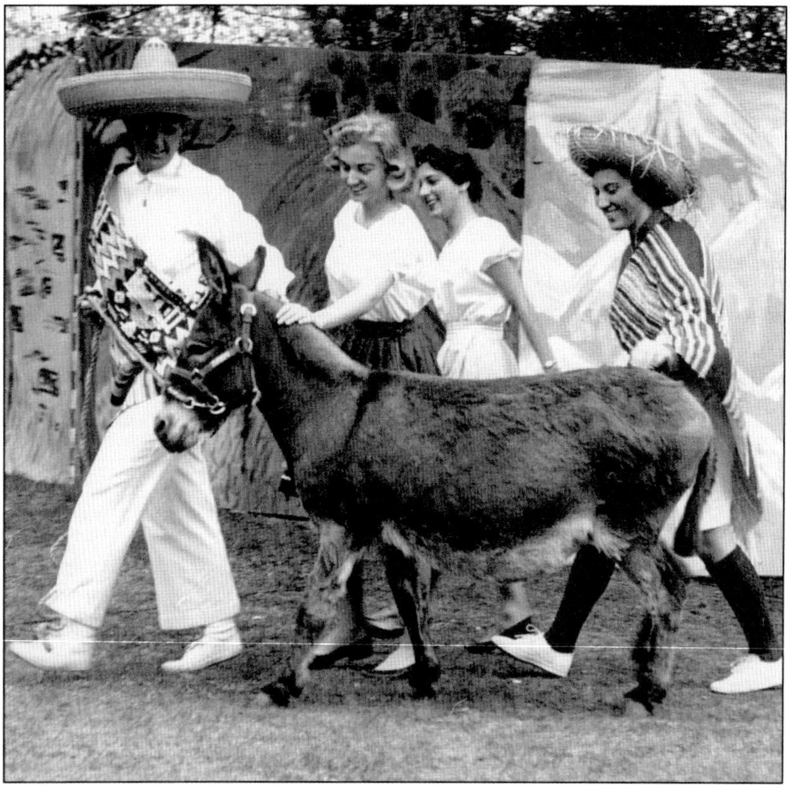

MAY DAY, 1959. Donna Curtin, Judy Ernst, Ruth DeCosta and Lois Ciafardini parade around with a pregnant donkey at the May Day festivities in 1959. Life was simpler in the 1950s—little did the students know how radically times would change over the next decade.

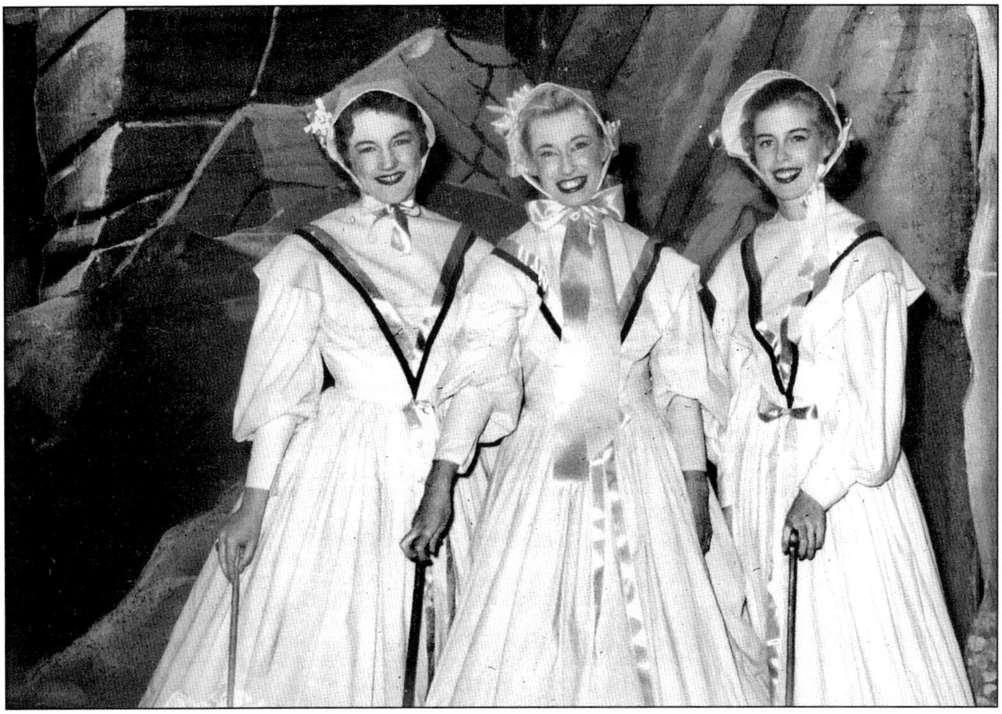

***The Pirates of Penzance*, 1961.** Judy Thatcher (left) leads the cast in this performance of Gilbert and Sullivan's well-known opera. The tradition of performing school plays continued over the course of many decades, with dedication and hard work remaining as the standard.

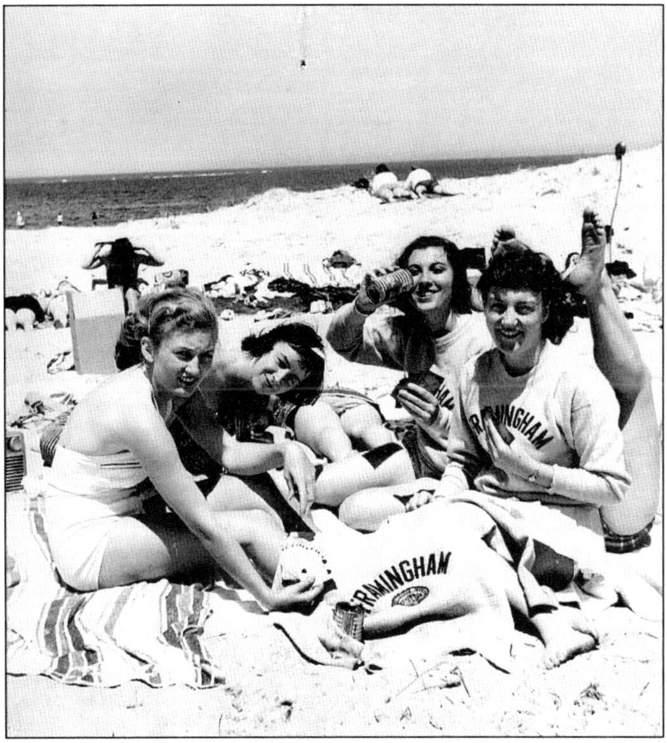

A Trip to the Beach, 1960. At the beach, from left to right, are Judy Ernst, Olive McDonald, Lois Ciafardini and Judy Thatcher, with the Framingham State College banner proudly on display. The students of the Class of 1960 were less formal than those of earlier generations—their children, however, would revolutionize the concept.

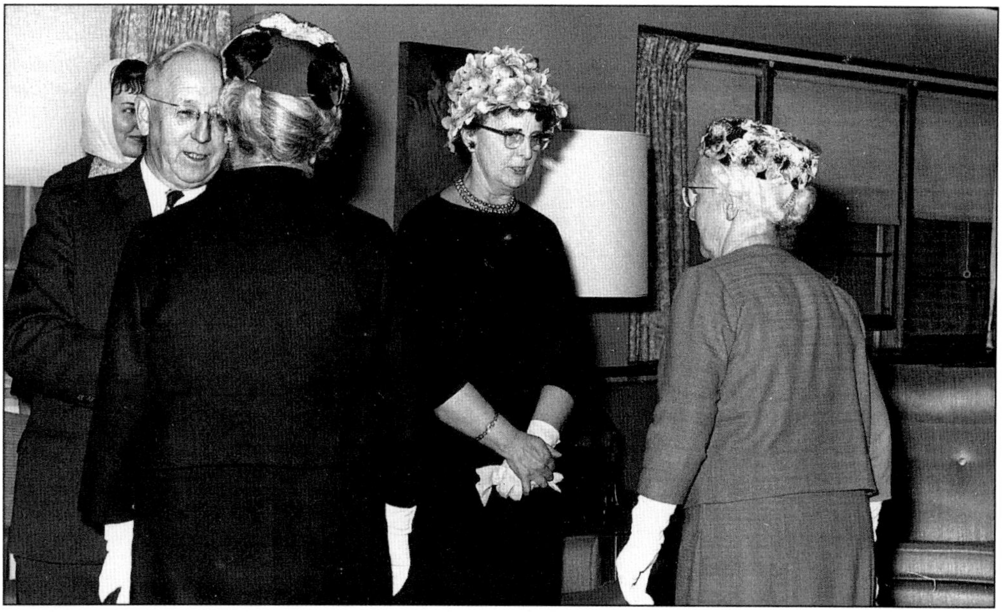

THE HEMENWAY LOUNGE, THE LATE 1950S. Over the years, the Hemenway Lounge hosted many functions for the Home Economics and other departments. The man pictured is Raymond J. Callahan, a member of the College Advisory Board, the precursor to the FSC Board of Trustees. His son, the Reverend Raymond J. Callahan Jr., was also a trustee, serving for 10 years, from 1981 to 1991.

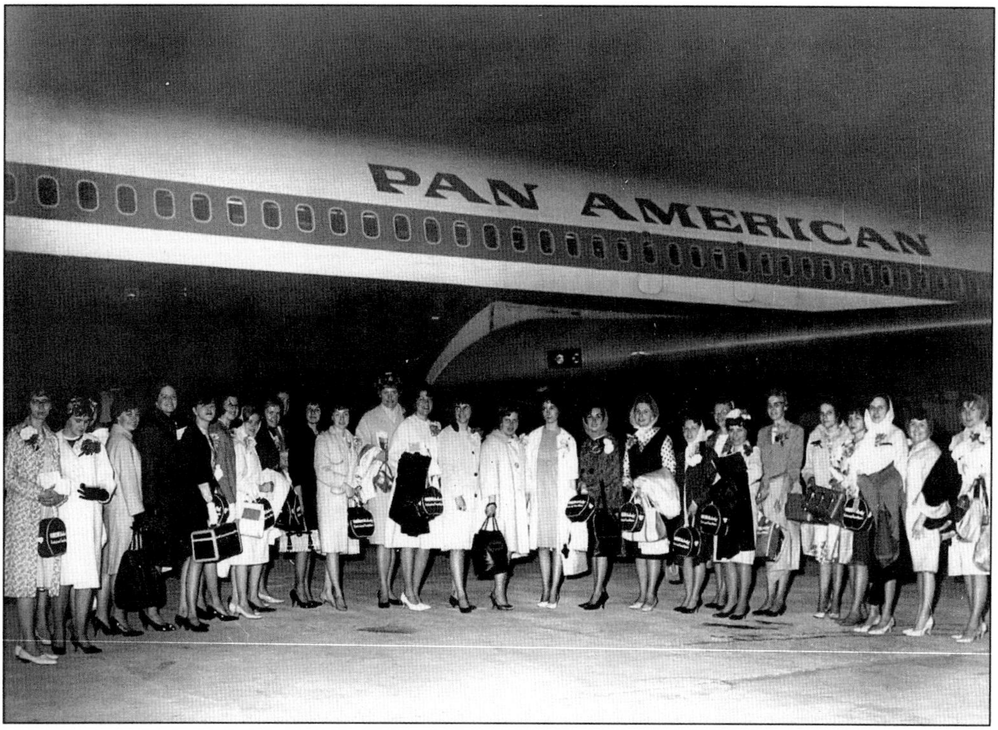

A TRIP TO BERMUDA, *C.* THE 1960S. From time to time, the college hosted overseas trips for the students. Here is one group of young women boarding a plane for Bermuda.

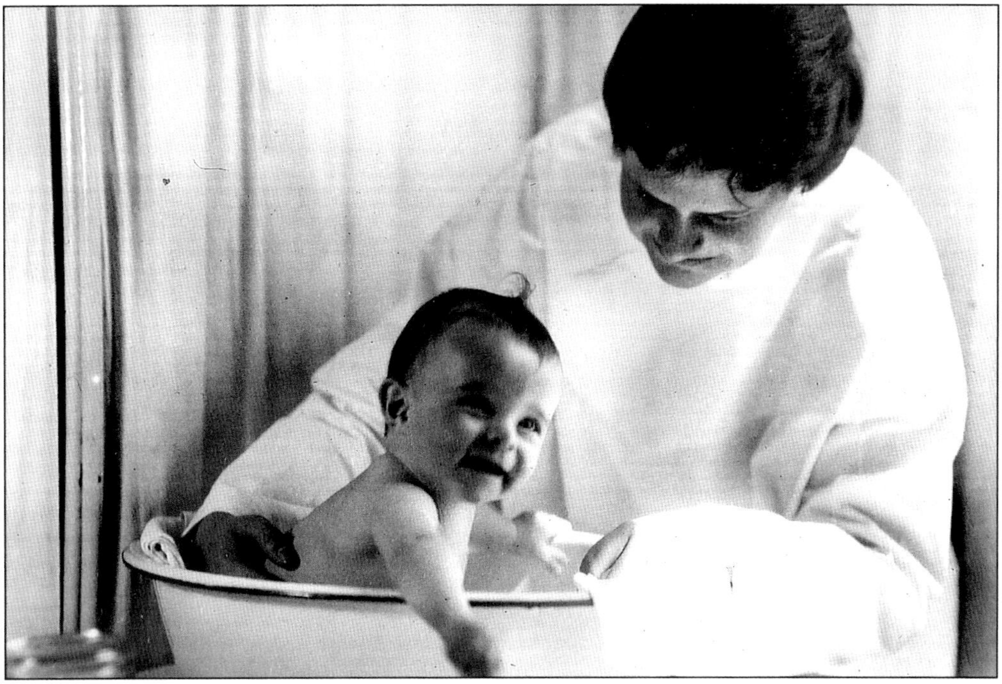

A Baby in a Tub. This photograph embodies the spirit of the college students and the young children with whom they deal. With the passage of time, the ages of the children the students interacted with became younger and younger. The school continues to be at the forefront of recognizing the changes in child development theory.

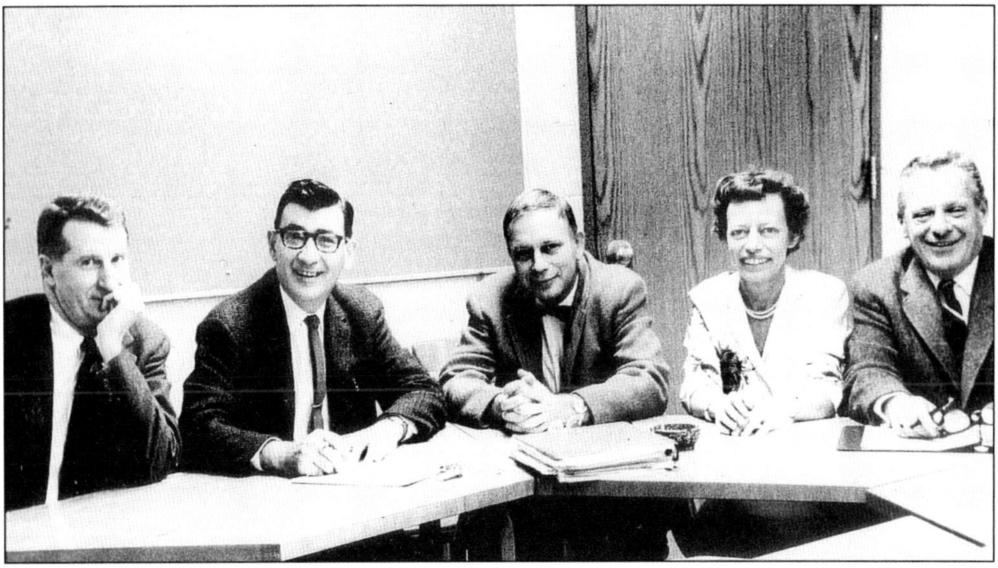

The Graduate Committee, *c.* the 1960s. Members of the committee, from left to right, are Dr. John Bowler, Dr. Joseph Palladino, Dr. Dana Jost, Dr. Constance Jordan, and Dr. Gail Cosgrove. There was significant change in the administration during the 1960s. Cosgrove came from Boston State College to become head of the FSC Elementary Education Department and director of the part-time Graduate and Continuing Education Departments, replacing Jost, who returned to teaching biology full time. Jordan was named head of the Home Economics Department.

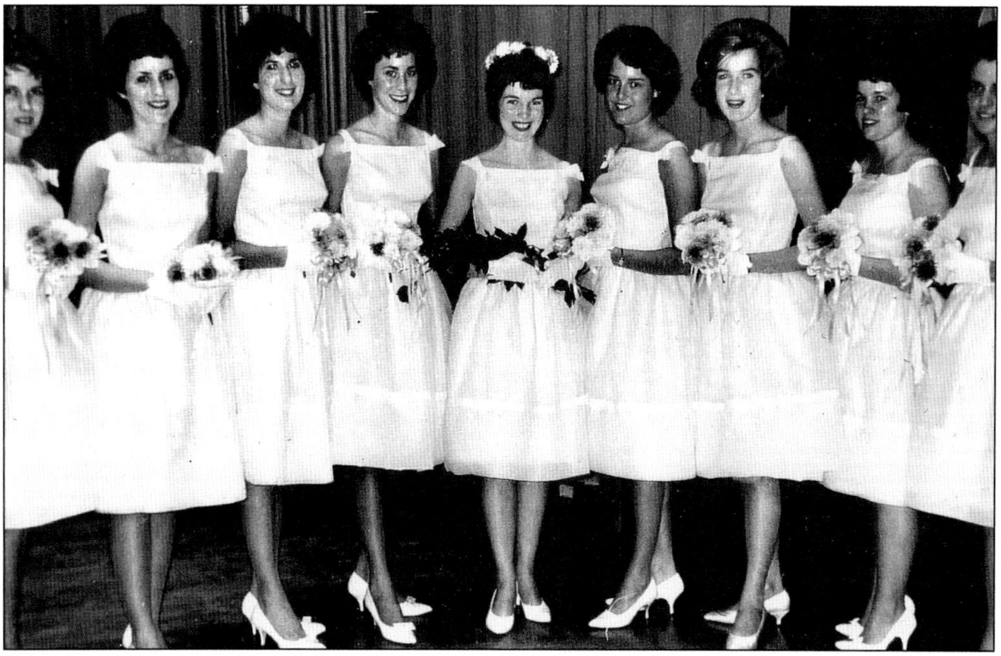

Nine Women Dressed to the Nines. As the school celebrated its 125th anniversary in 1964, many changes were afoot. The baby boomers were coming of age, making demands upon schools throughout the nation. From 1960 to 1968, the school was known as the State College at Framingham.

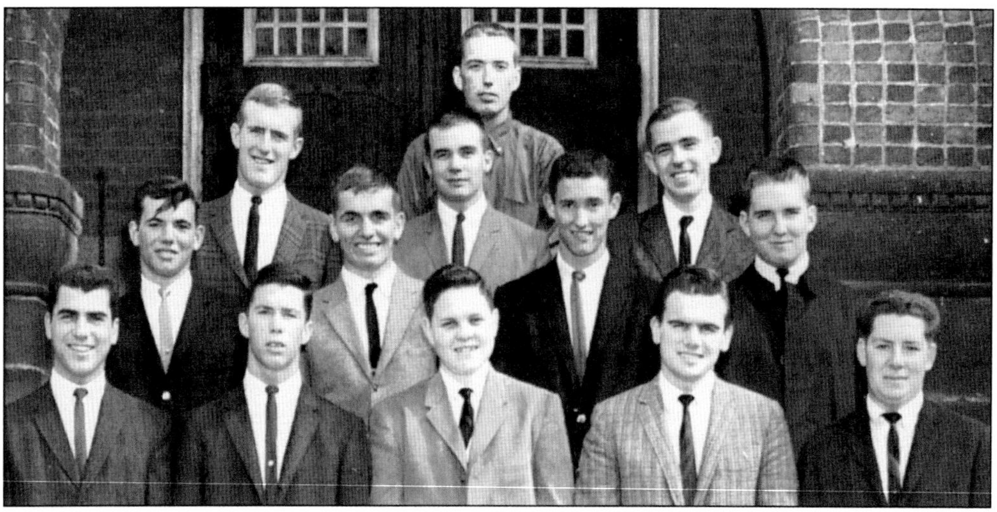

The First Men's Class. In 1964, after 125 years, the college admitted men for the first time. Interviews with incoming female students indicated that some had decided to attend the school because males had been admitted. Women, however, still comprised the overwhelming majority of the student body, at 98.8 percent.

Eight

THE RICH AND FAMOUS VISIT

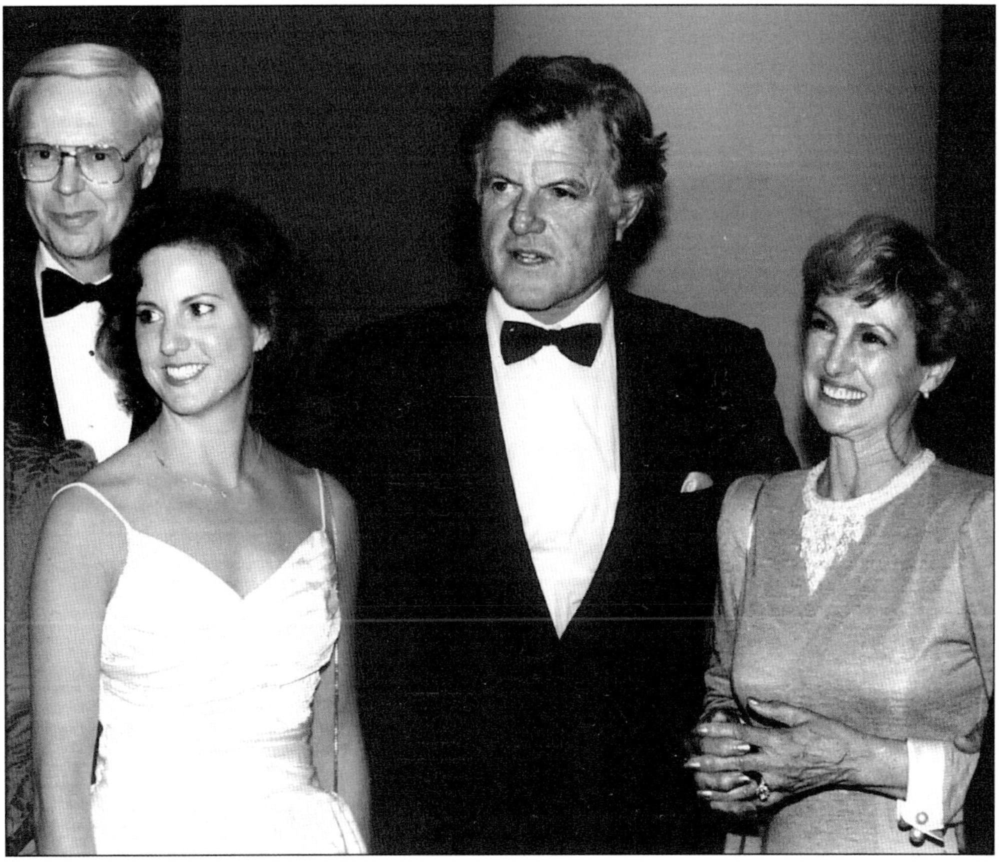

PRESIDENT WELLER WELCOMES GUESTS, 1987. At the first McAuliffe Dinner, Paul Weller (left), president of Framingham State College, greets, from left to right, Lisa Bristol, sister of Christa McAuliffe; Sen. Ted Kennedy; and Grace Corrigan, mother of Christa McAuliffe. Following in her daughter's footsteps, Grace Corrigan graduated from FSC in 1979.

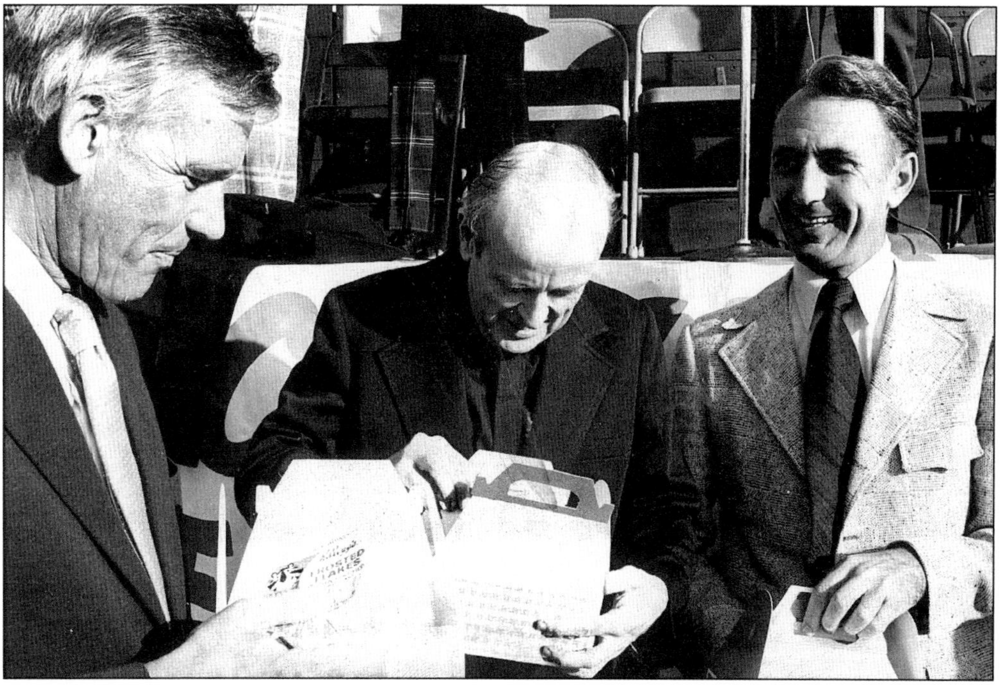

GOV. FRANCIS SARGENT, REP. ROBERT DRINAN, AND BOB COUSY, 1975. The three attended Stick-up for Breakfast Day, a nutrition program sponsoring healthy breakfasts. A moderate Republican, Francis Sargent was finishing his term as governor. Priest, lawyer, and politician, Robert Drinan served as a congressman for 10 years, starting in 1971. Hall of Famer Bob Cousy played for the Boston Celtics, retiring in 1963, after helping lead them to numerous championships.

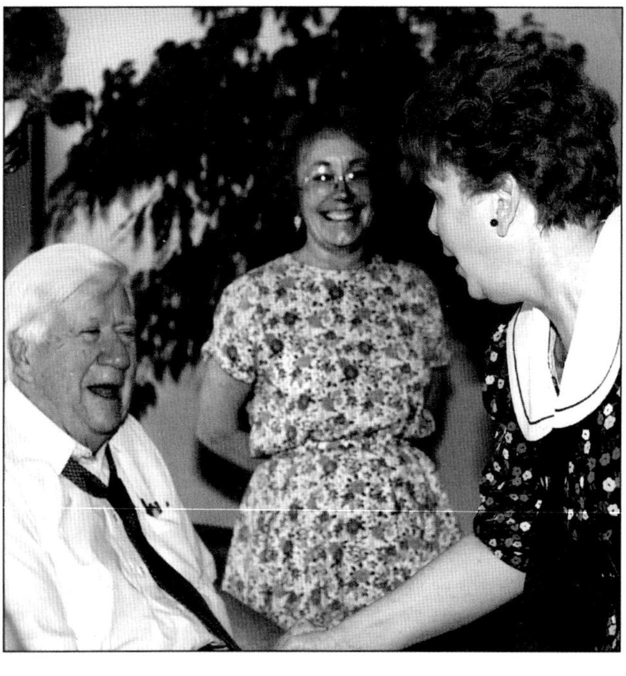

TIP O'NEIL, 1989. Joining the House of Representatives in 1953, Thomas P. "Tip" O'Neil rose to become its speaker in 1977, a post he held for a decade. In 1991, he received the Presidential Medal of Freedom. Pictured here preparing to accept an honorary degree at the college, O'Neil is joined by school official Martha Flinter (center) and curriculum librarian Mary Burns.

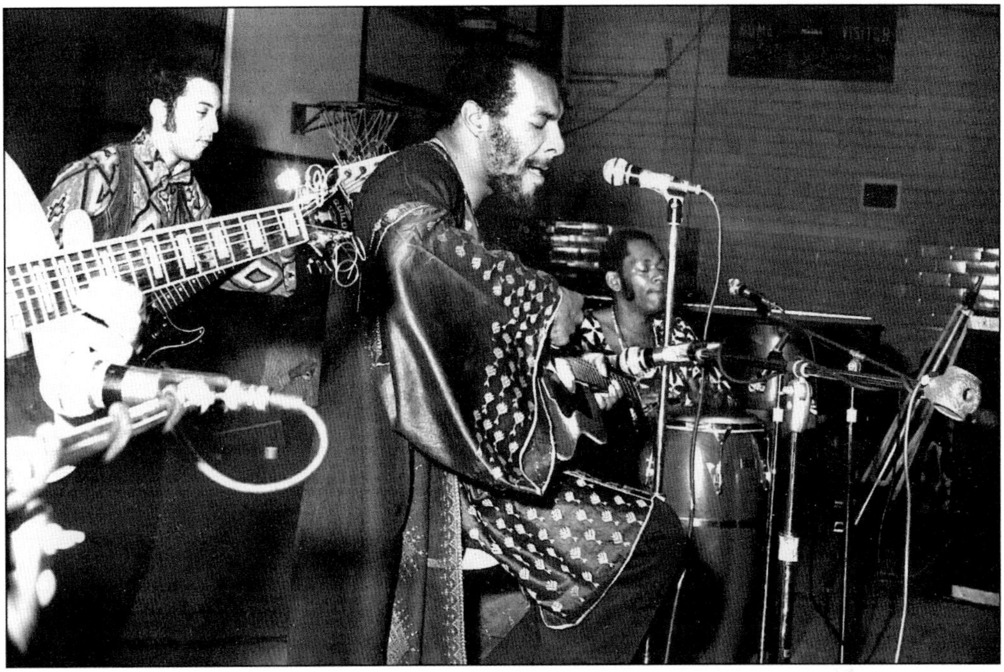

Richie Havens. His singing of "Freedom" at Woodstock in 1969 made him a legendary figure. He returned to Woodstock to play at its 30th anniversary. Before and after that, he toured throughout the world, singing and entertaining, as he did at Framingham State in the 1970s.

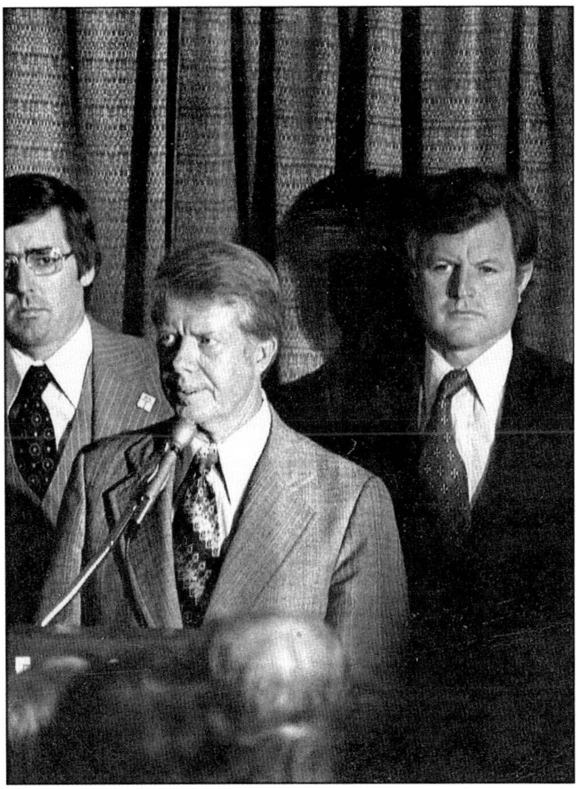

Jimmy Carter, Ted Kennedy, and Charlie Flaherty, *c.* 1976. A future president, a senator, and a future Massachusetts speaker of the house campaigned together in Framingham at an event many in the local college attended. From left to right are Charlie Flaherty, a national and state Democratic State Committee member who became speaker of the Massachusetts House (1991–1996); Jimmy Carter, who ran for and won the presidency in 1976; and Sen. Ted Kennedy.

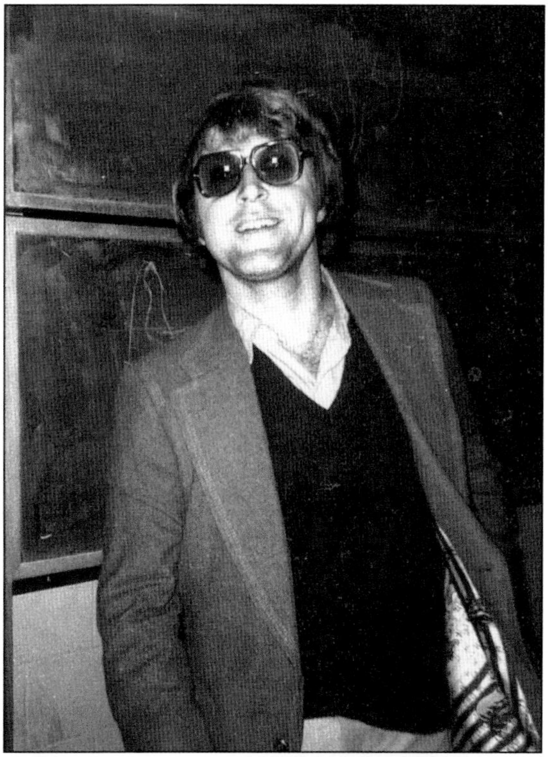

Bruce Schwoegler. Meteorologist and television fixture Bruce Schwoegler graduated from the University of Wisconsin with a degree in meteorology and naval science. While there, he was a member of the football team, playing in the 1962 Rose Bowl. Having written a book and numerous articles on the environment, he spoke to a science class at the college.

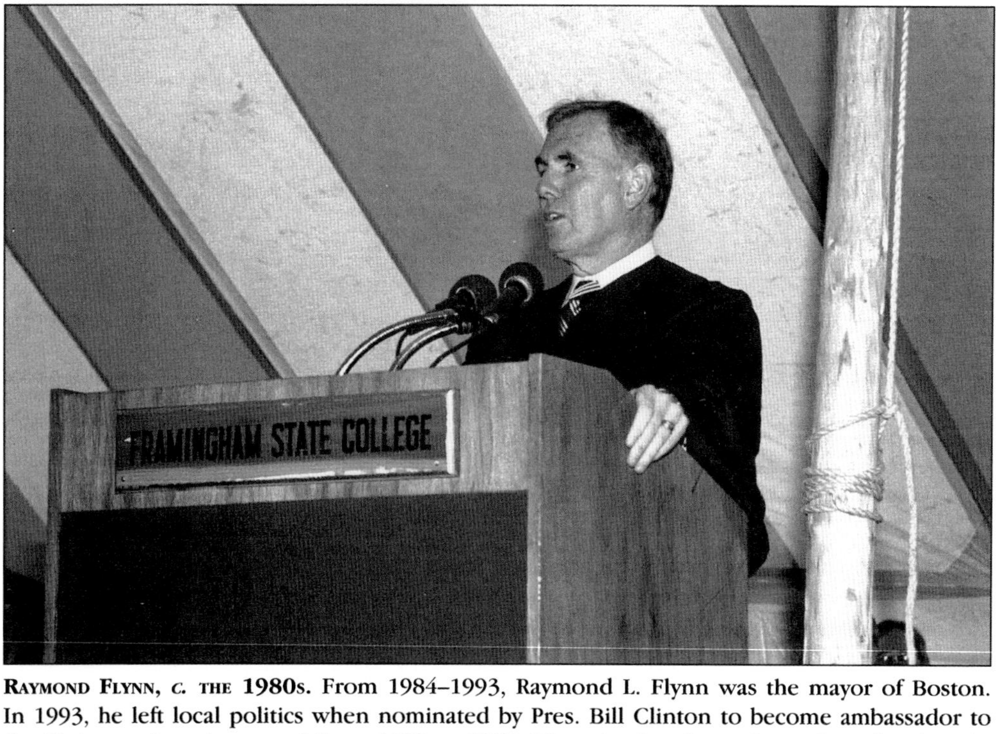

Raymond Flynn, c. the 1980s. From 1984–1993, Raymond L. Flynn was the mayor of Boston. In 1993, he left local politics when nominated by Pres. Bill Clinton to become ambassador to the Vatican, where he served from 1993 to 1997. Flynn is also the author of two books: *The Accidental Pope* and *John Paul II: A Personal Portrait of the Pope and the Man*.

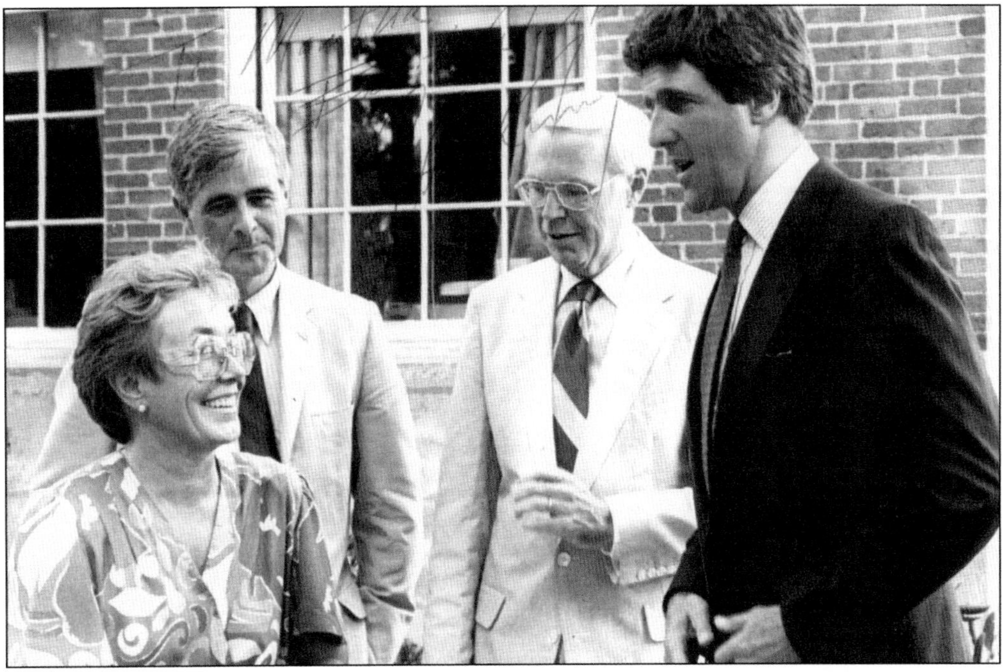

JOHN KERRY, *c.* 1988. Sen. John Kerry (right) visits the college to discuss higher education issues with students, faculty, and staff. He landed by helicopter on Dwight Field (now the Athletic and Recreation Center). Greeting him, from left to right, are Martha Flinter, director of the International/Study Abroad programs; Philip Dooher, vice president of enrollment management and dean of admissions; and Paul Weller, president of the college.

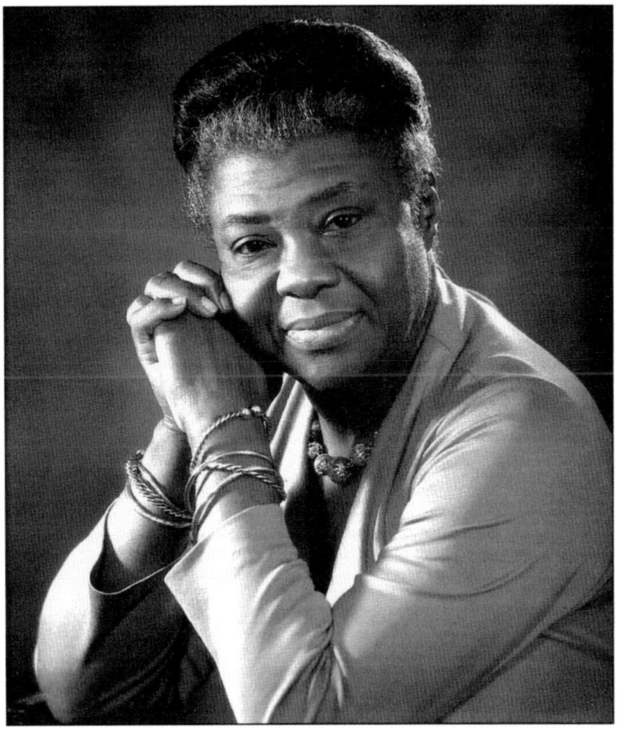

ELMA LEWIS. Elma Lewis was the founder of three performing and visual arts centers: the Elma Lewis School of Fine Arts, the National Center of Afro-American Artists, and the Museum of the National Center of Afro-American Artists. Among her many awards was the 1983 Presidential Medal for the Arts, commemorating her work enriching the cultural life of the African American community. Lewis received an honorary degree from the school in 1982.

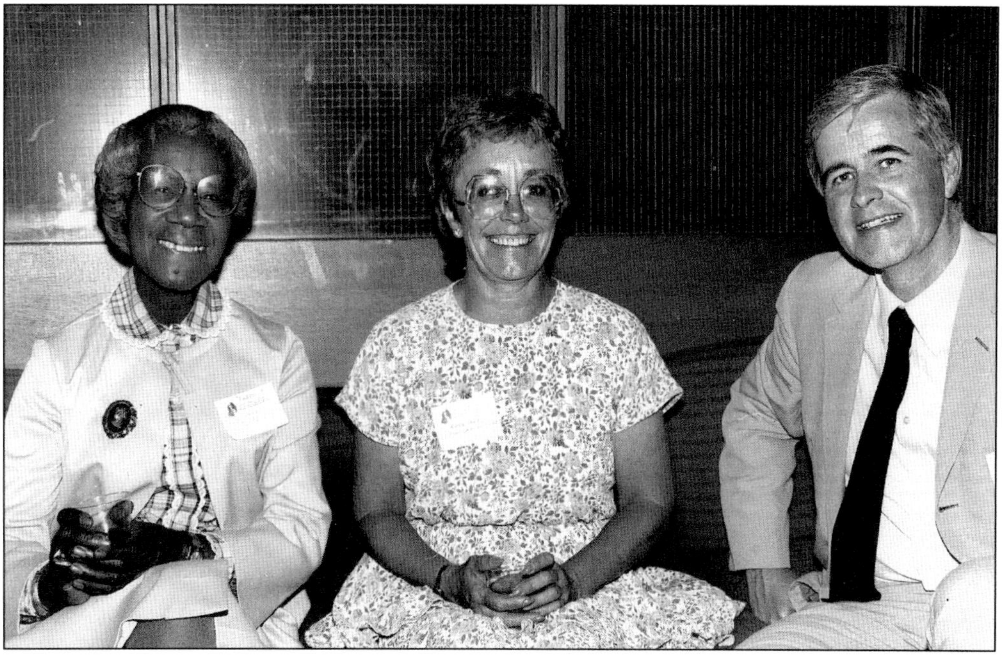

Shirley Chisholm. Rep. Shirley Chisholm (left) is welcomed to FSC by college officials Martha Flinter and Philip Dooher. With a bachelor's degree from Brooklyn College (1946, sociology) and a master's from Columbia University (1952), Chisholm became the first African American woman elected to Congress (1968), where she served for more than a decade. She concentrated her efforts on advancing the rights of women, the poor, and minorities.

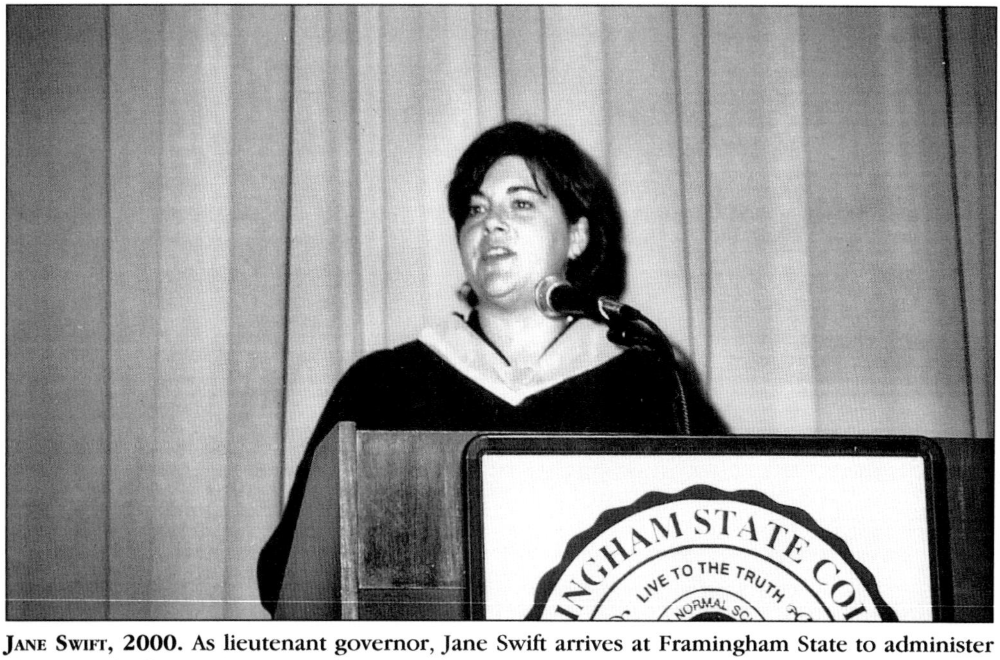

Jane Swift, 2000. As lieutenant governor, Jane Swift arrives at Framingham State to administer the oath of office to the new college president, Dr. Helen Heineman. At the age of 25, Swift was the youngest woman ever elected to the Massachusetts state Senate. She became acting governor on April 10, 2001, when Gov. Paul Cellucci resigned to become U.S. ambassador to Canada.

Nine

SPORTS

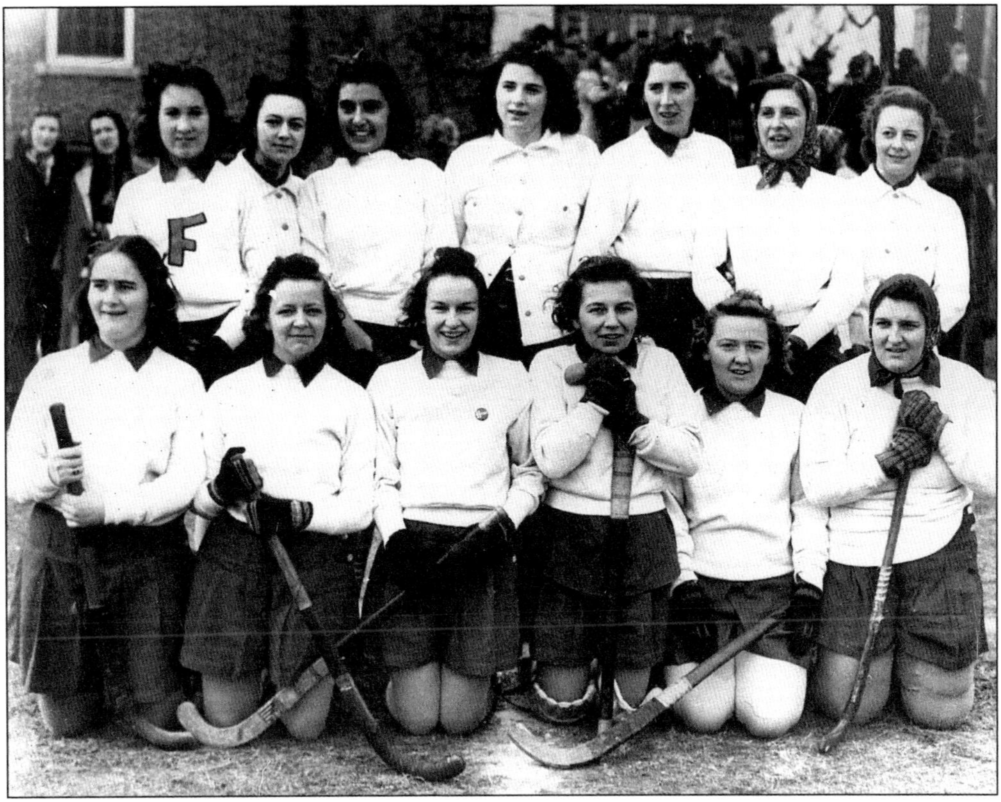

THE FIELD HOCKEY TEAM, 1940. During this period, the annual Harvard-Yale weekend, featuring field hockey competitions and other activities, was one of the highlights of the year. From left to right are the following: (front row) unidentified, Joanna Hazlett ('41), Marion Blood ('41), Mary Durfee ('40), Marion Brigham ('41), and Sylvia Parker ('43); (back row) Florence Totilas ('42), two unidentified players, Jeanne Arbuckle ('40), Barbara Stinson ('41), unidentified, and Helen Murphy ('40).

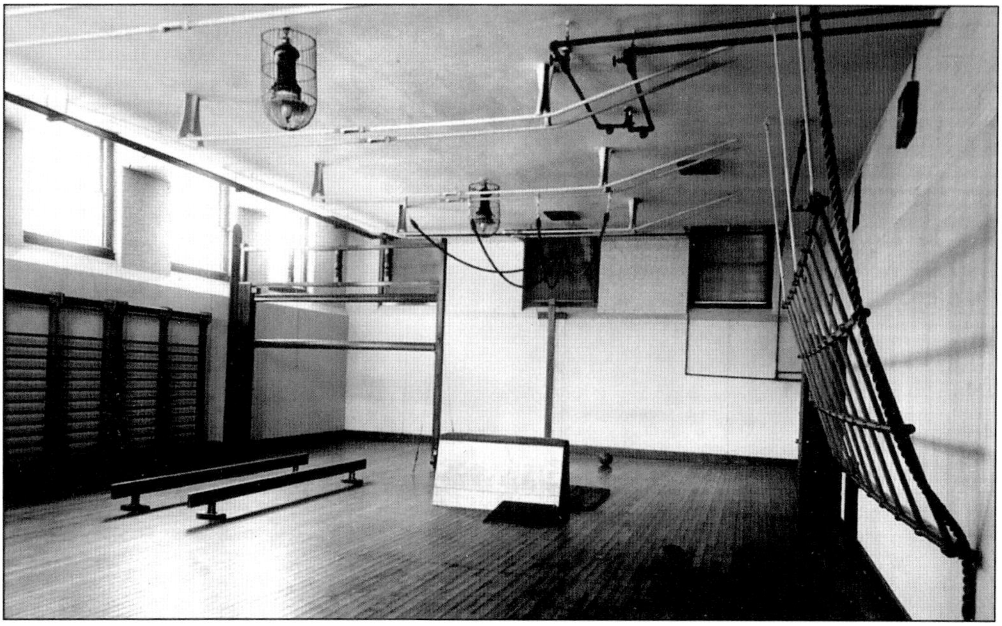

THE GYMNASIUM, THE 1890s. Gyms have changed dramatically since this little bandbox in May Hall. Since the construction and opening in 2000 of the new Athletic and Recreation Center, featuring high-tech equipment, the number of applications to the school has risen noticeably.

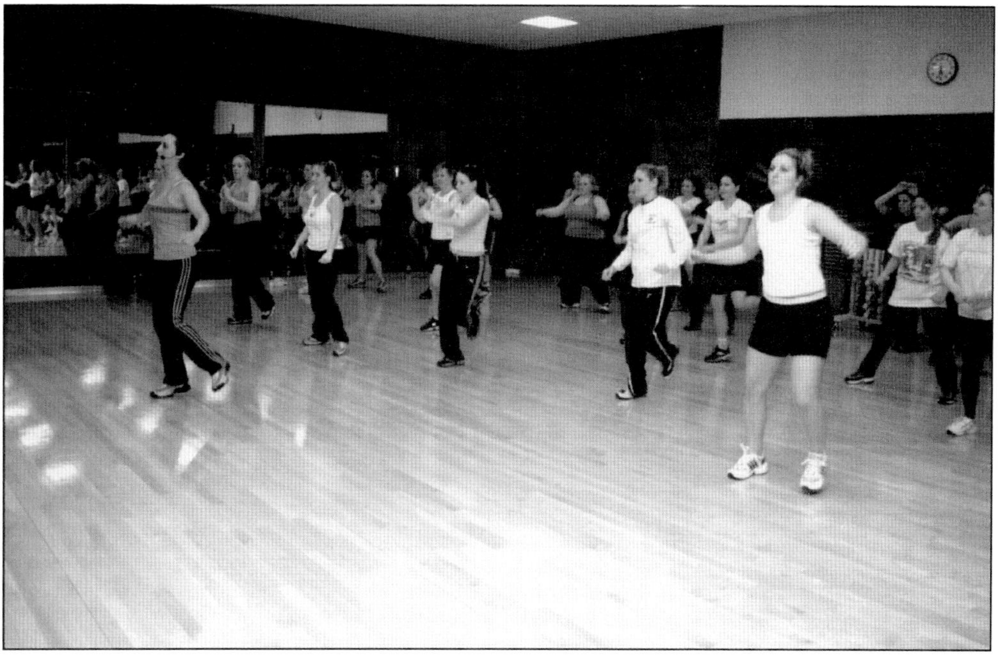

THE GYMNASIUM, 2002. Katherina Guttman (left) instructs a cardio-kickboxing class in the gymnasium of today. Along with this activity, students today have a multitude of athletic opportunities that their mothers and grandmothers never envisioned, such as aerobics, step aerobics, spinning, yoga, tae bo, pilates, core board, and a variety of weight machines, treadmills, bikes, stair climbers, and rowing machines—to name but a few.

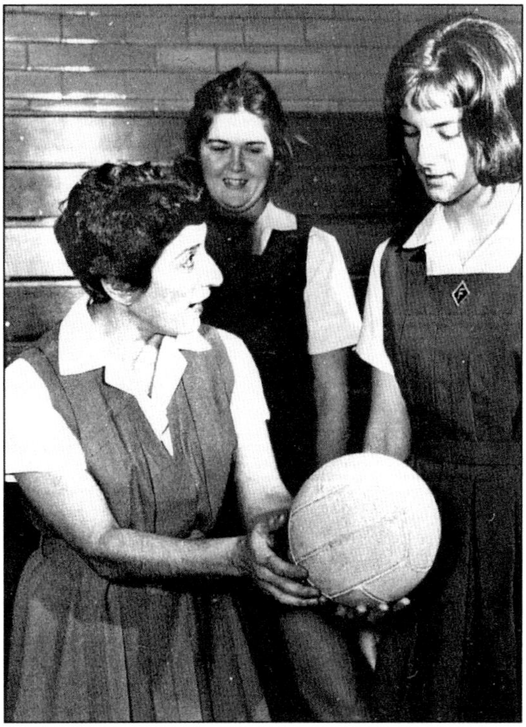

VOLLEYBALL, THE MID-1960S. Marie Salvucci (left) instructs two students on the finer points of volleyball. Salvucci received a B.A. and Ed.M. from Boston University. She was an assistant professor of physical education from 1961 to 1990, teaching classes in physical education, child health, health and fitness for children with learning disabilities, and dance.

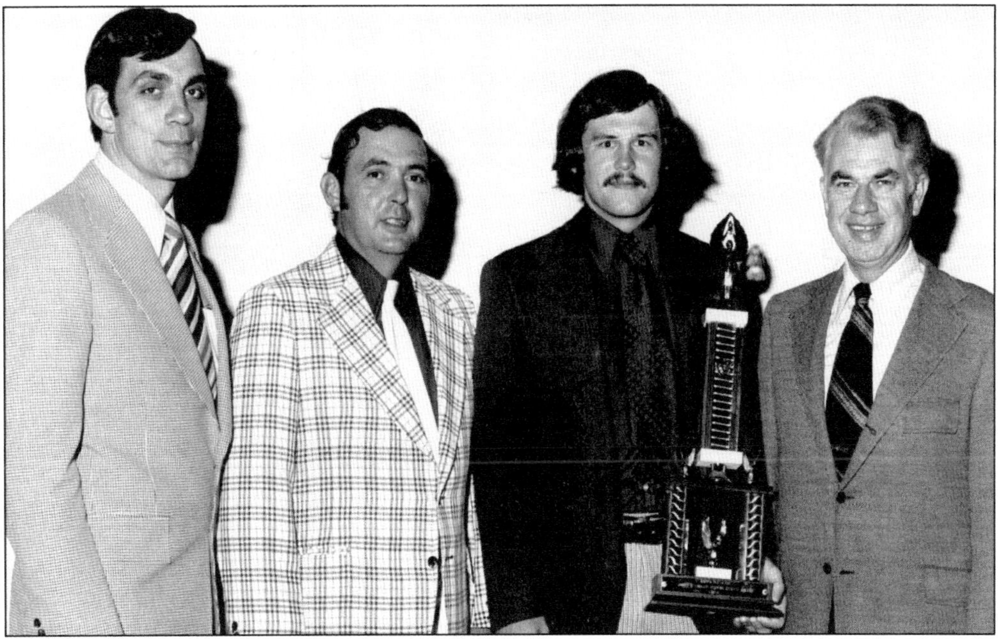

BILLY RIGNEY, STUDENT ATHLETE, 1974. Billy Rigney (third from left) receives the Student Athlete Award. Rigney (B.S. Biology, 1974) played end for the football team for three seasons. With him, from left to right, are Dennis Golden, dean of students and head football coach; Steve Ryder, assistant professor of physical education (1971–1975), director of athletics, and former baseball player in the Milwaukee Braves system; and Dr. D. Justin McCarthy, college president, making the presentation.

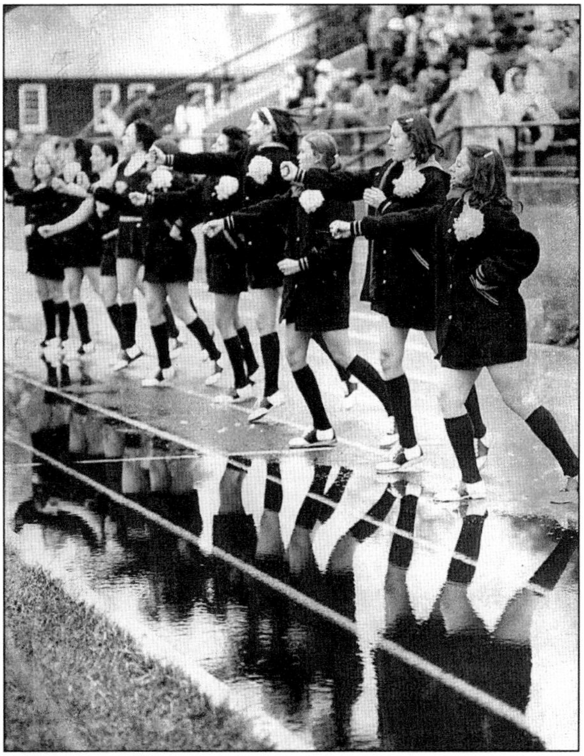

The Cheerleaders, October 19, 1975. The cheerleaders brave inclement weather to cheer on the FSC football team in the Homecoming Day game against Massachusetts Maritime Academy. Day. Their reflections are seen in the puddle in front of them.

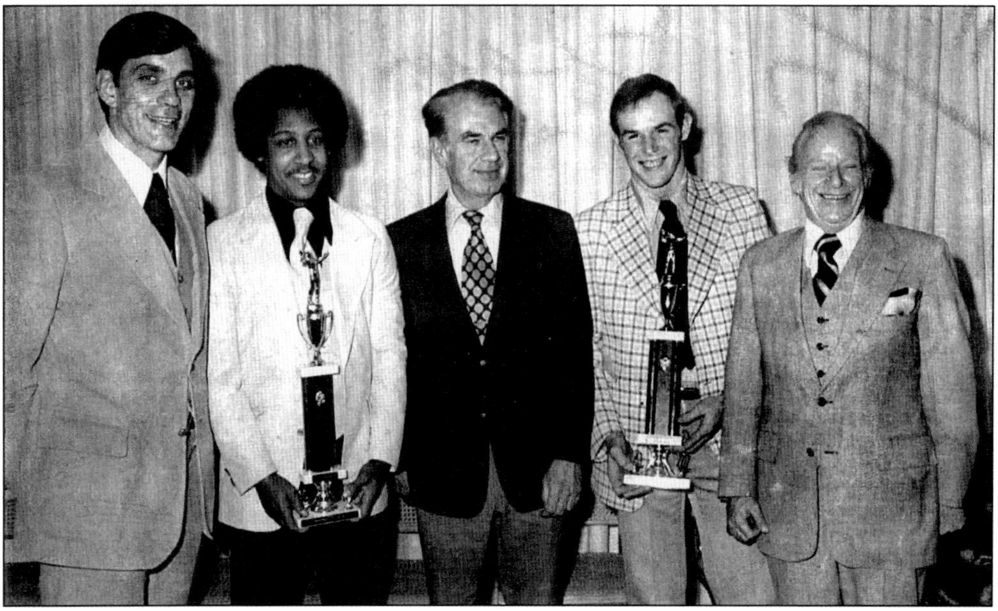

An Awards Ceremony. Holding their trophies, football players Tim Tolber (second from left) and Jay Britten are recognized for their outstanding athletic ability. Tolber (B.A. Sociology, 1979) played in 34 straight games and won Massachusetts State College Athletic Conference (MASCAC) and other All-Star honors as a defensive back and kick returner. Standing with Tolber and Britten (B.A. Geography, 1978), from left to right, are Dennis Golden, dean of students and football coach; Dr. D. Justin McCarthy, college president; and Gail Cosgrove, executive vice president.

RUGBY. Fran Foley (third from left) was a football and rugby player for the college, graduating in 1984 with a degree in English literature. After graduation, he was an assistant football coach at Colgate, the Citadel, Rutgers, and Boston College. In 1994, he joined coach Tom Couglin and the Jacksonville Jaguars of the National Football League (NFL), eventually serving as the Jaguars' director of pro personnel from 1998 to 2003.

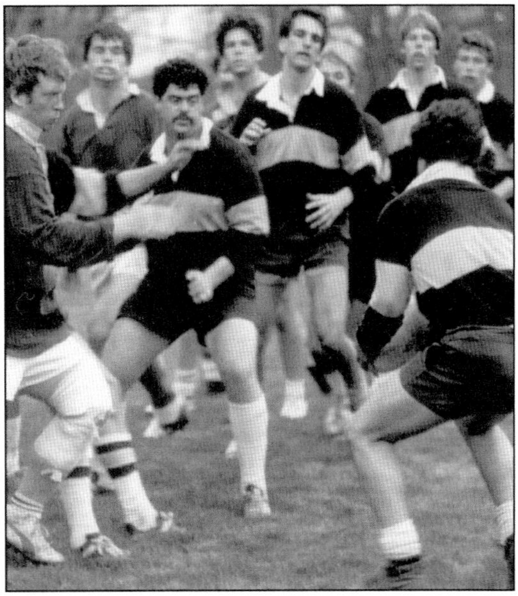

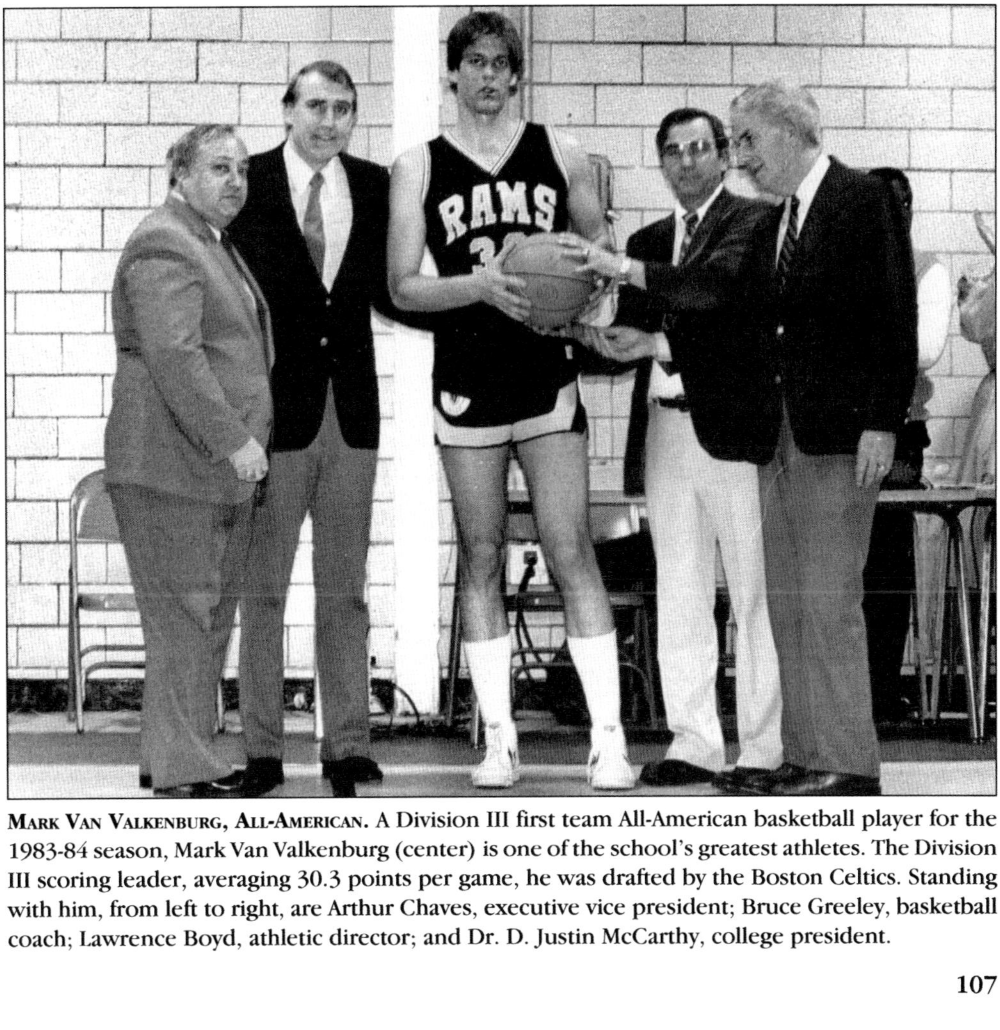

MARK VAN VALKENBURG, ALL-AMERICAN. A Division III first team All-American basketball player for the 1983-84 season, Mark Van Valkenburg (center) is one of the school's greatest athletes. The Division III scoring leader, averaging 30.3 points per game, he was drafted by the Boston Celtics. Standing with him, from left to right, are Arthur Chaves, executive vice president; Bruce Greeley, basketball coach; Lawrence Boyd, athletic director; and Dr. D. Justin McCarthy, college president.

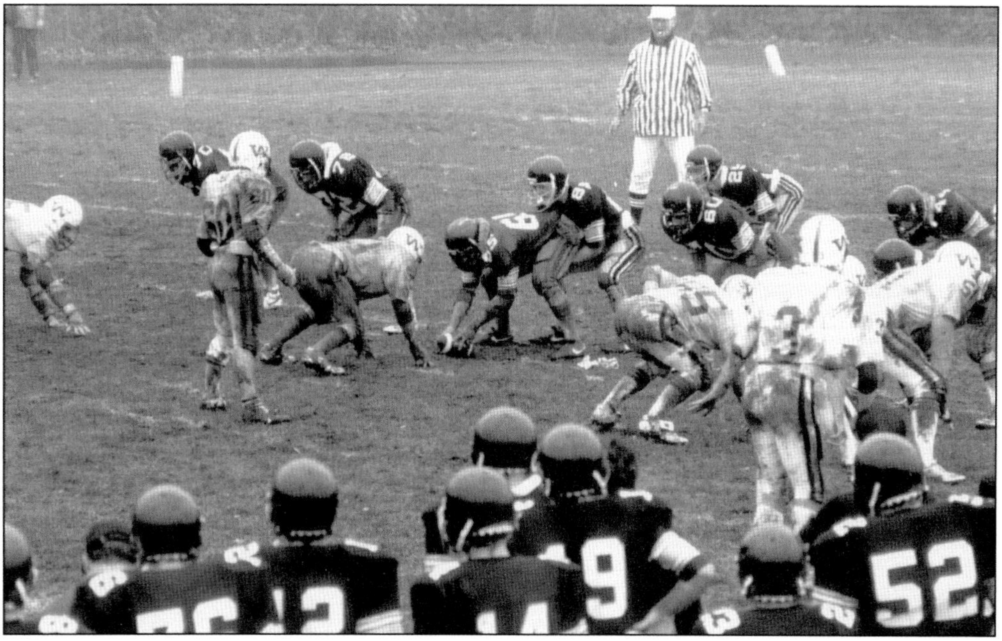

Homecoming, 1985. Quarterback Mike Hocking calls the plays in a 12-0 Homecoming victory against Westfield State College. Jack Flinter, Steve Megee, Chris Horblit, and Dave McDermott were the team captains for the 3-6 1985 Rams. Bright spots for the team included Tom Reusch being named New England Football Conference Player-of- the-Week; Bob Curran, Dave Wagman, and Steve Condon, joining captains Flinter and Horblit, as league honorable mentions; and Megee and Condon setting school records.

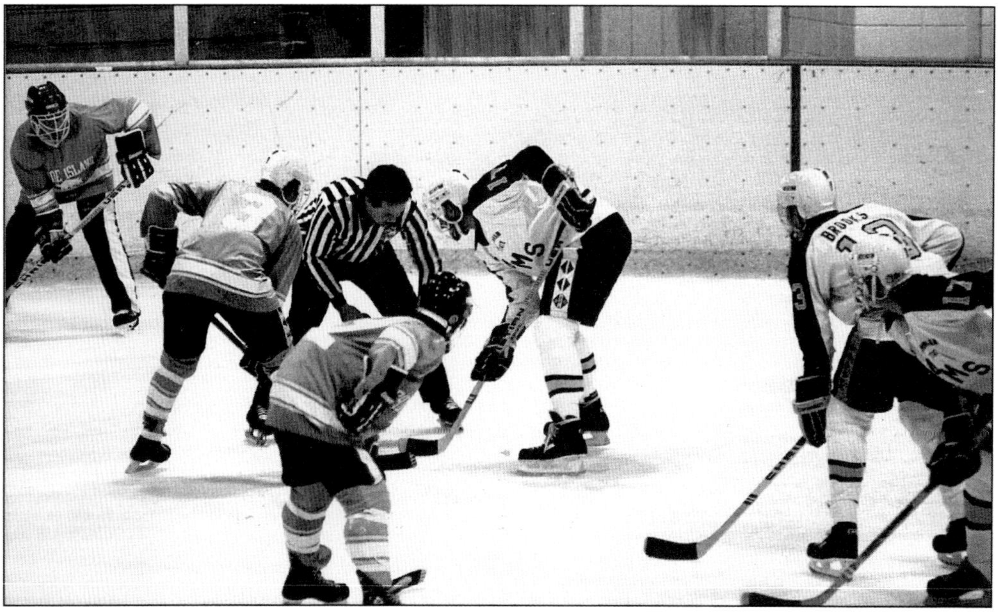

Hockey, 1986. As center Eric Hagen faces off against the University of Rhode Island, teammates Dave Brooks and Bill Flynn stand ready. The team was a solid one, making it to the Eastern Collegiate Athletic Conference (ECAC) semifinals. Eric Donaghey led the league in scoring, and Rick Morrisey was named second-team All-Conference.

Softball, 1986. One of the leading hitters in the league, cocaptain Shelly Cummings smacks another hit. The team, coached by Tom Kelley (see page 110) and Larry Mosher, finished with an overall record of 14-11 (5-7 in the league), qualifying for the Massachusetts Association of Intercollegiate Athletics for Women (MAIAW) tournament.

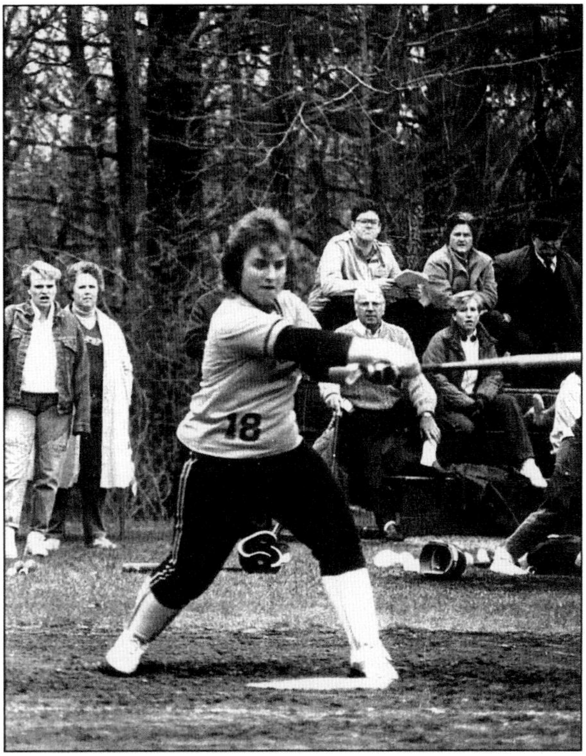

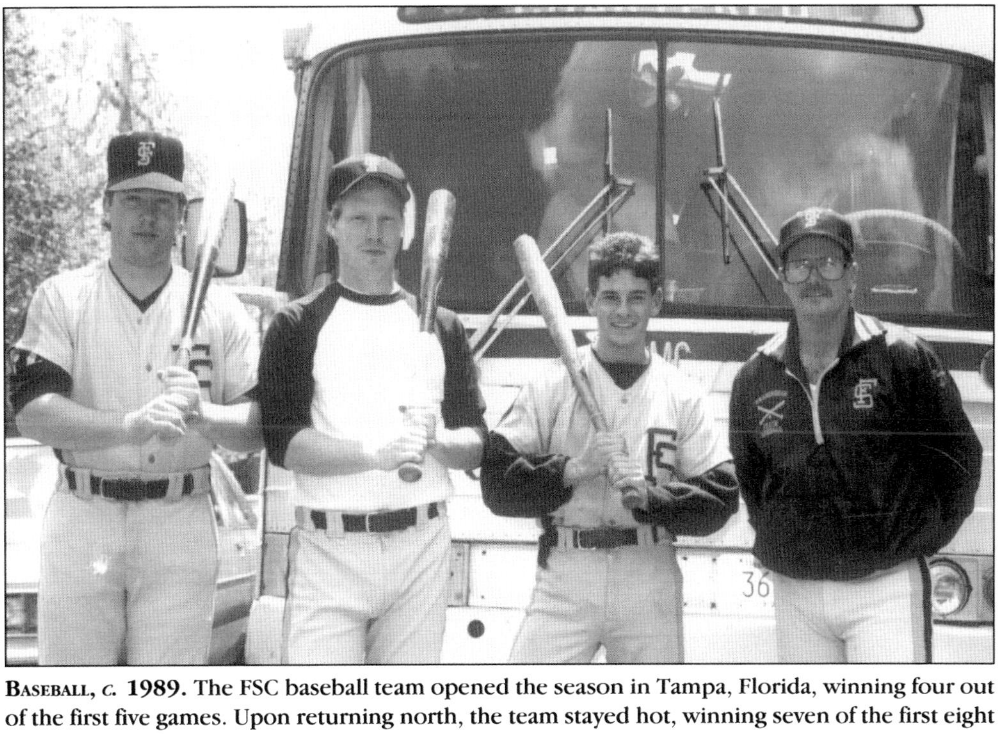

Baseball, *c.* 1989. The FSC baseball team opened the season in Tampa, Florida, winning four out of the first five games. Upon returning north, the team stayed hot, winning seven of the first eight and going on to the conference quarterfinals. From left to right are cocaptain Keith McMahon, David Lorenzen, Noel Frattazio, and coach John O'Connor.

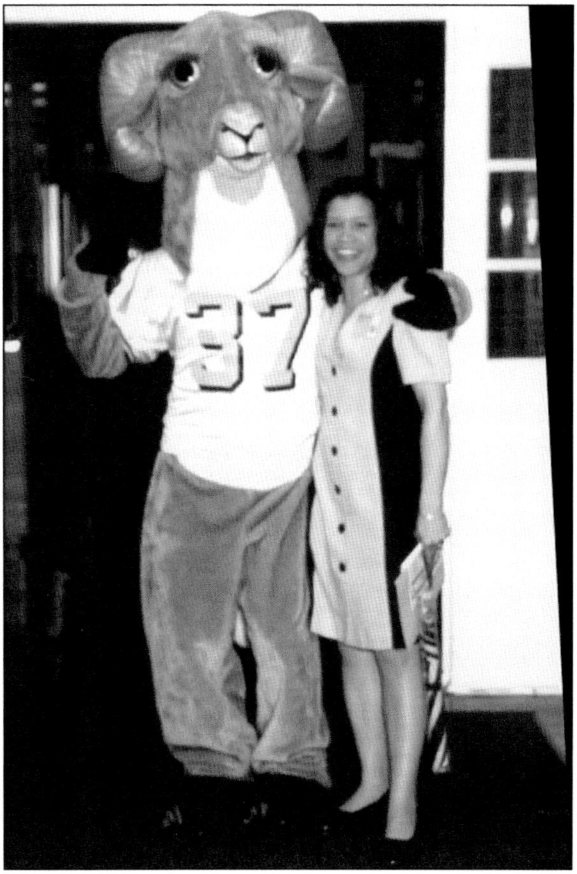

The Ram Mascot. The mascot came into existence in the mid-1960s, with the explosion of sports teams. At a 2003 reception for newly accepted students, the ram hugs Heather Porter Adamson ('91), assistant dean of admissions.

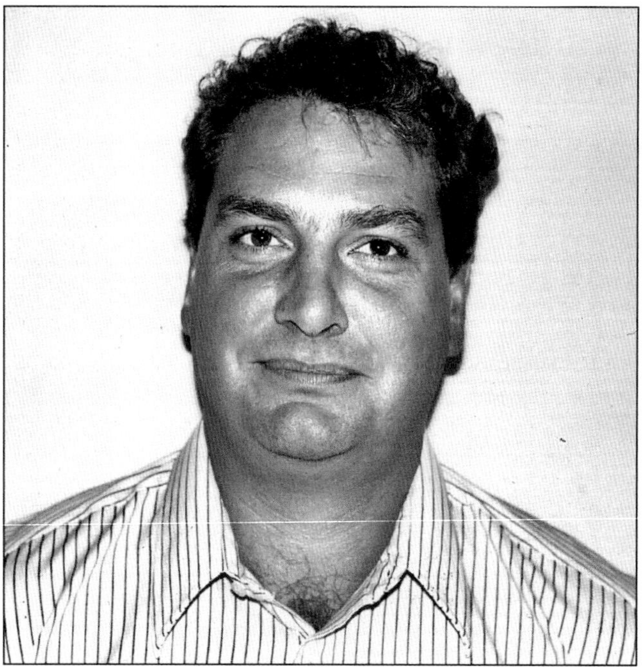

Tom Kelly, Athletic Director. Tom Kelley graduated in 1976 with a degree in sociology. He coached various sports, including football (1981–1983), working his way up to his current position as athletic director. He also found time to earn a master's degree. An admired figure at the school, he remains as good-humored and good-natured as he was as a student.

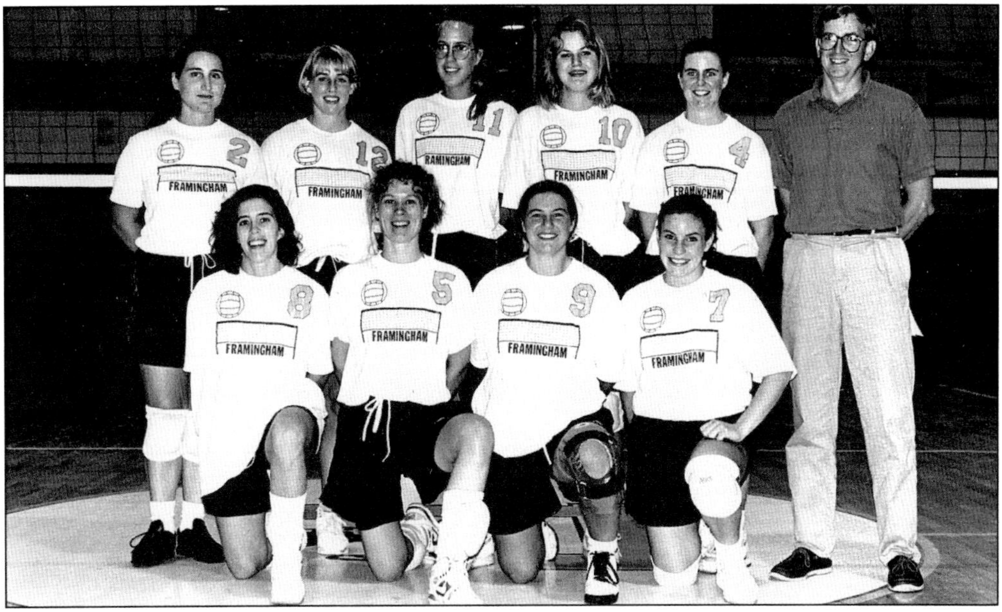

THE WOMEN'S VOLLEYBALL TEAM, 1993. This team played more than three fourths of their games on the road. From left to right are the following: (front row): Megan O'Brien (8), Cheryl Morin (5), Michelle Lowe (9), and Lisa Masiello (7); (back row): Dayna Del Gaizo (2), Laura Hartlen (12), Kristen McCarthy (11), Dotty Catton (10), Laura Jean Walsh (4), and coach Guy Tucker. Assistant coach Barbara Marshnik is not pictured.

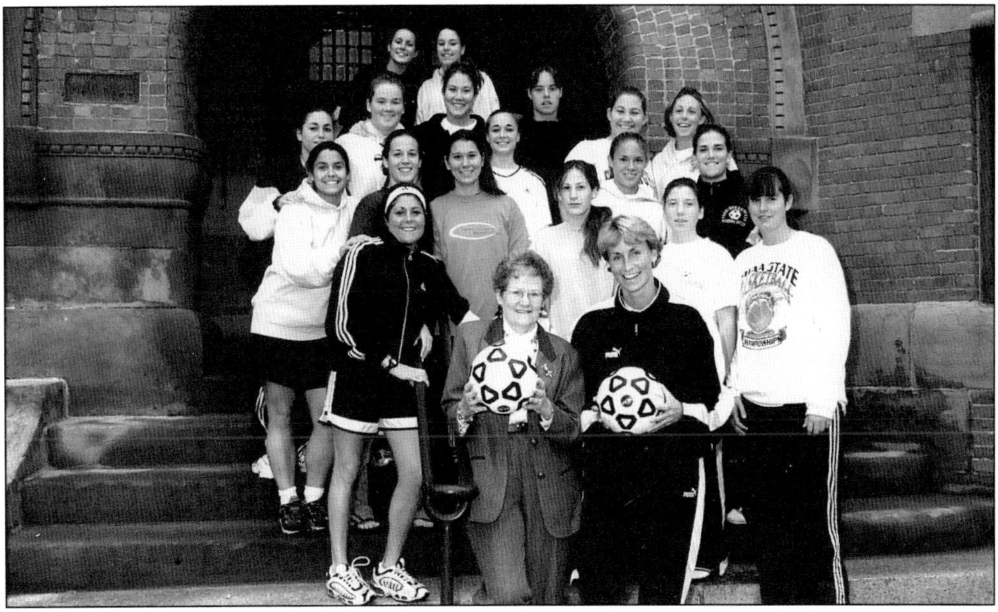

SARA BEHN. Leading the tournament-bound women's soccer team is Sara Behn (right foreground), one of the state's greatest high school (Foxboro) and college (Boston College) basketball players. A college All-American, she was the second leading scorer in the nation one year and is the all-time leading scorer in the Big East, men and women. She coached both basketball and soccer at FSC and, in 1999, was named MASCAC Coach of the Year. Beside her is Dr. Helen Heineman, college president.

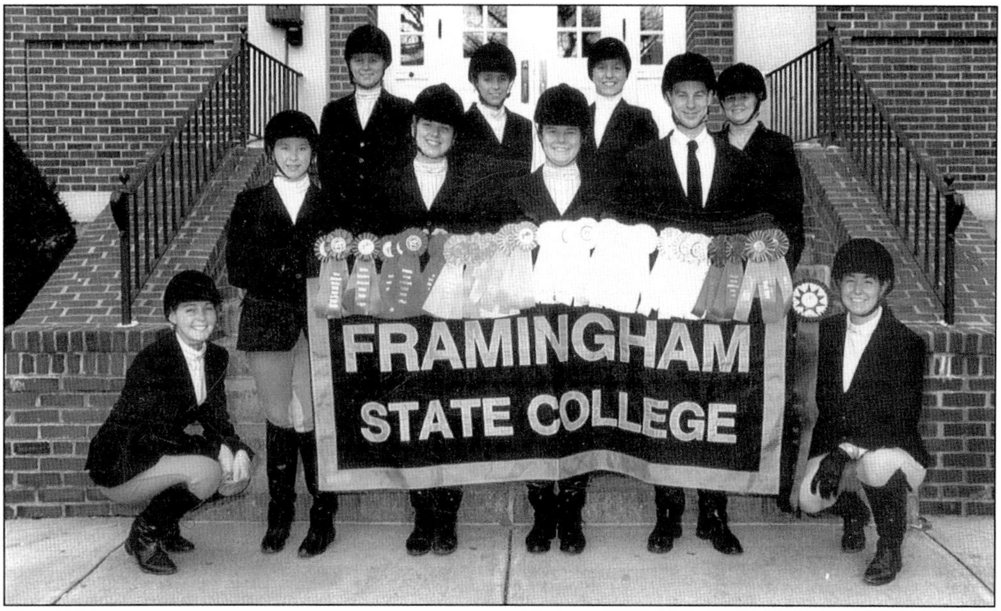

The Equestrian Team, 2000. Members of the equestrian team show off the ribbons they won during their season. From left to right are Beth Luccini, Tania Novak, Grace Cardwell, Amy Scott, Tracy Gauvin, Lea Lacross, Carl Secore, Kyra Maryeski, and Amy Aho. Not present are Gigi Singh and Samantha Bowles. With their horses, team members led the procession during the inauguration of college president Dr. Helen Heineman. Equestrian is a club sport sponsored by the Athletic Department.

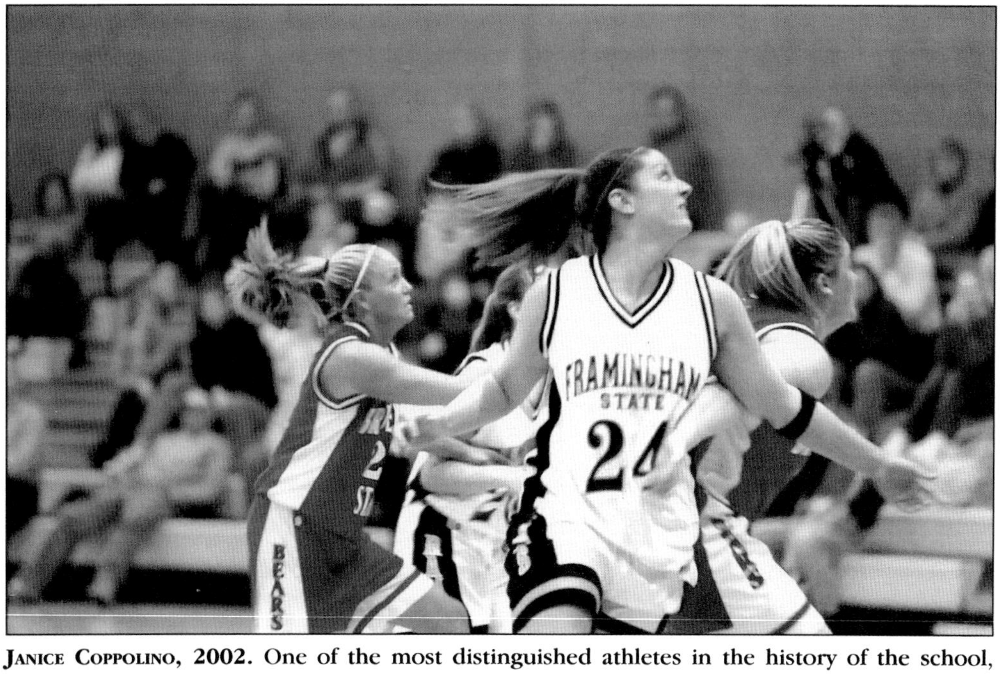

Janice Coppolino, 2002. One of the most distinguished athletes in the history of the school, Janice Coppolino was named the MASCAC Basketball Player of the Year in 2001–2002, during her junior year. A center, she holds the school record for rebounds, having made her 1,000th board on January 25, 2003. She was also a first team all-league volleyball player.

Ten

The 1970s Onward

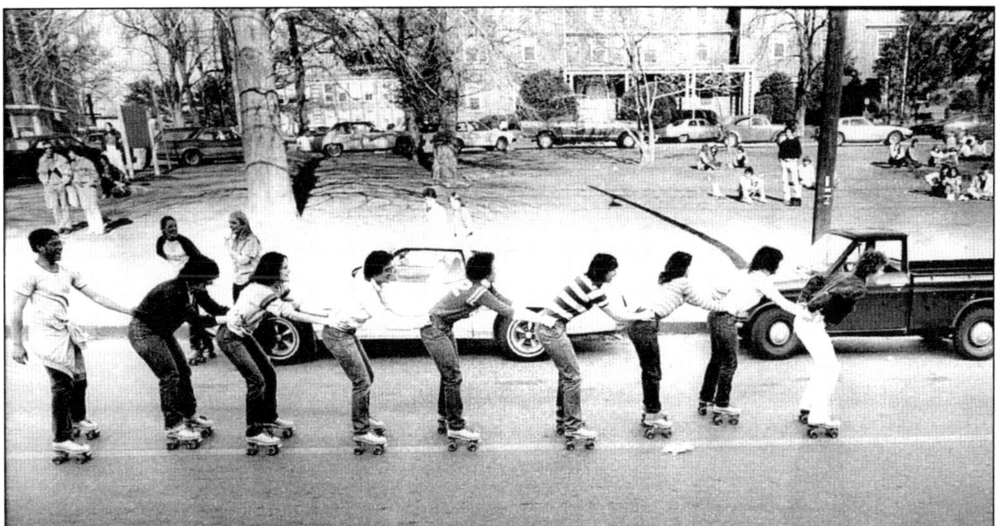

A Skaters' Chain, 1980. On April 17, 1980, a group of students, taking advantage of the spring weather, form a chain and skate around campus. They are shown on State Street, in front of Crocker Hall.

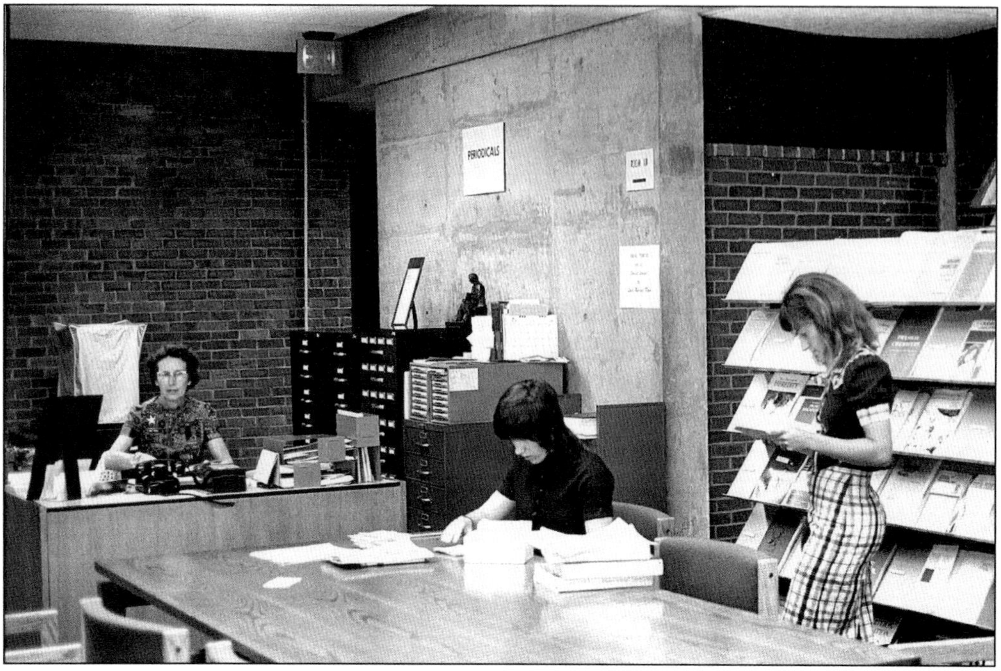

The Periodicals Library, 1970. Eloise Doten, the periodicals librarian, works at her desk in the Whittemore Library while two students do some research. The library has advanced over the years, meeting the challenges of computerization and technology.

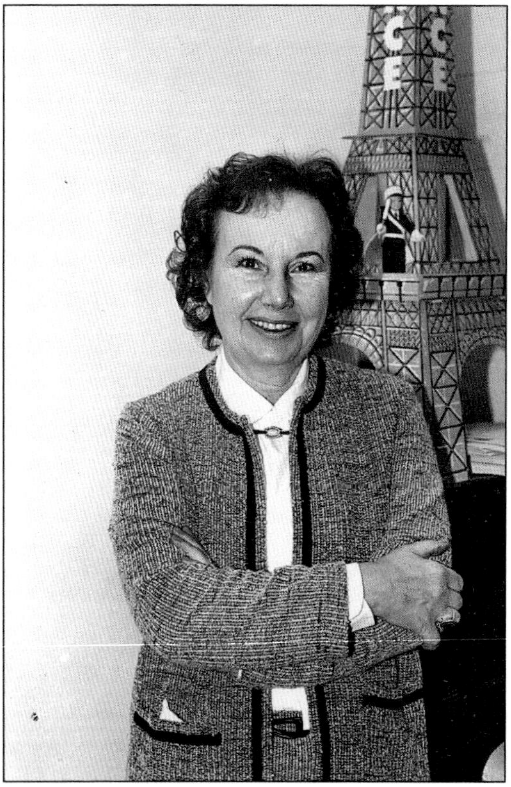

Marise Thompson, the 1970s. Marise Thompson studied in France, receiving her B.A. and M.A. from the Université de Toulouse and her Ph.D. from the Université de Paris. She taught French from 1968 to 1987 and was head of the Modern Languages Department from 1979 to 1986.

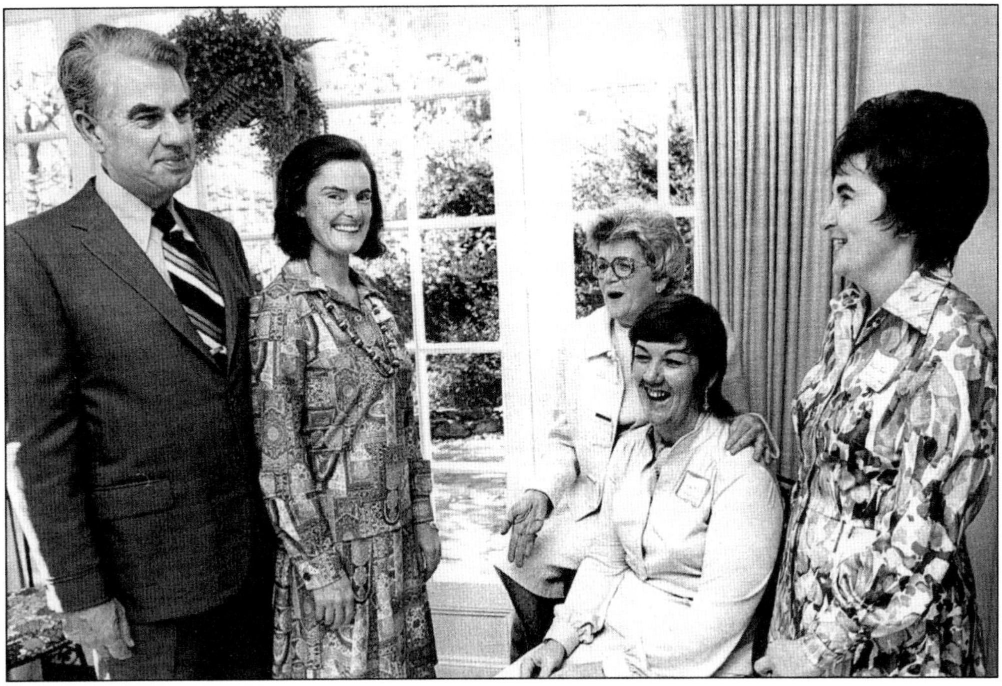

An Alumni-Faculty Reception, September 28, 1975. College president Dr. D. Justin McCarthy and his wife, Rosemary (left), entertain Rita Baker ('47), Lillian Buckley ('62), and Marilyn Fole ('58). It is only with the strong support of the alumni that the spirit of a school lives on.

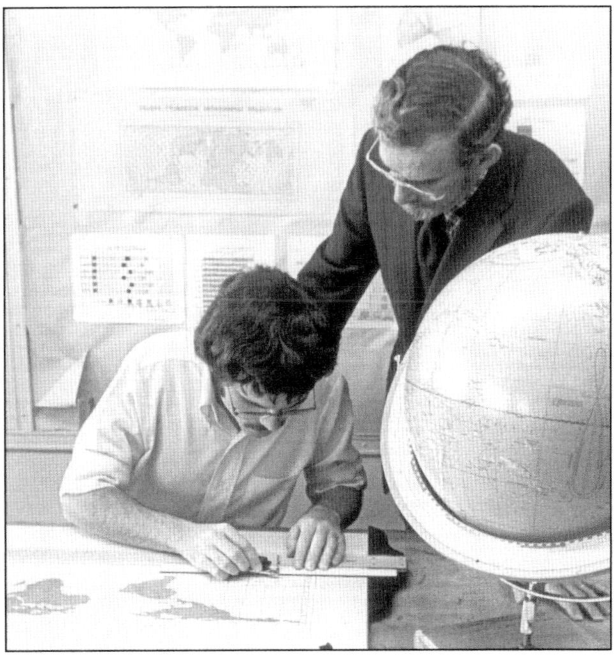

Cartography, Fall 1974. Cartography, the production of maps, is one of the many fields for geography majors at FSC. Prof. Howard Hirt supervises student George Hall, who is working on a map project. Students of the department produced an area map of the town of Franklin.

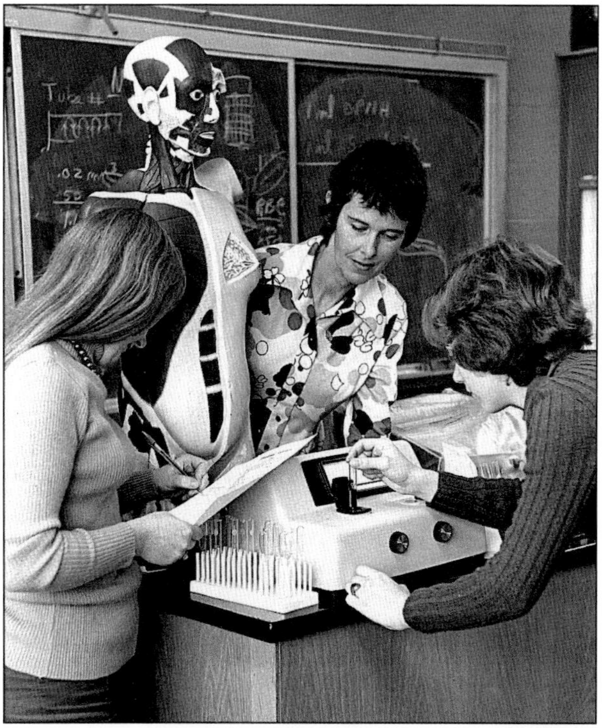

Medical Technology, Fall 1974. Students Alison Morse (left) and Laurene Bourassa (right), under the supervision of instructor Nancy Tanner, test serum for cholesterol determination, all part of their training as medical technology majors.

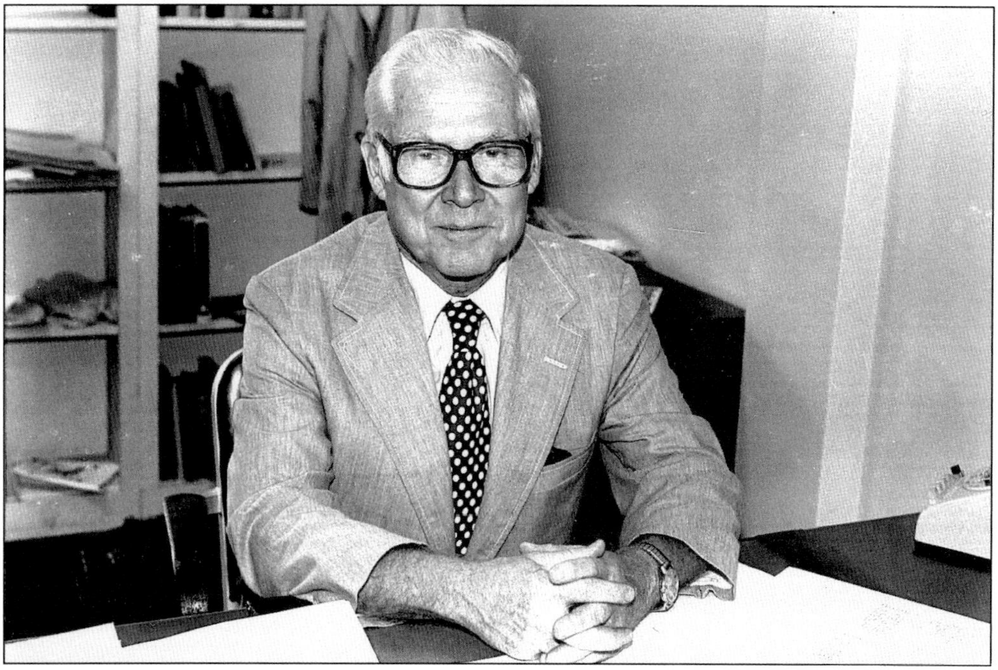

Elmer W. Salenius, the 1970s. From 1952 to 1985, Elmer Salenius was a professor of the English Department, which was established under his leadership. He served as the department's chair and also as head of the Liberal Arts Division. He was responsible for the development of many courses in literature and writing. A graduate of Maynard High School in 1935, he received his B.A. and Ph.D. from Boston University and an M.A. from Harvard.

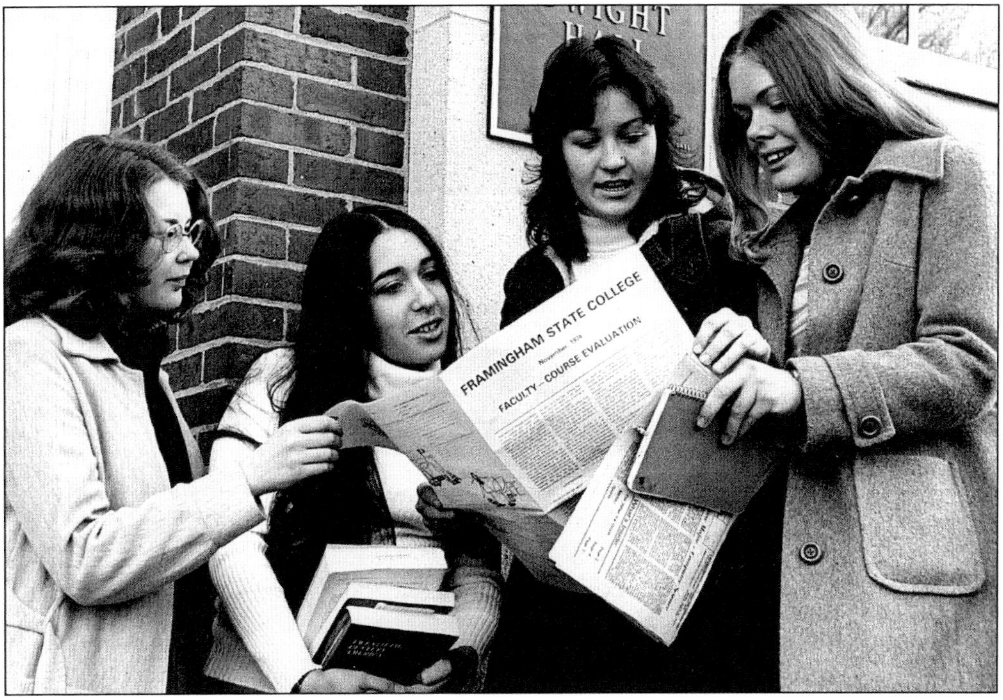

International Students, 1974. These four British students eventually returned to England after spending a semester at FSC as part of an exchange program with Sheffield City College. From left to right are Rosalie Vingoe, Siaeds Warsama, Linda Billington, and Daphne Barrie.

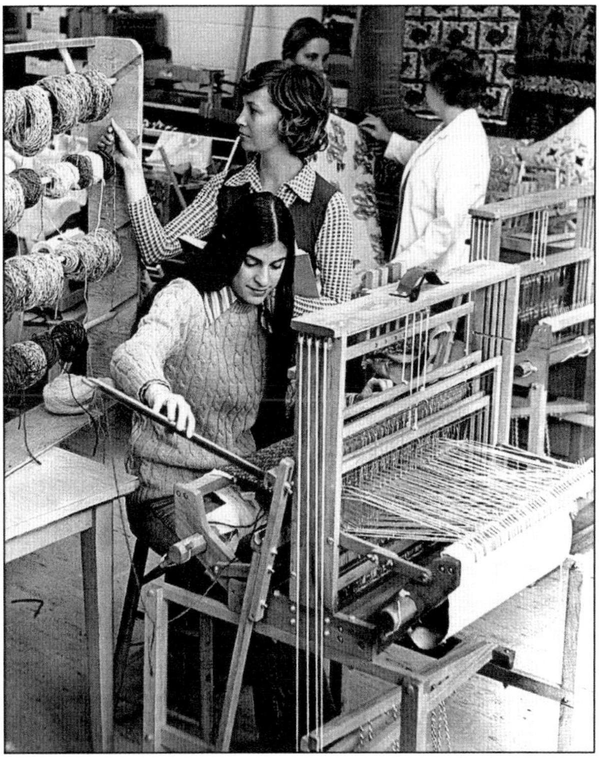

Fabric Design, c. 1975. Fabric Design is one of the many courses necessary for a bachelor's degree in Clothing and Textiles. Diane Beers, sitting at the loom, and Karen Dickey, standing directly behind her, try their skill on the loom, while Janice Liljestrand and Prof. Eleanor Gawn decide on the patterns for a project.

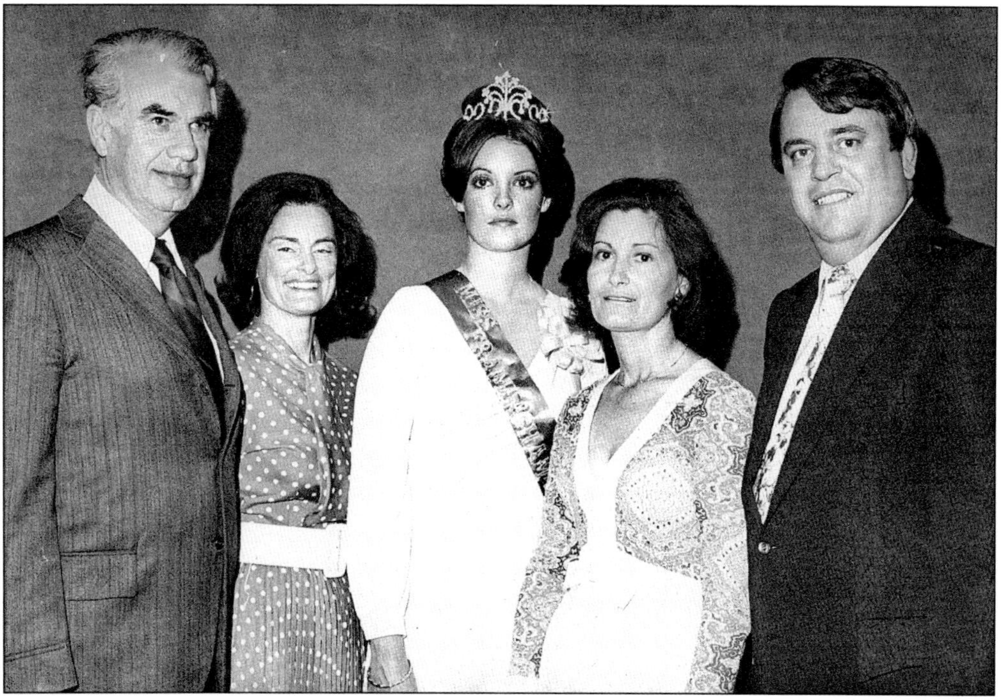

Miss Framingham of 1975. Over the years, the school has enjoyed a warm relationship with the town of Framingham. Taking part in the town's 275th anniversary banquet at the Chateau de Ville on Saturday, June 7, 1975, from left to right, are college president and toastmaster Dr. D. Justin McCarthy and his wife, Rosemary McCarthy; Kathleen Harding, Miss Framingham; and banquet chairman Mary Ann Croatti and her husband Donald J. Croatti, the town assessor. In 2000, the college awarded a special honorary degree to the town of Framingham for its 300th anniversary.

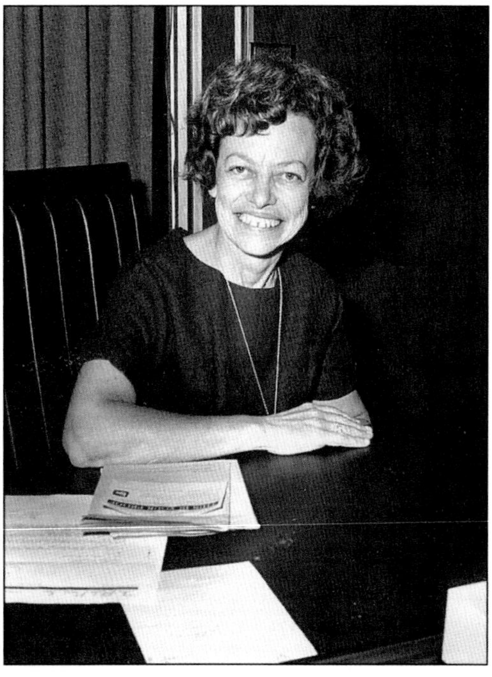

Dr. Constance Jordan, 1979. A 1941 Household Arts graduate, Constance Jordan received a master's in public health from Harvard and a Ph.D. in food and nutrition from Cornell (see page 83 for an earlier picture of her). After teaching at the University of Rhode Island, she returned to FSC as head of Household Arts. Dean of Graduate Studies from 1973 to 1978, she retired from teaching in 1983. Today, she is a member of the FSC Board of Trustees.

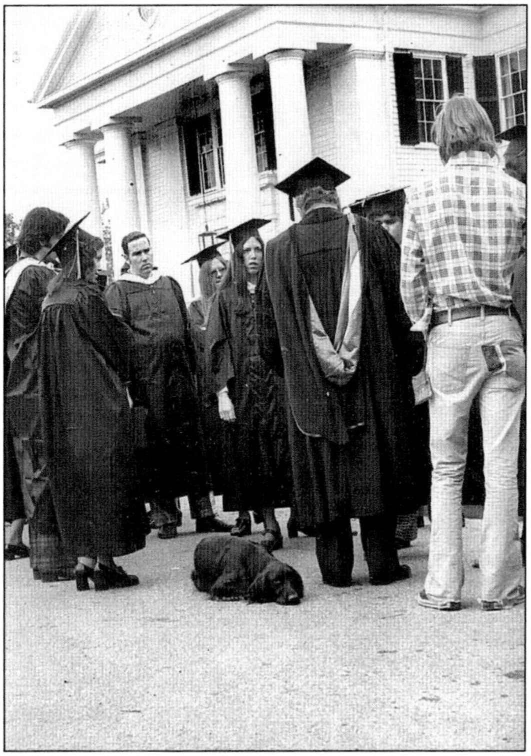

It's a Dog's Life, *c.* the 1970s. The college has held its graduation ceremonies outdoors, under tents, on the Framingham Centre Village Green since 1972. The building behind the students is known as Village Green and also as the Town Meeting Hall. Built in 1834 as a building for town meetings, it currently is used for social and civic functions.

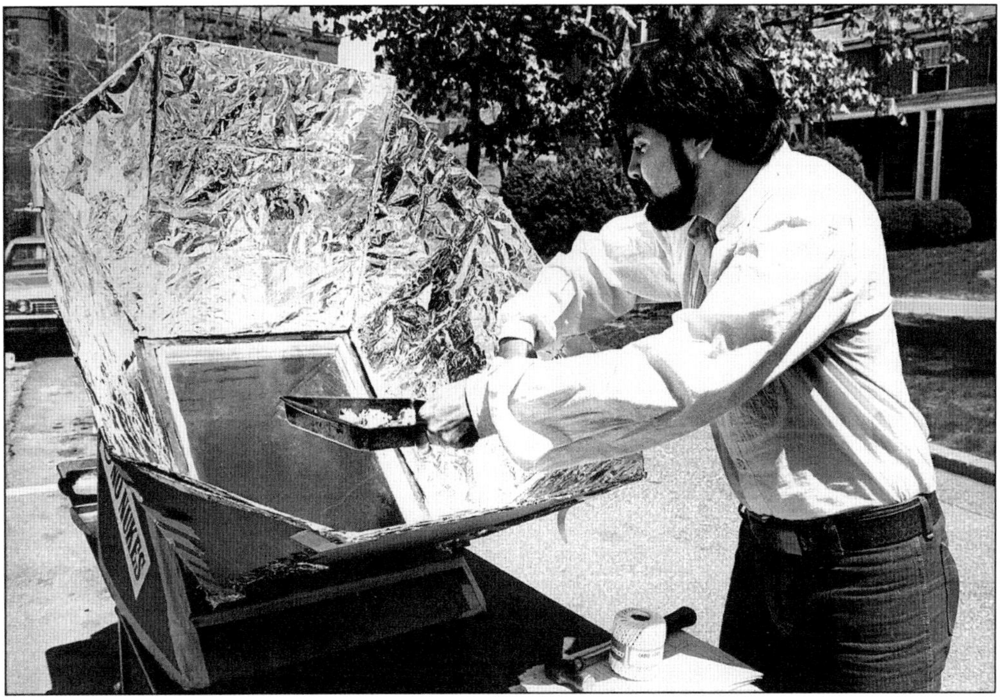

Cooking Cookies, 1979. Greg Reppucci of Topsfield participates in an Energy Awareness program held at FSC. He demonstrates how to prepare chocolate chip cookies, using the heat generated by the sun.

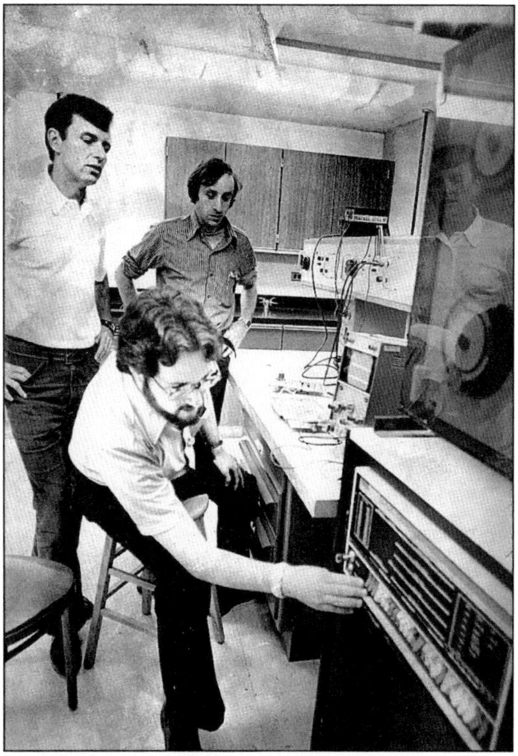

Computers Then. Joe Nicholson of Millis, a senior, works with a computer donated to the school in 1978. Looking on are Dr. Arthur Doyle (left), chair of the Physics Department, and Bernard Rosman, chair of the Computer Department.

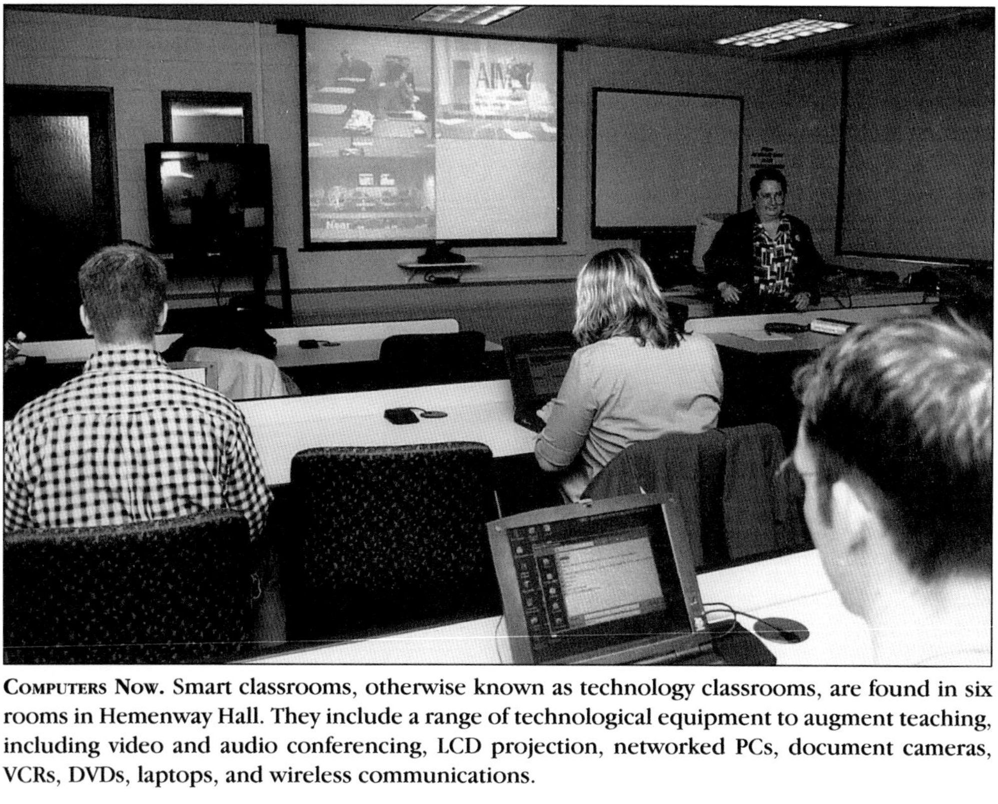

Computers Now. Smart classrooms, otherwise known as technology classrooms, are found in six rooms in Hemenway Hall. They include a range of technological equipment to augment teaching, including video and audio conferencing, LCD projection, networked PCs, document cameras, VCRs, DVDs, laptops, and wireless communications.

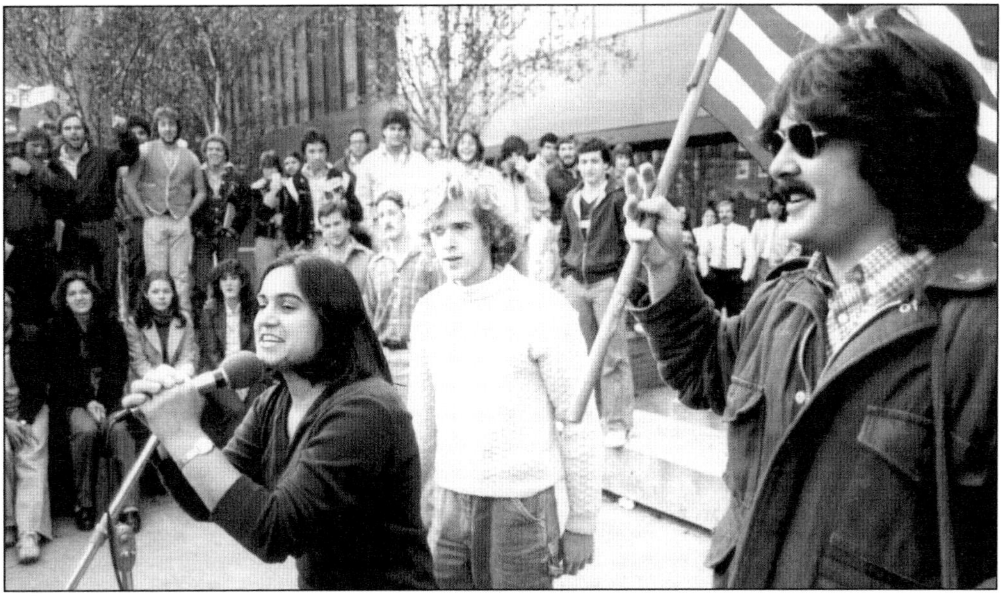

Democracy in Action, November 19, 1979. Students gather to protest Iran's holding of American hostages seized at the U.S. embassy in Tehran on November 4, 1979. This photograph depicts a flashpoint during the gathering, when FSC student and Iranian native Mahfam Alamian (left foreground) is booed and heckled by the crowd as she speaks her opinion that the hostages were taken to protest U.S. policy toward the former Shah. Alamian graduated from FSC in 1983 with a degree in biology.

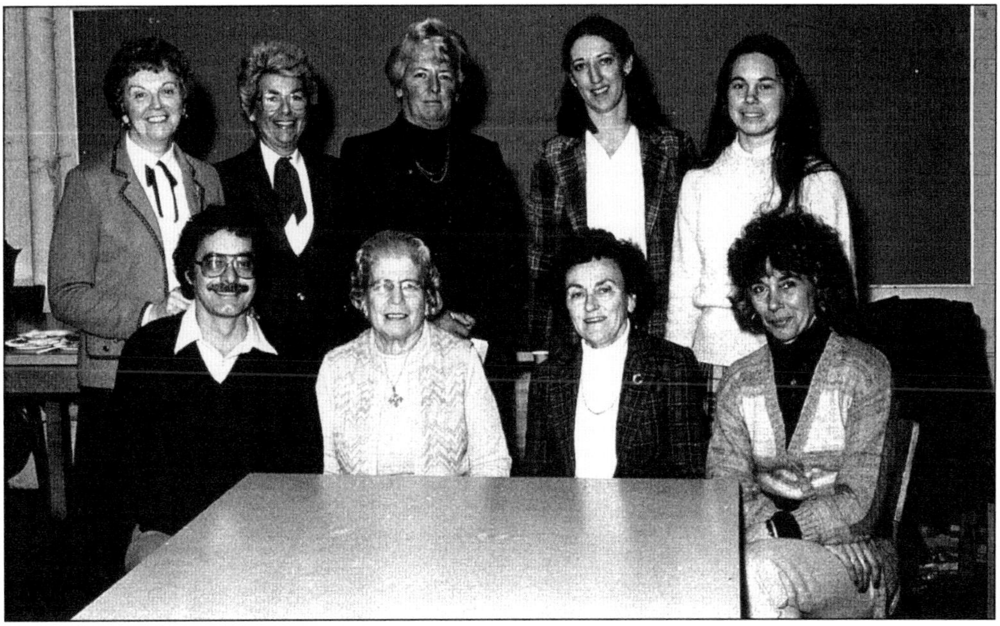

The Education Department, 1982. Members of the Education Department, from left to right, are as follows: (front row) Dr. Walter H. Klar, Dr. Mary K. Carter, Dr. Mary B. Brassard, and Jean M. Woodes; (back row). Dr. Elizabeth A. Mahan (chair), Jan Jorgensen, Dr. Dorothea J. Kunde, Dr. Cathleen Buydoso, and Michele Heist.

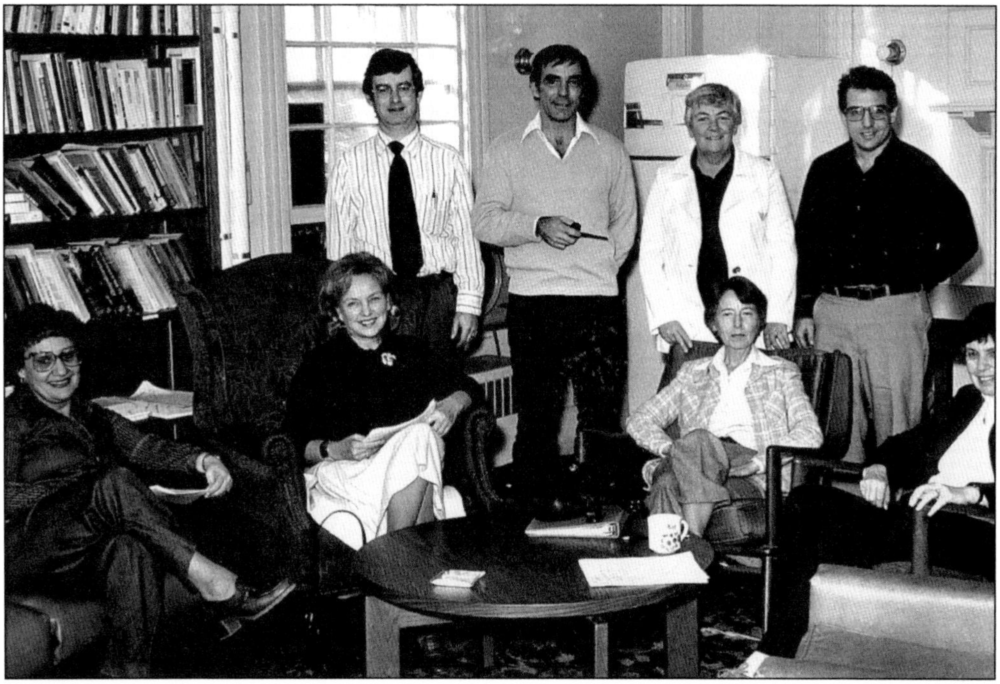

The Psychology Department, 1982. Members of the Psychology Department, from left to right, are as follows: (front row) Dr. Lorraine Low, Dr. Miriam Wilton, Dr. Beverly Weiss, and Dr. Katherine Stannard; (back row) Dr. Harold O. Kiess (chair), Dr. Leonard Flynn, Dr. Geraldine Guertin, and Dr. Barrie Westerman.

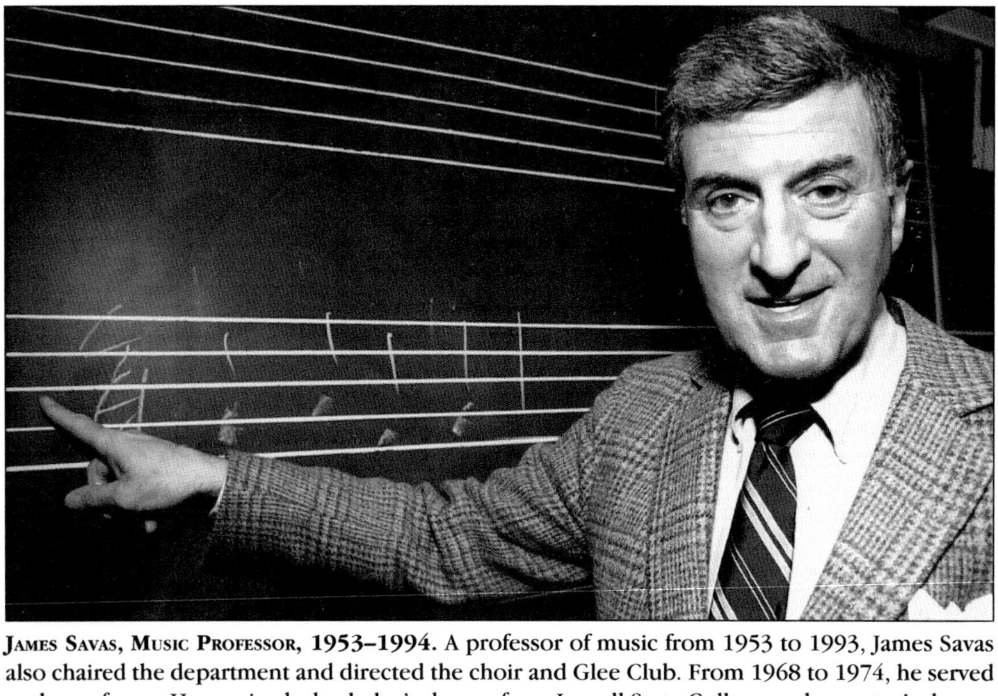

James Savas, Music Professor, 1953–1994. A professor of music from 1953 to 1993, James Savas also chaired the department and directed the choir and Glee Club. From 1968 to 1974, he served as dean of men. He received a bachelor's degree from Lowell State College and a master's degree from Columbia University.

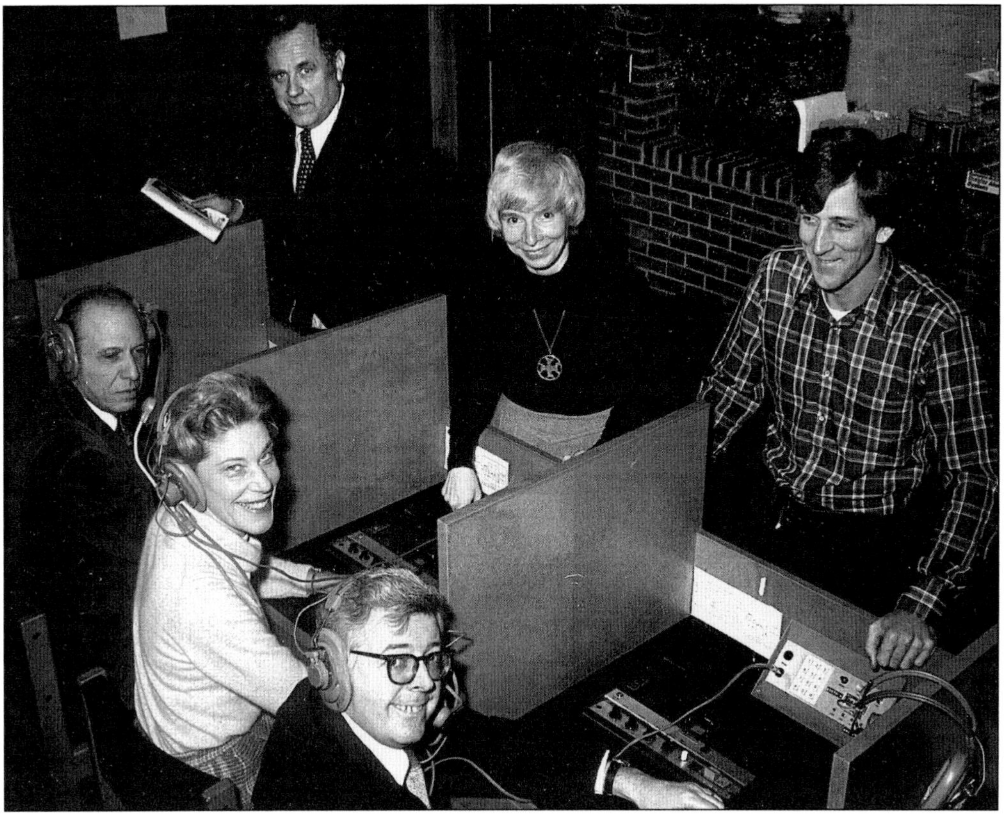

Faculty Members, 1986. Members of the faculty, from left to right, are as follows: (front row) Stephen Fiore (music), Joan Horrigan (speech), and Edgar Langevin (French); (back row) Walter Koroski (director, media communications), Josephine Reiter (music), and Michael Kovalis (technical staff).

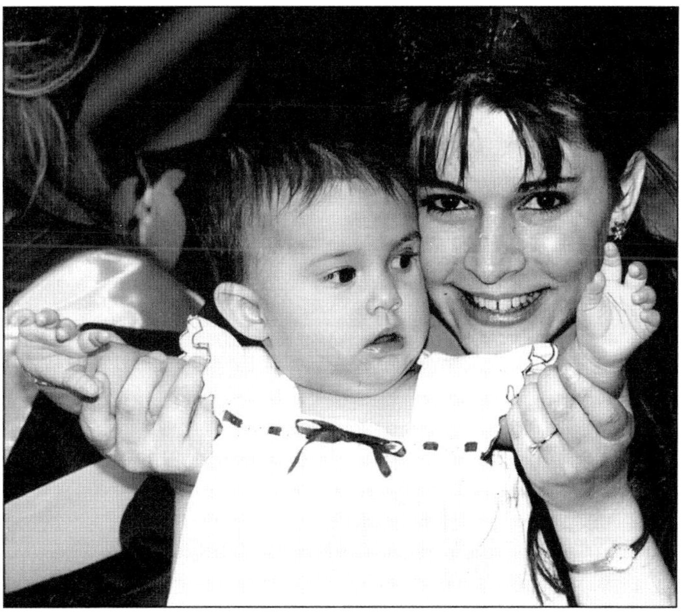

Graduation, 1989. Proud graduate Angela Calabro, an elementary education major, poses with a child who might just be a 2008 graduate. In 1989, approximately 5,000 students attended FSC.

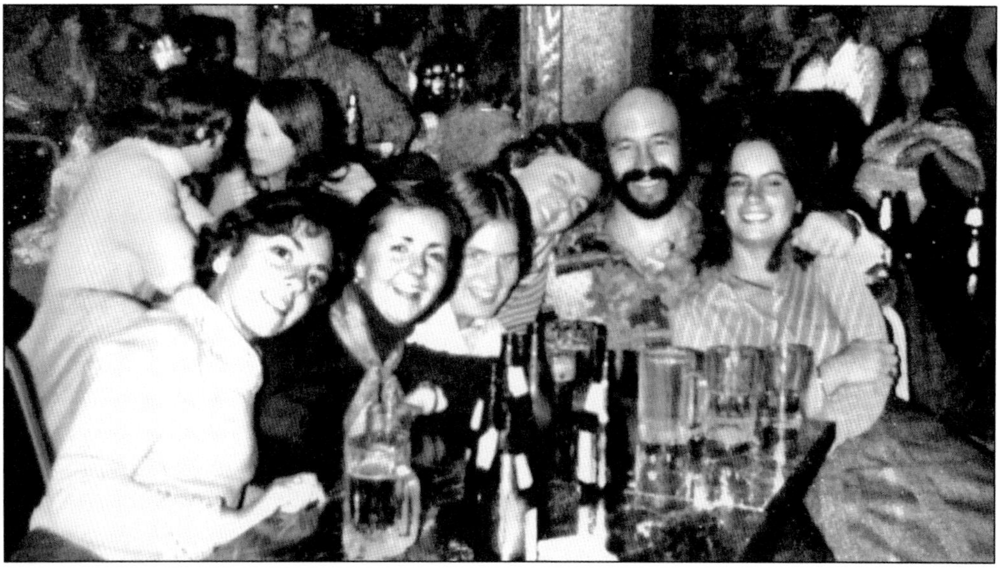

Friends, Class of 1976. College often establishes lifelong friendships. Attending a John Morgan concert in September 1976, from left to right, are Diane Talanian, Cindy Burns, Chrissy Ridder, Rosemary Bransfield, singer John Morgan, and coauthor Marianne Larson.

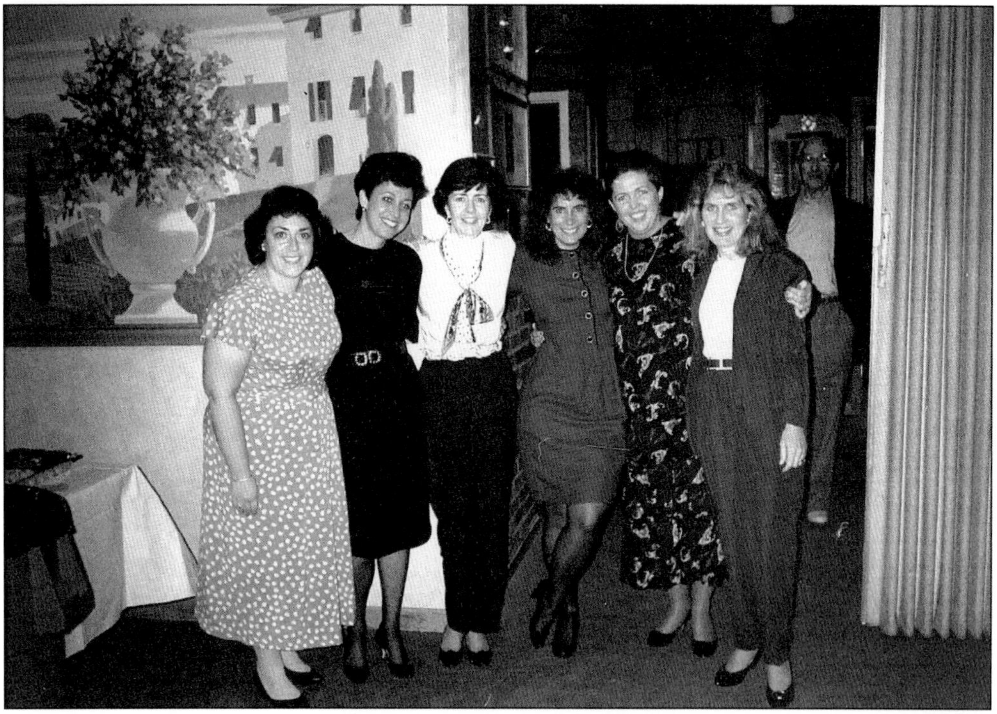

Still Friends, 1990. To this day, the friendship remains strong. Attending the 40th birthday party of coauthor Marc Kantrowitz, from left to right, are Diane (Talanian) Krueger, an elementary school assistant principal; Michelle Trunfio of San Francisco; Cindy (Burns) Howard; Marianne Larson, wife of Marc Kantrowitz; Rosemary Bransfield, family and consumer education teacher at Burlington High School and a McAuliffe Award nominee; and Chrissy (Ridder) Hastings. In the background is Theo Kantrowitz, father of Marc Kantrowitz.

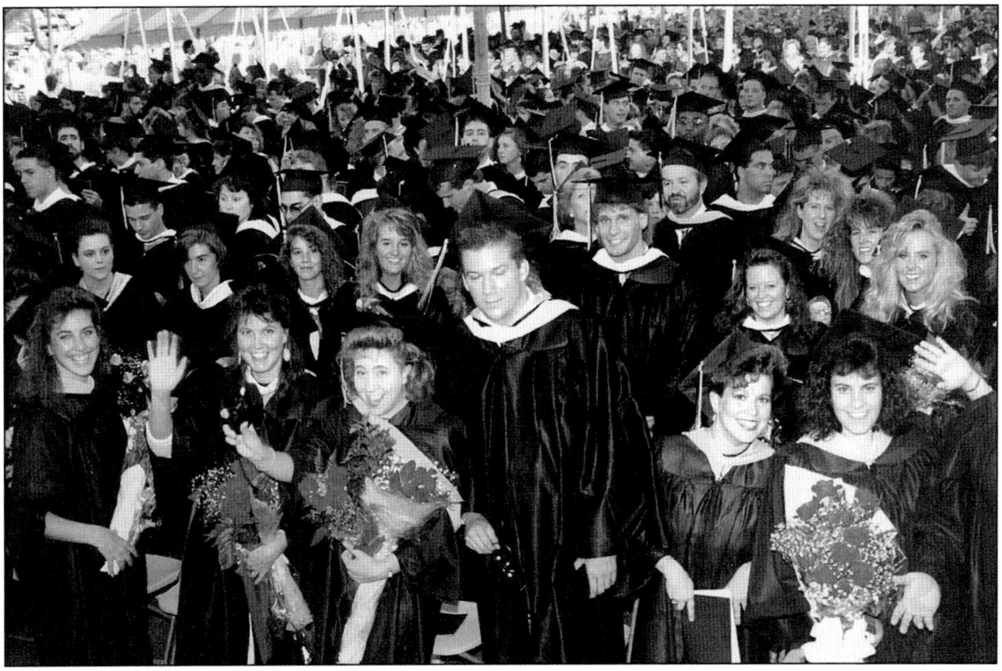

The Class of 1990. The officers of the Class of 1990 were Marianne O'Brien, president; Suzanne Floyd, vice president; Mary McLaughlin, secretary; and Tom Shea, treasurer. Cathy Mantegani, Stacy Iwanski, and Bob Gardiner were Student Government Association senators.

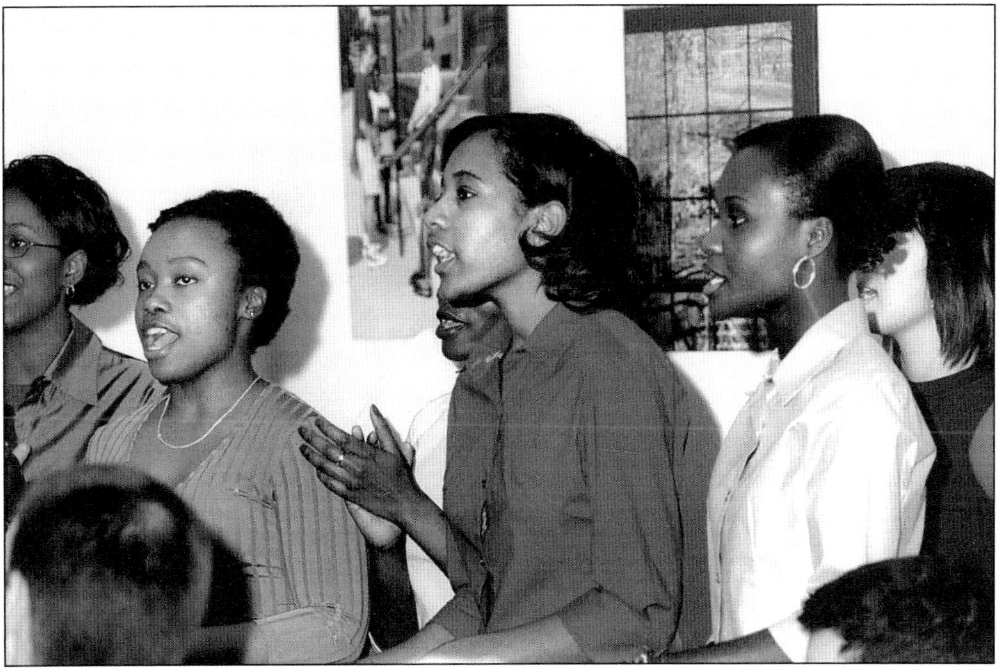

Diversity Awards, 2000. Recognizing the rights and accomplishments of women and minorities has been at the forefront of the school since its inception. Attending the Diversity Award ceremonies, from left to right, are Echine Orcel, Shelly Laine and Sandra Anim, who also sang with the United Voices of Praise.

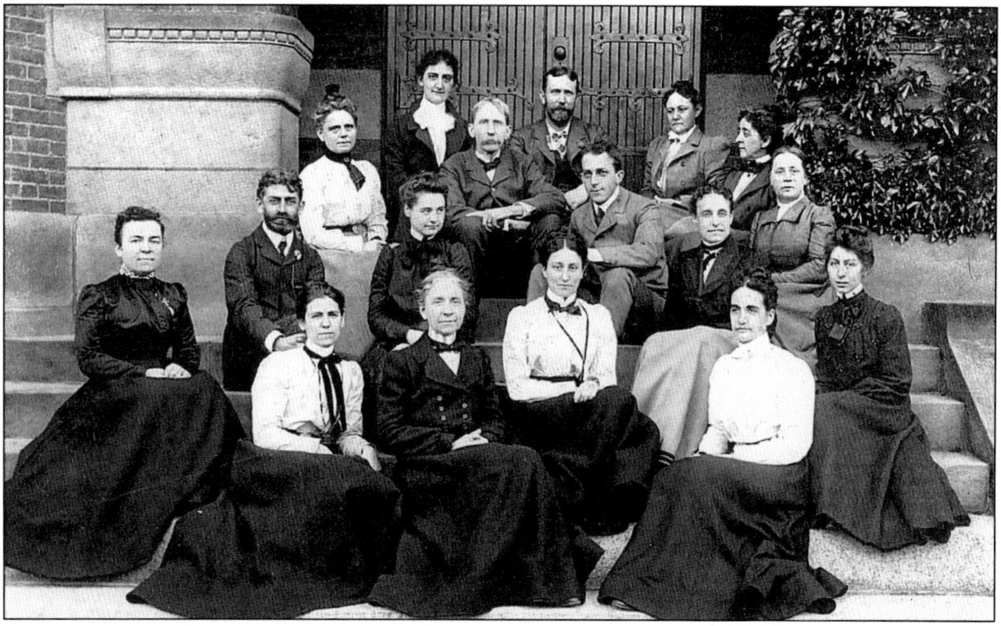

The Faculty, c. 1900. The faculty of 1900 is presided over by the principal, Henry Whittemore (second from the left in the next-to-the-back row). Although these men and women of a century ago were more formal than most professors are today, they shared the same love of teaching and passing knowledge on to the next generation.

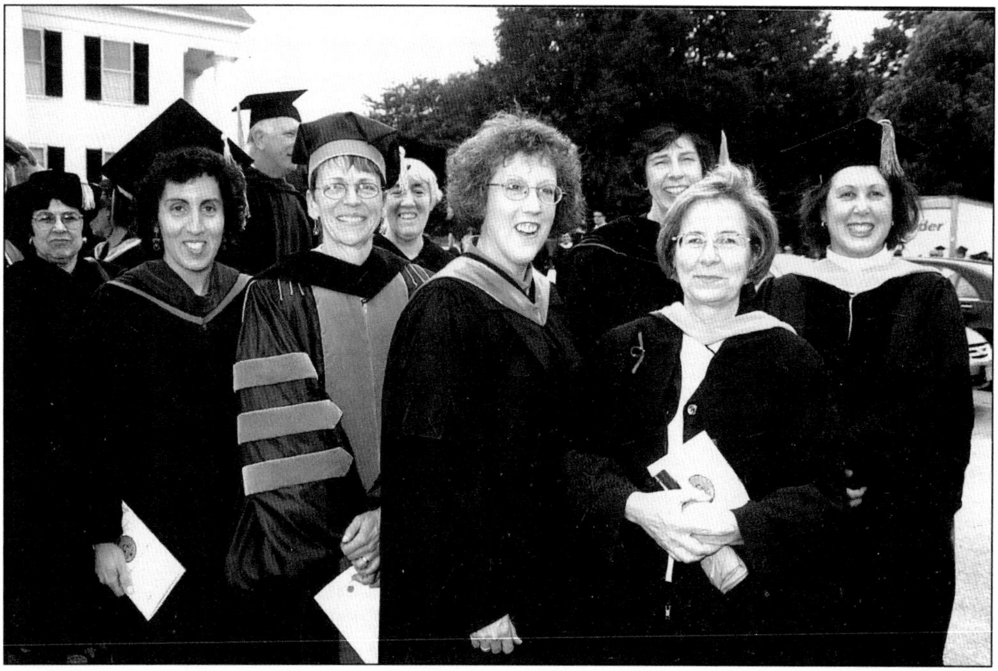

The Faculty, c. 2000. Today's faculty is far larger, nearly 10 times so, than its predecessors. On the far left is Carol Russell of the Chemistry and Food Science Department, who is joined by Family and Consumer Science Department members (foreground, left to right) Susan Massad, Jessica Hodge, Rebecca Taylor, Arlene Handschuch, and Marilyn Abernethy.

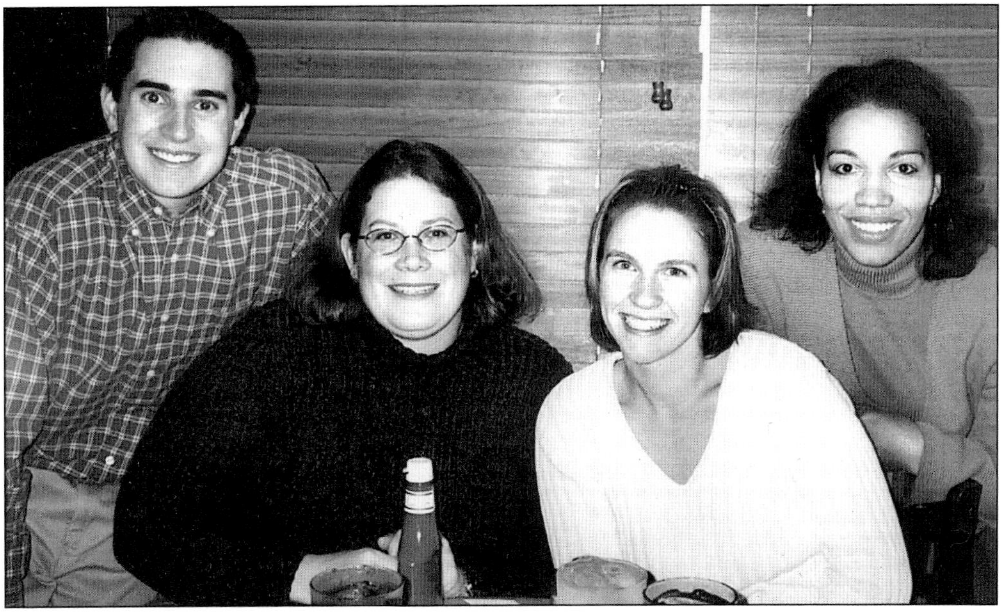

The Young Lead the Young. Youthful administrators hold various responsible positions working with the student body. From left to right are Matthew Robbie, program coordinator, Student Involvement (2001–2002); Carey Williams, assistant athletic director (1999–present); Rachel Lucking, director, Student Involvement (2000–present); and Angeline Lopes, assistant dean, Student Services, Multicultural Affairs, (2000–2002). (Courtesy of Rachel Lucking.)

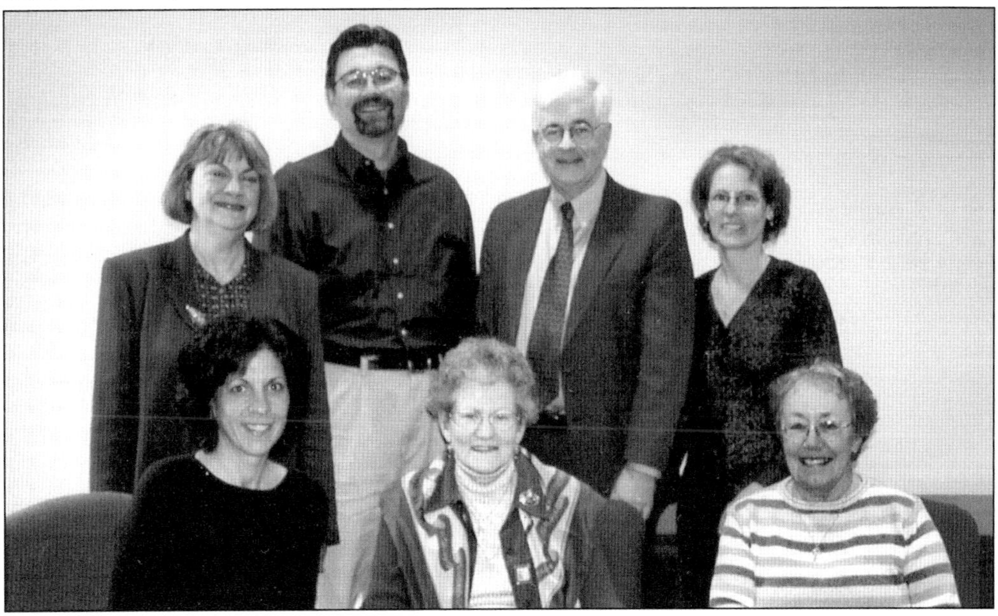

Those Who Made This Book Possible. The people who made this book possible, from left to right, are the following: (front row) Teresa Pagliuca, multimedia coordinator; Dr. Helen Heineman, president; and Martha Flinter, director of the International/Study Abroad programs;(back row) Margaret Storch, director of college publications; Chris Carden, special collections librarian-archivist; Philip M. Dooher, vice president of enrollment management and dean of admissions; and Bonnie Mitchell, director of library services.

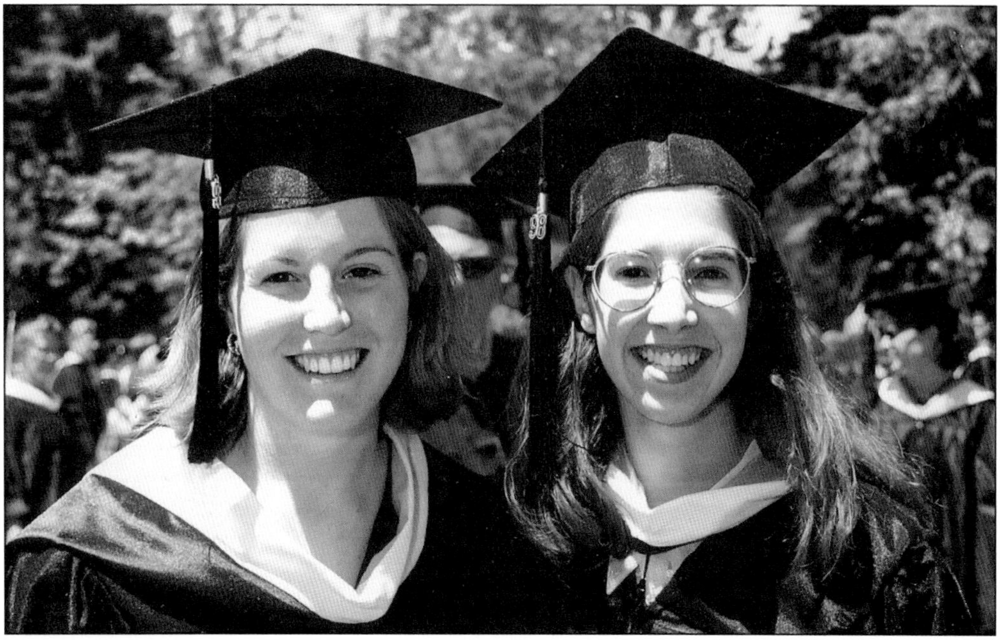

Graduation, 1998. Shayna Bailey Cameron (left) and Christine Miscia are the happy graduates in this photograph. They, like hundreds of their fellow students, enter the working world, walking in the footsteps of thousands who passed before them, all sharing an excellent education from a school dedicated to their needs.

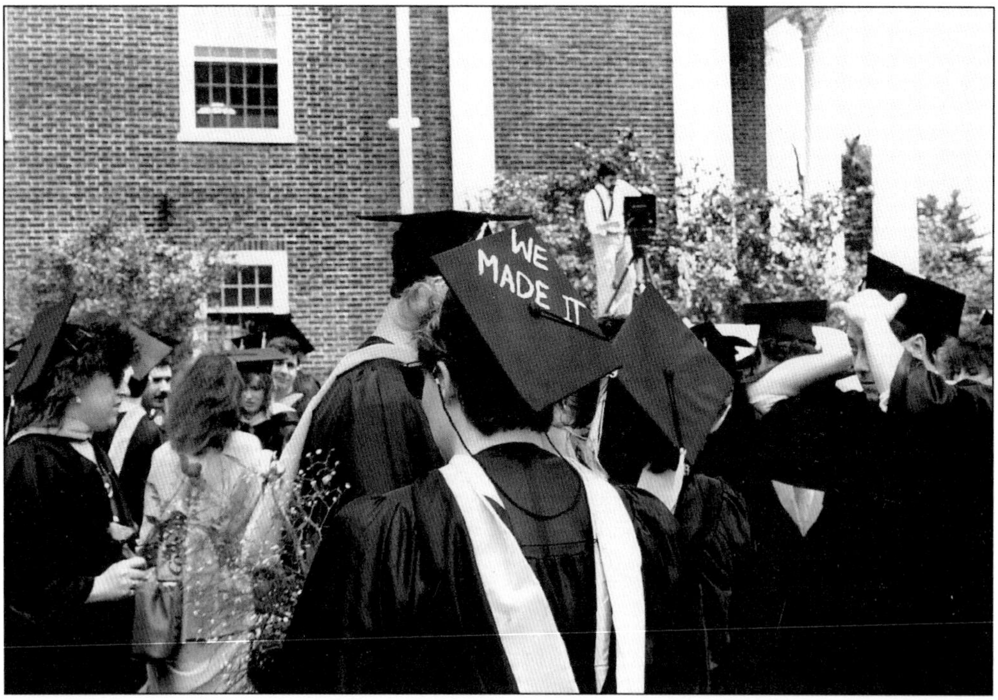

"We Made It." A chapter ends in the young lives of those who graduate. A new chapter is on the horizon, beckoning and challenging them. They are at the start of a new journey, where we can only hope that their dreams and wishes will all be realized.